NORTH KOREA
IDEOLOGY, POLITICS, ECONOMY

Edited by

HAN S. PARK

University of Georgia, Athens

Prentice Hall, Englewood Cliffs, New Jersey 07632

Library of Congress Cataloging-in-Publication Data

North Korea : Ideology, politics, economy/edited by HAN S. PARK
　　p. cm.
　　ISBN 0-13-102161-3
　　1. Political culture—Korea (North)　2. Communism—Korea (North)
3. Nationalism—Korea (North)　4. Korea (North)—Economic policy
5. Korea (North)—Foreign relations.　I. Park, Han S.
JA84.K6N67　　1995　　　94-48394

Acquisitions editor: *Mike Bickerstaff*
Project management and interior design: *Edie Riker*
Buyer: *Bob Anderson*

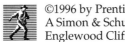

©1996 by Prentice-Hall, Inc.
A Simon & Schuster Company
Englewood Cliffs, New Jersey 07632

Printed in the United States of America

10 9 8 7 6 5 4 3 2 1

ISBN 0-13-102161-3

Prentice-Hall International (UK) Limited, *London*
Prentice-Hall of Australia Pty. Limited, *Sydney*
Prentice-Hall Canada Inc., *Toronto*
Prentice-Hall Hispanoamericana, S.A., *Mexico*
Prentice-Hall of India Private Limited, *New Delhi*
Prentice-Hall of Japan, Inc., *Tokyo*
Simon & Schuster Asia Pte. Ltd., *Singapore*
Editora Prentice-Hall do Brasil, Ltda., *Rio de Janeiro*

CONTENTS

4

THE IMPACT OF *JUCHE* ON LITERATURE AND ARTS 51

Vladimir Pucek

Charles University, Praha

5

IDEOLOGY AND WOMEN IN NORTH KOREA 71

Kyung Ae Park

University of British Columbia

PART TWO
POLITICS AND ECONOMY
OF INDIGENOUS SOCIALISM

6

POLITICS AND IDEOLOGY IN THE POST COLD WAR ERA 87

Vasily Mikheev

The Academy of Sciences, Moscow

7

THE POWER BASE OF KIM JONG IL:
FOCUSING ON ITS FORMATION PROCESS 105

Takashi Sakai

Ministry of Justice, Japan

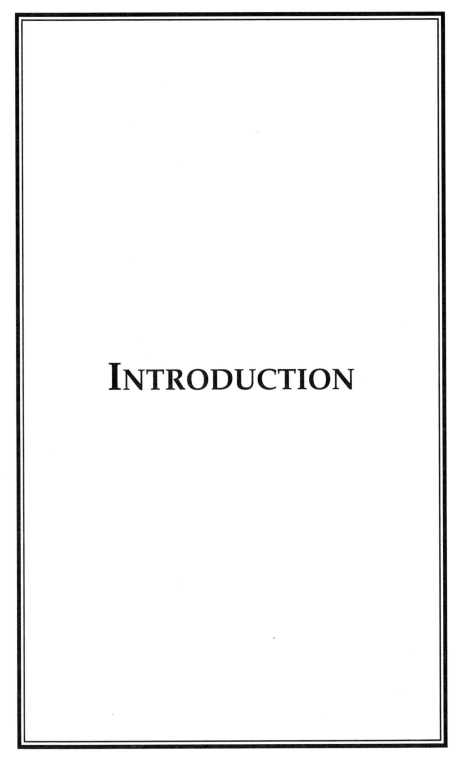

INTRODUCTION

The decline of the Cold War world order has resulted in profound changes in all of the surviving socialist regimes, especially the ones established under the guidance of the Soviet Union. The Democratic People's Republic of Korea (North Korea) is a country that was indeed established under the occupation of the Soviets, and yet the demise of the USSR has not prompted any fundamental changes in North Korea. This resiliency (or lack of sensitivity) may be attributed to the extremely closed nature of the society and the self-centered political culture. However, one wonders how long the North Korean political system and its mass beliefs will be able to avoid the tide of democratic revolutions that swept the communist bloc in the late 1980s. Due to the increasing significance of the Korean peninsula in international affairs, these complex issues and questions relating to North Korea must be addressed. Ironically, while North Korea plays an important role and presents a difficult strategic challenge in the international arena, little is known about the system.

North Korea has undergone a long period of seclusion from the world. This seclusion followed the partition of Korea in 1948 that was preceded by a period of colonial rule under Japan (1910–1945) following its annexation of the last kingdom of the Yi dynasty. As such, North Korea has never experienced a legitimate form of republicanism. The masses have not witnessed a regime turnover or leadership change since the inception of the government of the Democratic People's Republic of Korea (DPRK), with the exception of a hereditary power succession following the death of Kim Il Sung in the Summer of 1994. During the long hibernation, North Korea has managed its own life through the development of a peculiar national character and ideology. Although the political system is said to have been founded on the premises of Marxist socialism, there is little similarity between North Korea and other Marxist regimes. Indeed, North Korea has made itself politically centrist, ideologically paternalist, economically collectivist, ethnically racist, diplomatically isolationist, and culturally nationalist. These characteristics have become crystallized with the advent of the *Juche* (self-reliance) belief system.

Juche was initially put forth as an adaptation of Marxism-Leninism to postwar Korea. Under the tutelage of the Soviet Union, North Korea began the development of an ideal socialist state. Yet, conflicts with both China and the Soviet Union, in addition to the particular domestic situation, led to a transformation of *Juche* into a philosophy and political belief system that is quite unique to North Korea. Much of *Juche* thought can be better understood when one acknowledges the fact that the theory was developed in a nation that has experienced long periods of foreign domination and exploitation. There was a perception that the existence of foreign domination led not only to the commission of great acts of cruelty against the Korean people but also to practices that somehow robbed the Korean nation of its essential nature and character and particular place in history. Thus, one finds that central to the *Juche* belief system is a strong belief in nationalism and *chajusong* (individualism, or an independent social being). Ardently rejected in *Juche* thought is the notion of *sadaejuui* (loosely translated as *flunkeyism* or subservience to a foreign power).

The strong nationalism promoted in *Juche* and the simultaneous efforts to promote a belief in self-reliance and the superiority of Korean culture led North Korea down a path of increasing isolation from, if not hostility toward, the outside world. In addition, *Juche* was increasingly used to build and strengthen the personality cult of the Great Leader Kim Il Sung, and more recently his son, the Dear Leader Kim Jong Il. Due to these alterations, *Juche* is no longer simply a political ideology in which the North Koreans have emulated the Soviet or the Chinese models of Marxism. It indeed may have evolved into a form of a religious doctrine. It appears, at the very least, that *Juche* has come to permeate all aspects of North Korean life, and it seems to have taken hold of the thought processes and belief systems of the people. Should this be the case, one may not be able understand North Korean behavior, including policy orientations, under accepted Western assumptions such as rationality in decision making.

To better understand North Korea we must develop a great deal of knowledge from the perspective of symbolic interactionism or the phenomenological interpretation of human behavior. One must make efforts to understand better the cognitive processes and perceptions of the North Korean people. Thus, for the sake of credible analysis one needs to delve into the North Korean mind-set. For the empathetic and thus more accurate assessment of this most unconventional society we should obtain information and knowledge provided by experts who not only have first-hand information but also more importantly, maintain value neutrality toward both of the Korean regimes. The present volume represents an ambitious step toward this goal.

The uncertainty about the current state of affairs and the future in North Korea has recently been exacerbated by the death of Kim Il Sung and the succession of his son Kim Jong Il. Much of our understanding of North Korea has been based on our understanding and our analysis of Kim Il Sung, and his death has, to a great extent, eliminated our primary point of reference for understanding North Korea. While it appears that Kim Jong Il has succeeded in carrying out a relatively smooth transition and consolidation of power, a scarcity of information on Kim Jong Il and his true power base in North Korea has made analysis of the current situation speculative at best.

To complicate these issues, North Korea is now believed to have the technological and physical capability to produce nuclear weapons in the very near future. This potential carries profound implications for inter-Korea relations, as well as for regional and global security. Yet, in addition to the transition in leadership, significant developments have occurred quite recently on the diplomatic front. Discussions over North Korea's nuclear capability have led to cautious first steps toward greater economic and diplomatic cooperation between North Korea and the United States, and more importantly, between North and South Korea. Early indications are that the regime under Kim Jong Il may be more willing to move toward greater participation in and cooperation with the international community.

The secrecy and resiliency of the North Korea regime are central themes running through all of the articles contained in this volume. While in most instances we see what appears to be a maintenance of the status quo, almost stagnation, in North Korean economics, politics and culture, the question keeps surfacing as to whether this trend can continue. To answer that question we must first answer a number of other questions. For example, are there sociocultural and ideological attributes so unique to North Korea that the system should be dealt with independent of the recent pattern of change in the Communist world? Will the apparent strength of *Juche* be able to survive the transition of power from Kim Il Sung to Kim Jong Il? Should we expect greater or reduced isolation under the new leadership? Is there the possibility that Korea might follow the experience of German reunification? Should the fact that both North Korea and South Korea are now members of the United Nations lead us to be more optimistic about the possibility of their reunification?

We should no longer tolerate our ignorance and heavily biased perceptions about North Korea. What we know about the system is generally based on information filtered through South Korea or propaganda material emanating from Pyongyang. This information is severely lacking in credibility and reliability. In the post-Cold War era in which North Korea is expected to reach out to the world in order to establish economic and diplomatic relations, it is imperative for us to study and enhance our understanding of this long isolated system and its people. It is this reality that prompted the publication of this book. In attempting to address this issue, this book will look at the process of political socialization and the structure of the mass belief system, and assess their implications for economic and social programs as well as national unification.

Some characteristic features of the book include the following. First, diverse sources of authorship perspectives are represented; the contributors to this book represent ten countries including the former Soviet Union, China, Poland, Czechoslovakia, Hungary, Bulgaria, Germany (formerly East Germany), Japan, Canada and the United States. Second, the volume contains a wealth of firsthand information as all the contributors have either visited or lived in North Korea. In fact, all of them have a command of the Korean language although only three are ethnically of Korean origin. Third, it is hoped that the volume will present a balanced view of North Korea with respect to the ideological orientation. Given the wide range of country origins and ideological diversity of the authors, it is fair to assume that their analyses as a whole might indeed be well balanced and evenhanded. Finally, whereas most treatments of North Korea are limited in scope, this book deals with a wide spectrum of the society including politics, economy, education, ideology, literature, and foreign policy. The book is divided into three parts: ideology and culture; politics and economy, and foreign and unification policy.

In the first part, "Ideology and Political Culture," four chapters examine the nature and process of socialization and the impact of *Juche* ideology on the people's cultural life. In my own contribution to this volume, I attempt to provide a comprehensive description and analysis of the *Juche* ideology. *Juche* is quite unique among communist ideologies. I argue that, in fact, *Juche* has developed into a complex system of ideas with multiple functions. While *Juche* is first and foremost a political ideology that provides regime legitimacy, it has also developed into a mass belief system and a theology. In order to understand North Korea and to analyze its politics and culture, one must first understand this ideological structure.

Göthel presents an informed reflection on *Juche* and the national identity. She begins by contending that ideology plays an important part in the lives of all people, but especially in the lives of people who have suffered from some form of colonial oppression, like the Koreans. In North Korea, *Juche* was used to mobilize the masses and to help them discover their own identity in the construction of the country as well as a means to cope with inner-party rivalries. Göthel discusses the positive and negative impact of *Juche* in the development of North Korea.

In his article on the educational system in North Korea, Jiangcheng He discusses the tremendous improvements North Korea has achieved in providing universal education to the people. He describes the four major educational reforms carried out by the North Korean regime and then analyzes the content and methods of North Korean education. According to Jiangcheng He, the North Koreans have been extremely successful in improving education and have been especially successful in using the positive teaching method in education as a tool for political education and indoctrination.

Pucek presents us with a description of literature and the arts in Korea. According to Pucek, literature and the arts have registered some positive development over the past forty years. Overall, though, *Juche* as the pervasive ideology of North Korea has had a negative effect on culture and the arts. The isolation of the nation, its rigid ideology, and the strict control the government has exerted over the humanities have limited artists and authors and it does not appear that this trend will be reversed in the near future.

In an analysis of the status of women in the revolutionary system of North Korea, Kyung Ae Park examines the way in which socialist policies engineered the course of social change affecting the role and status of women that had traditionally assumed inferior status under the Confucian social order. She observes that while the lot of women has improved significantly in the areas of labor force and political voice, North Korean women still lag behind their male counterparts in important power positions.

In the second part of the book, "Politics and Economy of Indigenous Socialism," a set of five chapters examine the various aspects of indigenous socialism as it is manifested in political dynamics and economic strategies.

In his article on ideology and politics in the post-Cold War era, Mikheev points out that education and thought are tightly controlled in North Korea and the people remain highly isolated from the rest of the world. Changes in international relations as well its domestic economic situation will force the regime in North Korea to reevaluate its position and to find new ways to cope in the post-Cold War world. In this period of crisis, the two main mechanisms of North Korean totalitarianism, propaganda and repression, have intensified. Yet what North Korea might need, he argues, is to accept more open and civilized dialogue within the international arena.

Sakai provides a detailed account of the power base of Kim Jong Il, especially in the areas of cultural life and the military. His study suggests that Kim's power base might be broad and stable. In view of the scarcity of information on Kim Il Sung, Sakai's contribution is especially timely and significant.

Shenying Shen discusses the policies and strategies for economic development in North Korea. Shen argues that feudalism and Japanese colonialism retarded Korea's economic development for a long time. Shen then discusses three significant stages in North Korea's economic development, while focusing on the third stage of Socialist Construction. Shenying Shen shows that the economic policy has been rather consistent over time and concludes that despite the pressures for change, one should not expect any major reversals in North Korean economic policy in the near future.

In her article, Marina Trigubenko points out that North Korea is one of the few remaining nations that adheres to socialism and its traditional economic policy. While both internal and external pressures for change exist, the North Korean regime is still strong enough militarily and ideologically to maintain the status quo. Trigubenko goes on to analyze the development of the current economic situation in North Korea with particular emphasis on the liability of some of North Korea's socialist allies for the problems the nation experiences today.

In his article, Karoly Fendler highlights economic assistance given to North Korea from socialist nations. He shows that this assistance was fundamental in shaping the form and structure of the North Korean economy. For that reason, according to Fendler, in order to better understand the prospects for Korean reunification and North Korea's place in the world, a better understanding of the impact of these programs is essential.

In the final part of the book, "Foreign and Unification Policy," the complexity of North Korea's policy goals and strategies are discussed from various perspectives and areas. Koh argues that due to North Korea's unique military and political position in the world, an in-depth understanding of its foreign policy is necessary. He describes three dimensions of North Korea's foreign policy: goals; constraints, and prospects. Through his analysis Koh shows that while some change is occurring in North Korean policy, the change has been slow and cautious.

Iuli Banchev discusses the economic foreign policy making of North Korea. In his article he argues that the globalization of economics and the changing nature of the world order are leading toward the rationalization of regional economic orders. Unfortunately, on the Korean peninsula, politics and ideology are interfering with the dialogue between the two regimes. Perhaps what is needed, he concludes, is an effort toward systematic cooperation between them.

In his article on North Korean reunification policy, Cyrzyk states that the reunification of the two Koreas has always been the supreme goal of the Pyongyang regime; yet the specific approaches and policies have changed over time. Cyrzyk looks at the four categories of reunification proposals and concludes that changes in the international environment as well as in North Korea's domestic political and economic situation make it necessary for North Korea to reevaluate its policy in the 1990s.

In the final chapter of this book, I present the case of the nuclear controversy. It is contended that Pyongyang's nuclear program has resulted from a rational calculation on the part of the Kim Il Sung regime and that a negotiated settlement will require a comprehensive package deal that includes security, economic, and face-saving cultural elements.

The underlying premise of the book is that North Korea is not an ordinary socialist system that will adhere to the conventional norms and historical experiences as seen in the former Soviet Union and Eastern European countries. It is a system that has established a peculiar ideological structure through an effective political socialization in the contained environment. A proper understanding of the ideological system must precede any meaningful analysis of the social, economic, and political dynamics. This book is an attempt to show the interplay between the ideology and the rest of the political system.

I would like to express gratitude to the contributors for their timely submission of manuscripts. Initially, earlier versions of the chapters, except my own contributions, were presented at the First International Conference on North Korea sponsored by the Dongwha Research Institute held in Seoul, South Korea in the Spring of 1991. Without the painstaking efforts of the institute and its president Kyung-nam Lee as well as Sung Chul Hong, this book would not have been possible. I would also like to recognize Donald Rodgers and Zhongyi Wu for their contribution to translation and editorial assistance. The views expressed in this book are those of the writers of the various chapters, and they are solely responsible for the content.

1

THE NATURE AND EVOLUTION OF *JUCHE* IDEOLOGY

HAN S. PARK

University of Georgia, Athens

As a system of values, *Juche* is commonly translated as "self-reliance" which has become the blueprint of North Korean society and the central guideline for policies. It has evolved through various phases ranging from a mere political slogan to a comprehensive *Weltanschauung*. We will examine the nature and structure of this value system in terms of what it does and what it is.

JUCHE AS POLITICAL IDEOLOGY

Juche is first and foremost a political ideology. A political ideology is an institutional means designed to help the ruling elite solidify its power base, integrate the political community, and achieve national consensus in order to make governance easier. The ideology, then, provides the regime with legitimacy. As long as the legitimization of a regime is a function of ideology, the fact that an ideology does perform this role in a given political system should not be considered abnormal or subjected to criticism and condemnation. The role of ideology as the provider of legitimacy can be witnessed in every form of government even including participatory democracy.

North Korea is one country that has most effectively and forcefully employed a political ideology for the purpose of solidifying the power base and integrating the political community. For that matter, no system can be said to have achieved such a degree of political indoctrination as completely as has North Korea. Only when one understands *Juche*, will he be able to ascertain the motivation and attitudes of the masses that made such indoctrination possible. All policies are given justification as concrete manifestations of *Juche* philosophy. Indeed, the realization of a *Juche* society in which members are completely immersed into *Juche* ideas is the ultimate goal of the government. The self-reliance idea has become the underlying principle of all areas of public policy ranging from economic plans to cultural life.

As a legitimizing tool, *Juche* has been an effective means to secure public compliance to government policies and to generate a broad base of support for the regime. This has been possible through a structured and rigorous process of political education and indoctrination. By keeping the society tightly closed from outside political education effectively shields off any source of doubt about the truthfulness of *Juche*. In the most isolated environment, political socialization takes place at all levels of education. The *Juche* belief system is the backbone of education as its ideas are effectively integrated into teaching materials and work-study programs. The belief system itself has been refined and advanced by organized efforts of leading scholars who are estimated to be several hundred in number. In conjunction with the advance of the "social-political life" doctrine of *Juche*, the Academy of *Juche* Sciences was instituted in 1987. At this institution, leading scholars devote their full time to advancing and teaching the ideology, at times, by inviting foreign scholars. Then, what is the essence of the belief system?

MASS BELIEF SYSTEMS

Juche has a professed *weltanschaung* with respect to a set of desirable (ideal) relationships in the life world. Just like any other ideology, it is meant to guide behavioral orientations for the individual, patterns of institutionalization for the society, and policy directions for the government. For a mass belief system instilled by the government to be effective in guiding the course of action at various levels of the society, it needs to be congruent with the prevailing sociocultural condition seen in the context of the historical milieu.

The sociohistorical milieu surrounding *Juche* ideology can be characterized in terms of national independence, the Sino-Soviet relations, the global politics of the Cold War era, and national division. These historical and contextual events have made a decisive impact on shaping the belief system of *Juche*, and as a result, it has attained much ideological attributes as militant nationalism, human centeredness, spiritual determinism, and human creativity. We shall examine these attributes and analyze the way in which they have influenced the process of mass education and political socialization.

Militant Nationalism

The most salient factor in the belief system of *Juche* has to be nationalism as it invokes hostility against foreign hegemonism and promotes supremacy of the Korean heritage and its people. *Juche* views Korea as a chosen land as the people are told consistently that world civilization originated from the Korean peninsula, a theme that is portrayed emphatically in the massive thirty-three volume history books (*Choson Jon Sa*). When history is viewed as having been designed and devoid of any accidental development, a sense of predestination sets in. Coupled with this. the notion that a people is predestined to inspire and "lead the world's oppressed peoples" makes North Korean nationalism ultra ethnocentic and uncompromising.

In a Marxist socialist system, politics is supposedly guided by class consciousness but it is national consciousness that has guided North Korea since the introduction of the *Juche* ideology. Indeed, national consciousness supersedes all other forms of beliefs. Political purges and power solidification have been pursued in the name of nationalism. North Korean nationalism, however, was firmly founded on the repudiation of foreign powers, beginning with colonialist Japan and eventually "imperialist" America. The negative foundation of nationalism carried the Kim Il Sung regime through regime crises and eventually to the adoption of *Juche* as the official ideology.

Juche in its present version is far more than a form of anti-foreignism; it has acquired a quality of self-affirmation. The "self" in this case is the nation as an indivisible and deified sacred entity. The notion that individuals are not worthy of living if they are deprived of their nation has been promoted so pervasively that complete loyalty to the nation is considered natural. In the initial stage of the building of nationalism, the concrete historical reality that Japanese colonialization of Korea forced the Korean people to live a subhuman life helped the solidification of nationalism. Furthermore, Kim Il Sung's leadership position was reinforced by the fact that he was known as a leader of the independence movement.

The nationalist sentiment is evidenced in all areas, especially in the cultural and aesthetic life. As will be discussed later in the context of the *Juche* art, the quality of art is judged by its expression of and contribution to nationalism.

Human Being as the Locus

The notion of "self-reliance" was initiated to convey the doctrine that Korea as any other nation should be self-subsistant without having to rely on external resources or power. But this exclusive nationalism or anti-foreignism has proved to be counterproductive and even detrimental to the economic and technological development. More recently, therefore, *Juche*'s "self-reliance" is being reinterpreted as meaning a human-centered world-view. The perception that "man is the master of nature and society and the main factor that decides everything"[1] is the cornerstone of the *Juche* world-view. *Juche* theoreticians maintain that "society consists of people, social wealth, and social relations. Here man is always master. Both social wealth and social relations are created by man and serve him."[2] As such, man should not be subjected to enslavement of any kind, whether it is due to economic poverty, political subjugation, or military domination by fellow human beings. North Korea's emphasis on technological development as part of the heralded "Three Revolutions Campaign"[3] is intended to convey the theme that technology should contribute to the emancipation of man from the constraints of nature and society. *Juche* theoreticians consider technical revolution to be "an important political task to help the working people [be] relieved of exploitation and oppression, to cast off the fetters of nature. . . as a part and parcel of the cause of human emancipation."[4] Kim Il Sung himself maintains that "the technical revolution is a momentus revolutionary task which will relieve our people, free of exploitation from hard work, enable them to produce more material wealth while working easily and ensures them a richer and more cultural life."[5] Furthermore, human beings, according to *Chajusong*, should never be manipulated by institutions, material conditions, or mythical beliefs such as religious dogmas. The doctrine that man is the master of the universe suggests that society along with its many institutions is created by man and should serve the well-being of its members. This, however, is not to suggest that North Korea does not promote the collectivist view in the relationship between society and individual members. What it suggests is that the nature of a society should be determined by the ideals and "consciousness" of the people, although isolated individuals detached from the society are given no *raison d'etre* for existence (this theme will be elaborated upon later).

Spiritual Determinism

It is a supreme irony that *Juche* as an ideology of socialist and self-proclaimed Marxism is in defiance of the material determinism of history. The Marxist premise of economic or material structure as the substructure upon which all superstructures will be founded is unequivocally denounced. Instead, it is the spiritual consciousness that determines the course of history and it alone underlies all other structures. In fact, *Juche*'s fundamental deviation from Marxism begins at this point. According to this doctrine, human behavior is guided not by the conditions of mode and relations of production but by the direct guidance of the brain. Likewise, social change occurs in accordance with the command of the society's "brain" (*Noesu*), as opposed to being dictated by the forces and relations of production. In this way, a direct analogy is made between the human body and social organism. This analogy enables the theory of the "socio-political life" in which a triangular relationship is advanced involving the people, the Party, and the Great Leader. The Leader in this case performs the function of the brain that makes decisions and commands actions for the various organismic parts of the body, the Party as the nerve system that mediates and maintains equilibrium between the brain and the body, and finally the people themselves who implement decisions of the brain and channel feedback to the Leader.

The central concept in this context is *Uisiksong*, roughly translated as "consciousness." According to *Juche*, it is this quality of man that makes human beings unique and distinguishable from all other living species. *Juche* theoreticians perceive consciousness "in relations to man's independent and creative abilities to reshape and change the world." They define consciousness as "a mental activity, a special function of the brain which directs man's independent and creative activities in a unified way."[6]

Man is meant to be conscious about his place in the universe as dictated by the aforementioned *Chajusong* that guides all forms of relationships in the life world, and concerns of problems in the existential historical situations. In fact, this theory of human quality is based on the *Juche*'s interpretation of human nature. According to this doctrine, man consists of the body and the spirit. It is the spirit that enables man to cultivate and develop consciousness. And it is also the spirit that ultimately commands the body, not the converse. Consciousness, however, will not develop without concerted efforts by the individual through education and continuously internalizing the collective will of the society as represented by the guidance of the Leader and the Party. In this way, *Juche* adheres to a logic of dialectical synthesis among the three entities in order to create the "socio-political body" of the life world.

Creativity (*Changuisong*)

While *Uisiksong* or consciousness refers to metaphysical or spiritual preparedness toward the development of human nature, *changuisong*, which may be translated as creativity, is an integral component of human nature that is an active, mobile, and engineering force of human action. If *uisiksong* is static and philosophical, *changuisong* may be understood as dynamic and scientific. This quality of man enables him to apply abstract principles to concrete reality by creatively adapting the principles to the specific condition of the society. Kim Il Sung defines creativity as "a quality of man who transforms the world in keeping with his independent aspirations and requirements."[7] Accordingly, *Juche* maintains that it is this quality of man that has developed Marxism-Leninism to work in the peculiar indigenous situation of Korea, thus advancing the ideological system to a greater perfection. Conversely, if political ideologies and institutional arrangements are copied from foreign experiences without adjusting them creatively to the concrete indigenous condition of each society, they will exhibit irregularities and ill-symptoms. Therefore, a society of creative people must not blindly adopt foreign values or institutions. In order to be creative in this regard, one must first study one's own society scientifically and understand fully the historical and cultural condition. This encourages further the nationalistic perspective in educational programs and cultural activities. Then, how do North Korean theoreticians understand the Korean history and cultural heritage? This is a question so central to the understanding of the *Juche* idea itself that an elaborated discussion will be made later.

JUCHE AS THEOLOGY

With the advent of the "sociopolitical body" in 1986 and the ensuing establishment of the *Juche* Academy of Science, the ideology of *Juche* has been rapidly transformed into a religious doctrine or theology. An obvious question in this context is whether the "sociopolitical body" will be maintained when the leader, in this case Kim Il Sung himself, passes away. Although his son Kim Jong Il will succeed him as the brain of the "body," no matter who the occupant might be, the life span of the "body" must coincide with the physical existence of the leader. Thus, the "religionization" of *Juche* is inevitable as the leadership as the brain of the "body" is sublimated into the realm of immortality. Hwang Jang Yop, widely regarded as the architect of the ideology and its most profound theoretician, commented to this author that "*Juche* will not be perfected as a philosophical system without being 'religionized,'" a point that was never made until late 1992. Indeed, without acquiring a religious character of sorts, the theory of "sociopolitical body" will be self-destructed when the Leader disappears from the scene.

It is in this context that one must understand the fact that the Pyongyang leadership has not only allowed Christian churches but many *Juche* theoreticians have also been deeply involved in studying the possible linkage between the ideology and Christian theology. One should not be surprised by the fact that *Juche* theoreticians have even advanced the "theology" of an eternal life as well as the concept of a supernatural being or God of sorts. The eternal life proclaimed here is attained when a biological (isolated) individual acquires a social life by overcoming innate human desires and egoistic life style through integrating himself thoroughly into the life system of the national community, thus, becoming part of the immortal social life. An example of this is found in people who have sacrificed their lives for national and social causes and are remembered throughout history. In this way, martyrdom is sanctified as a path toward the eternal life. As to the nature of the supernatural entity, *Juche* theoreticians envision that such a being is embodied in a symbolic construct that can be inferred from the perfected personhood that cannot be realized but only be imagined. Li Ji-soo, another leading theoretician and the director of the Academy of *Juche* Science, conceptualized that the spiritual and moral quality of man has made steady improvement over the course of history as evidenced by the fact that the killing of a fellow man in a fight is no longer institutionalized as was the case for the medieval knight. If, as expected, human moral quality develops continuously despite inevitable fluctuations in the short run, we can envision a situation in the remote future where human nature can be perfected. It is this imagined state of perfected humanhood that helps us portray the characteristics of "God." According to Li, man should strive to expedite the process in which human nature is perfected. It is the *uisiksong* that enables man to extend his imagination beyond the existential constraints and be able to envision "God." In this sense, one might infer that human development or the quality of man in this ideological system is seemingly assessed in terms of the proximity to that perfected state of human nature. This human development is thus induced and represented by *Chajusong*.

The difference between political doctrine and theology is that the latter addresses itself to the question of human mortality. A doctrine that has an organized theory concerning "after-this world" distinguishes itself as a religious doctrine from a political ideology. It is in this sense that North Korea's *Juche* has indeed acquired a theological quality.

The term "the eternal truth" has long been used to refer to the ideology but the notion of "eternal life" is relatively new. However, it has become the cornerstone of the theological aspect of the belief system. According to *Juche* theoreticians, a biologically mortal human being will acquire an immortal life when his or her existence is integrated into the society itself. The society unlike the individual does not perish with a finite life span. It endures and outlives individual members of the society. Thus, individual achievement, whether it may be intellectual, material, or political, will evaporate "just like the morning fog" with little meaning and value unless the achievement is integrated into the life of the society itself. Then, what does one have to do to become immortal and where does the eternal life exist? The immortal life is gained when one's individual life is felt by the society and history. In other words, when one makes a lasting contribution to the society, one's presence will not disappear just because his or her biological existence is terminated. Then, essentially, the eternal life is a life that is in the minds of members of the society not only at the present time but also into possible eternity. In this sense, national heroes, martyrs, artists, intellectuals, workers, and even peasants who have made tangible and enduring contributions to the social life itself can attain the eternal life. In this perception of eternal life, there may be several important questions: Are there varying degrees of eternal life depending on the magnitude and significance of the contribution? If one's contribution is not noticed by other members of the society at the time but it can become recognized later in the future, will such a contribution acquire immortality at the time of rediscovery or at the time of the work itself? What if a potential contribution is never recognized due to accidental disappearance of the pertinent record or because of insensitivity or ignorance of people? These questions have never been addressed as of now.

Nevertheless, the notion of eternal life is apparently concrete and realistic to at least the mass public of North Korea. North Koreans are told that the state of human nature is ever imperfect and that one can improve the quality of human nature by cultivating a quality that the image of "God" calls for. Their God is inseparable from human beings. In fact, God is the extension of man in that a perfected man is the realistic perception of the ultimate embodiment of the transcendental being. According to *Juche*, God is caring, compassionate, and above all loving, rather than commanding or controlling; nor does He have a grand blueprint for a predestined human history. They view that human beings have made steady improvement over the long course of history in terms of compassion and loving as being perceived as an admirable quality, although there have been short-term fluctuations. In the early and medieval times, physical coercive capability was the sole determinant of leadership; but as history progressed, humans have found the virtue in living together through love and compassion. What ties the society together is no longer sheer power but persuasion and legitimacy by certain respectful values such as liberty and equality. The scientific mind of humankind has made even more dramatic progress toward perfection. Here, the perfection may never be attained but always pursued and approximated; the imagined perfected stage, however, represents the quality of God, thus He is and grows within and by humankind itself. When I attempted to convey to a leading *Juche* theoretician that Christian God supercedes human achievement in the society, he asked me how can one maintain an unwavering faith in such a God when He is so vague and cannot be explained scientifically. Their God in this sense is experiential because He is inferred from the existential nature of human beings. Their God is also practical and functional because He makes people improve the quality of life. To the extent that an individual becomes perfected as he or she attains "social life" through becoming an integral part of the community, human development is a process of acquiring the eternal life.

There may certainly be numerous logical inconsistencies and philosophical inadequacies but the issue is not in the "objective" persuasiveness of this "theology;" the central issue here is whether or not the masses in North Korea believe in the doctrine. If so, who are the true believers and how many could there be?

Considering the rigorous requirement of ideological preparedness for members of the Korean Workers' Party, it might be reasonable to conclude that most of the party members are true believers, which accounts for 15 percent of the population. Additionally, the young people who have gone through a complete process of ideological education including the membership of the League of Young Socialist Workers could well be true believers. Even a conservative estimate suggests that 20-30 percent of the 22 million people might have developed unwavering faith in *Juche*. They are the fanatic supporters of the Kim leadership as well as the hereditary succession of power.

In short, *Juche* is more than a simple slogan. It may have started as a slogan but in the course of evolution, a system of beliefs and values has evolved into a grand ideological structure. To characterize the ideology as a convenient device with which to justify Kim's power and leadership is an inadequate understanding. It took a long time for *Juche* to be evolved into the present form. There was a time when the ideology was just a political slogan but to understand it only in that restricted sense is far inadequate to account for the recent reality of North Korean politics and policies.

NOTES

1. *Kim Il Sung Works*, Pyongyang, Foreign Languages Publishing House, Vol. 27, p. 491.

2. *Kim Il Sung Encylopaedia* (New Delhi, India: Vishwanath, 1992), p. 85.

3. The Three Revolutions Campaign includes science, technology, and culture. This campaign is believed to have been advanced by Kim Jong Il.

4. *Kim Il Sung Encyclopaedia*, p. 262.

5. *Kim Il Sung Works*, Pyongyang, Foreign Languages Publishing House, Vol. 15, pp. 178-179.

6. *Kim Il Sung Encyclopaedia*, p. 79.

7. Kim Il Sung, *Answers to the Questions Raised by Foreign Journalists*, Pyongyang, Foreign Languages Publishing House, Vol. 3, p. 285.

2

JUCHE AND THE ISSUE OF NATIONAL IDENTITY IN THE DPRK OF THE 1960s

INGEBORG GÖTHEL

Humbolt University, Berlin

The issue of national identity plays a very important role in the life of a great number of people throughout the world. This is especially true of people who have suffered from some form of colonial oppression at some time during their history. Given the history of the Korean people, national identity plays a significant part in their lives.[1]

Koreans from all walks of life—no matter whether they lived in Korea or abroad—put up massive resistance to their Japanese colonial masters, making huge sacrifices in the process. Although their resistance saved their national pride and honor, it did not serve to allow them to expel the colonial rule on their own, a fact that certainly has a considerable impact on their national self-confidence and national identity. Any strengthening of their national self-confidence was therefore just as important for every individual Korean as it was for the nation as a whole.

People in the Democratic People's Republic of Korea (DPRK) had to face extremely complex tasks in all spheres of life after the end of the Korean War. Given the tremendous obstacles faced by the people of the DPRK, including severe starvation, mass homelessness, and abject misery and despair, they could cope with these issues only if they were extremely organized and mobilized. This mobilization, though, could occur only if national confidence and identity were stimulated.

Although the country's towns had been completely destroyed during the war, the leaders of the DPRK generally did a good job of preventing the people from sinking into a severe state of collective melancholy in the postwar years. The country's leaders did indeed succeed in fostering optimism and belief in a better future, thus creating the mood necessary to engage in constructive economic and political activity.

Hundreds of thousands of rank-and-file members of the Korean Workers' Party were working countless unpaid hours on top of their normal duties in order to rebuild their country. It should never be forgotten that the DPRK would not have achieved the great economic success of those years if it had not been for the tremendous sacrifices made by the grassroots party members, efforts and sacrifices which undoubtably had an effect on the rest of the people.

After the war wreaked havoc on the country and brought untold suffering upon all of the citizens, people longed to be given new bearings and a new sense of self-awareness. There was an objective need for the conception of a new ideology to help restore the badly shaken self-confidence of the Korean people and to deepen their sense of national identity.

It should also be noted that beginning in 1946 and continuing through the postwar years there was an enormous degree of social mobility. The proportion of blue and white collar workers rose from 18.7 percent in

1946 to 40.9 percent in 1956.[2] Young men who had been released from the armed forces after the war, and young women from villages and small towns went to the centers of economic activity and reconstruction. In their new social environment, they learned many previously unknown trades and professions.

This new domestic situation, which was heavily influenced by the external situation—with the shooting war over but the Cold War continuing strongly—urgently required the discovery of new ways and means to strengthen people's national identity. The conditions which had emerged were ideal for people to absorb a new ideology which would serve that very cause. In addition, the intellectual and ideological climate of the DPRK was marked by a mixture of patriotism and nationalism.

On December 28, 1955, Kim Il Sung proclaimed the ideals of *Juche* to the public.[3] These ideals were established with the goal of making the country independent, self-confident, and self-sufficient. In proclaiming these ideals Kim Il Sung was satisfying an objective need for the people of Korea given the social and political realities of the day. The question remains, however, whether he proclaimed the ideology early enough.

The need for the pursuit of the aims of *Juche* first arose back in 1945, when Soviet troops had liberated the Koreans from Japanese colonial rule and had, in the process, received a great deal of encouragement from the Koreans. (The question of whether this continued to be true until the Soviet troops were withdrawn from the country in 1948 has yet to be investigated.) In 1945, the Commander-in-chief of the Soviet armed forces issued an appeal saying:

> Citizens of Korea! Remember that your happiness now lies in your own hands. You have been given your own freedom. Everything will depend on you now. The Soviet Army has created all of the conditions the Korean people need to embark on the road of free creative labor. You will now have to be the architects of your own future.[4]

In adopting the *Juche* ideology, the DPRK did what many other ex-colonial countries had done before, or were to do later: It rejected a foreign model. However, it did this more in words than in form and substance. In fact, it continued to rely heavily on many principles of Chinese politics, even though Sino-Korean relations were at a low ebb for a period of time.

Despite all of the public protestations to the contrary, *Juche* was not solely Kim Il Sung's brainchild for it was deeply rooted in ideas that had once been propounded by the scholars of Silhak, the most prominent of whom favored an increased ethnic self-awareness of the Koreans vis-à-vis

Manchurian rule in China, and opposed any kowtowing to China.[5] Although reliance on tradition was commendable, there were many problems involved in sticking to feudal ideals in a situation that was indeed very different from feudalism.

Whether *Juche* would produce more than just an ephermal effect was, in the last analysis, dependent on how well it was adapted to new needs. Only if we investigate the origins of *Juche* will we realize why any *Juche*-based policies were bound to be full of contradictions. We should not forget that what the DPRK had inherited from the Yi Dynasty and from the colonial era provided conditions that clearly favored the establishment of *Juche* in form and effect. The conditions included both the continuation of Confucianist behavior, which allowed for preaching what was called a "well-organized life style,"[6] and an inadequate understanding of democracy.

As a result of both Japanese colonial rule and the post-1945 developments in the country, North Korea had no bourgeois elements and no large number of progressive intellectuals. In addition, the country's young working class, though quite strong in numbers, was weak in terms of self-awareness. Therefore, the country did not contain any forces that could have helped the public at large to develop a proper understanding of democracy.

Above and beyond that, both the Korean War and the continuing Cold War proved to be additional obstacles to the necessary wide-ranging democratization of the country. Rebuilt cities like Pyongyang, Hamhung, and Sinuichu were mainly populated by nonnative inhabitants and therefore did not have the conditions they would objectively have needed to become centers of a democratic movement.

In its efforts to influence people's minds, the Korean Workers' Party was, in the 1960s, giving increasing prominence to the resistance that the Koreans had offered to Japanese colonial rule in the past. While *The History of the Modern Revolutionary Movement in Korea*,[7] published in 1961, spoke of only a few groups of Korean partisans fighting the Japanese, publications appearing later in the 1960s kept referring to the presence of a huge partisan army which, under the leadership of Kim Il Sung, was said to have managed to liberate Korea from its Japanese colonial masters. Despite this fuzzy history, slogans coined during the partisans' struggle and the Korean War were adapted to suit the new needs of mobilizing people to step up industrial and agricultural production.

The cultural tradition of the individual subordinating his own interests and desires to those of the group to which he belongs, coupled with the high degree on personal discipline attained during the Korean war, allowed *Juche*-inspired production campaigns to be run like military offensives. Methods of this kind left little space for resourcefulness and creativity, and proved to be a considerable obstacle to the efforts made by the well-trained engineers, doctors, philologists, and others returning from the European socialist countries. In fact, few of these experts were ever given senior posts.[8]

The use of methods developed in the 1930s in building a future that would lead into the third millennium was destined to cause numerous problems. The application of these methods was a clear manifestation of the educational level, life experience and world outlook of Kim Il Sung and his group, all of whom had first met as partisans. Unfortunately, it never proved possible to overcome the problems caused by the original concepts behind these methods, even though a lot of changes and very skillful adaptations were made in later years.

In April 1956, a mere four months after the *Juche* ideology had been proclaimed, the Third Congress of the Korean Workers' Party decided that the construction of socialism was to begin.[9] The interesting thing was, however, that Kim Il Sung made no mention of *Juche* in his report to the Congress.[10] Nor did the new statutes of the party, which were adopted on April 28, 1956, make any mention of *Juche*. Instead, they stressed that "the Korean Worker's Party relies in its activities on the theory of Marxism-Leninism."[11] It was only much later that *Juche* came to be used for uniting all social forces in the DPRK and mobilizing them to help achieve the chosen strategic goal, the construction of socialism.

Juche was the principle that was to inspire every effort to strengthen the country. It was, in addition, used as an ideology to fight against a substantial section of the country. Although the resultant contradiction was to be resolved by regarding the Republic of Korea as a colony of U.S. imperialism, it actually complicated the intellectual situation in the country. Apart from the unrealistic assessment given of South Korea, many problems were created by the notion of the same ideology being expected to mobilize people to fight colonialism on the one hand, and build socialism, on the other. This double purpose gave rise to even more contradictions, which badly needed resolving in later years.

In carrying out its strategy-forming function, *Juche* played an important role not only in mobilization, but also in domestic and foreign policy formation and decisions. Last but by no means least, it was *Juche* which made the DPRK turn its back on its closest allies, the Soviet Union and China, and permitted the DPRK's exclusion from the conflicts between them. *Juche* even permitted the DPRK to pursue a policy that, in accordance with its interests at any particular time, allowed it to move closer to the Soviet Union on some occasions and to China on others.

In the 1960s, *Juche* was gradually being turned into an immediate guide for political action and a ready set of behavioral standards. For this purpose, political and ideological education was stepped up throughout the country.

The main instrument used to step up this education was the use of radio programming, with community listening arranged in factories, villages, and residential areas all around the country. At the centers of construction, loudspeakers blared propaganda from five in the morning until midnight every day. In addition, everybody from school-age children to the most elderly citizen was obliged to attend political education sessions. These sessions were far more instrumental in providing political education than were the newspapers, which were hardly accessible to common people due to a severe shortage of newsprint.

Political education was considered to be as much a part of life as work and rest. This was demonstrated by the official division of everybody's day into "eight hours of work, eight hours of study, and eight hours of sleep." Since the amount of time allotted to work and study was never to be shortened, only sleep could be cut back. This policy was especially hard on working mothers. Since a constant lack of sleep threatens a person's very existence, many sessions of political education offered a downright grotesque picture, with a speaker talking to an audience fast asleep from exhaustion.[12] In spite of all of this, it was little short of amazing what *Juche* was capable of achieving in the 1960s. It inspired in people a belief in their own strength, gave them a heightened sense of national identity, and filled them with visions of future happiness.

The line adopted by the Fourth Congress of the Korean Workers' Party in 1961—that the living standard of the people in the DPRK should catch up with that of the people in the European socialist countries by the end of the 1961–1967 seven-year economic plan (there was even talk of overtaking Japan)—came to be believed by most people in the country, who were therefore inspired and prepared to work as hard as humanly possible. Making strenuous efforts, they also drew a lot of inspiration from the love that they held for their country. The difficulties arising even in those early years were usually attributed to foreign or external factors.

Juche was proclaimed at a time of and was closely related to considerable factional fighting in the party. In his speech entitled "On Some Questions of Party and State Work at the Present Stage of Socialist Revolution," presented at a plenary meeting of the Central Committee of the Korean Workers' Party on April 4, 1955, Kim Il Sung accused Pak Hon-yong, Yi Sung-yop, Pak Il-u, and others of factionalism in, and hostility toward, the party. Following this accusation, he was badly in need of an ideology which was suited, inter alia, to strengthen the position of the group with which he had surrounded himself.[13] He used *Juche* for this very purpose.

All of this confirms that *Juche* was not only meant to be an ideology used to mobilize the masses and make them discover their own identity in the construction of the country, but also a means of coping with inner-party rivalries, which, although the social conditions of the day were radically different from those in the past, were as fierce and merciless as those in the Korea of the Yi Dynasty.[14]

Preserving Kim Il Sung's power required stepping up the cult of his personality. It was not by any means accidental that *Juche*, which had proven to be a fine means of national identification, was integrated into the Kim Il

Sung ideology which began to be promulgated in the 1970s. Nor was it accidental that there were frequent references to the *Juche* ideals evolved by Comrade Kim Il Sung. A successful attempt was made to take advantage of the strong patriarchal beliefs for the purpose of creating a strong intellectual and emotional bond between Kim Il Sung and every citizen of the country.

Speaking at the Fifth Congress of the Korean Workers' Party in 1970 and very much in line with the spirit of the day, the Deputy Prime Minister of the DPRK, Pak Sung-chol, said, "for all members of our party and for our entire people, there can be no greater honor than to live and fight under the wise leadership of our beloved leader Kim Il Sung, the father of *Juche*. And there can be no greater pride than to have been born in the country that is the home of heroic *Juche*."[15]

Since any personality cult necessarily has a cumulative effect requiring increasing doses of propaganda, it was not enough for *Rodong sinmun*, the party's major newspaper, to insist that "people should be ever better equipped with Comrade Kim Il Sung's revolutionary ideas."[16] The paper went as far to say that "the coherent ideological system of the party must take ever deeper root in the entire party and entire society; it is a system that does not recognize any ideas but the revolutionary thoughts put forward by Comrade Kim Il Sung."[17]

The constant appeals for *Juche* to be spread ever more widely may have been an indication that the implementation of *Juche* in all spheres of social life in the DPRK ran into a large number of difficulties. In attempting to answer the frequent question about the reasons and conditions for the Kim Il Sung personality cult, one should never forget that the version of Marxism adopted in the DPRK was highly simplistic, with the adoption often being rather mechanical.

Like the Communist Party of Korea of the 1920s, the Korean Workers' Party got to know Marxism mainly through its acquaintance with Leninism. Although the North Koreans received Korean translations of works by Marx and Engels from the Soviet Union after 1945, many of them did not have a sufficient level of education to fully understand the works. Although early party statements and Article Four of the DPRK's 1972 Constitution said that *Juche* was a "creative application of Marxism-Leninism to the conditions of our country," this claim was far from true.

Juche overstates the importance of social consciousness and its activating role to the extent that it renders the temporal, historico-genetic and content-related primacy of matter practically meaningless. The question remains to what degree *Juche* ever sought to attain any of the important goals of Marxism at all, and whether it ever really tried to establish the conditions for an "association in which the free development of everybody individually is a condition for the free development of everybody together."[18]

Another factor encouraging the development of a personality cult was the patriarchal structure of the country's society. Although many people, especially young people, were hardly aware of the Confucianist traditions in their own actions and thoughts, several meetings of the Central Committee of the Party called for a struggle to be fought against the observance of negative Confucianist standards. This was especially ironic because the Korean Workers' Party actually managed to enforce many of its measures only because of the presence of traditional structures and modes of thinking which were the result of both the rigid application of Confucianist ideas during the Yi Dynasty and the oppression and severe discipline of the colonial era.

Even the Kim Il Sung personality cult itself is strongly reminiscent of Confucianist ideas. Since Confucianism placed excessive emphasis on both the ruler in society and the father in the family, Kim Il Sung was easily assigned the status of "Father of the Nation," a phrase first mentioned in a song written about him in 1967. The arrangement to which the song referred, of the working people as sons and daughters of Kim Il Sung, once again verifies the transfer of the hierarchical Neo-Confucian structure of the family onto the entire society. It reemphasized that absolute obedience and loyal humility toward father Kim Il Sung must be achieved just as to the father of the traditional Korean family. In this context, it is drummed into the heads of the citizens of the DPRK that they must be completely indebted to Kim Il Sung for any of their meaningful achievements in the building of the country. On April 16, 1967, *Rodong sinmun* printed, "You, our leader, you have given all brothers, all things, unselfish care and help. Because of you, we are able to free the Fatherland again."

Throughout society, despite constant protests, the traditional mentality persisted. It reached the ruling group of Kim Il Sung, which the Confucianist, or more precisely the Neo-Confucianist, influenced social psyches of the society to draw them into their politics and to aid in the success of the party. Kim Il Sung's group skillfully tied the declared Neo-Confucianism with the well-being of future generations. One of the commonly used policies of the time called for a struggle for the well-being of future generations and to pass to them a unified Korea. However, the heroic tasks of the citizens of the DPRK did not bring about the unification of Korea since they were not accompanied by analogous politics, not even in the 1970s when the ideas of coexistence and detente between East and West began to be widely accepted.

Manismus (cult of the ancestors) was given an important role in Neo-Confucianism. The strength with which the group of Kim Il Sung incorporated the active *Manismus* within the society was evidenced in the expansion of *Manismus* in the Kim family. Mangjondae, the birthplace of the "highly distinguished and loved leader," is described as the cradle of the Korean revolution, despite the fact that no revolutionary activity ever occurred in this tiny town near Pyongyang. During pilgrimages to this town, visitors view not only the birthplace of Kim Il Sung, but also bow to the burial mounds of his parents and grandparents who were laid to rest there in the 1950s. More recent historical accounts were revised to give Kim's parents, grandparents, and other relatives a leading role in the revolution, thereby creating a dynasty of revolutionaries which experienced its golden age in the 1970s with the election of the son of Kim Jong Il through the followers of Kim Il Sung.

In connection with the development of *Manismus* and the legitimation of the power of Kim Il Sung through *Manismus*, Kim Il Sung's group managed, in the summer of 1967, to create a "holy mother of the race," Kan Ban-sok, who willingly died in her thirties and declared her the Mother of Korea. The refrain of a song written about her brings simultaneous ignorance and false judgment of the situation in South Korea expressed as, "Oh Mother of the Homeland, Kang Bang-sok. You shine like a star in the hearts of all 40 million Koreans." Neo-Confucianism means that situations orient themselves around norms, but norms don't orient themselves around conditions. This belief does not imply a search for the absolute: its highest goal is much more so the fixation of social norms and ethical worth and in connection with this, the conceptualization of a model of humanity. This model of humanity, conceptualized by the DPRK asserts that all people have become loyal sons and daughters of Marshall Kim Il Sung.

Even the cult form of Kim Il Sung bears strong similarities to the worship of Confucius. On the occasion of the reestablishment of the influence of Confucius, a Ming ruler released an appeal in 1468 that is accepted without question. It states, "Confucius made the sky into a bell. If the sky hadn't borne Confucius then how would later generations have learned the lessons of Scha, Schun, Ju, Tang Wen and Wu?" Giving credit for the salvation of an entire culture to one person was carried from Confucius to Kim Il Sung. A 1962 party brochure asked, "Who, if not Comrade Kim Il Sung, would have been able to save and to rally to war and victory a homeland during its most terrible situation and a people in their darkest period of Japanese control." As in Confucianism, the Kim Il Sung ideology asserts the primacy of morals. The means of their acquisition is through the influence of the rhetoric of the Great Teacher of the nation, Kim Il Sung. As in the times of the Yi Dynasty the students were urged to memorize their texts. This did not involve only outstanding policies and quotes, but also entire speeches. On December 4, 1970, *Rodong sinmun* wrote that the leaders of the Union of Socialist Workers of Korea agreed that the "members of youth groups would memorize the historical lecture of Marshal Kim Il Sung on the day of the party."

Despite its often wholly embarrassing manifestations, the Kim Il Sung personality cult was closely related to national identity. The horrifying years of the Korean war, the postwar period with its extremely low standard of living, and the visible success achieved in the 1960s allowed strong links to be forged between national identity and the Kim Il Sung personality cult. Much of this can be attributed to a constantly growing propaganda campaign which constantly reiterated that the country's success was solely due to Kim Il Sung's art of leadership. He was a figure with whom people were prepared to identify, as was obvious in everyday life.

In the eyes of quite a few North Koreans, Kim Il Sung symbolized the country's economic progress. Many people shared in this progress in moving from huts to modern apartments and being able to send their children to university without spending a cent. Everybody believed that the international recognition that was extended to their "revered and beloved leader" was tantamount to international appreciation of their own efforts, an appreciation that was expressed again and again in speeches made by foreign politicians and statesmen visiting the DPRK.

On the other hand, the personality cult had a deleterious effect on national identity, since national identity is, in the long run, impossible to maintain without a consolidation of everybody's own identity and dignity, something which the personality cult serves to undermine. The Kim Il Sung personality cult also prevented ordinary people from becoming self-confident, especially since traditional views continued to be considered valid. Value judgments of the kind first accepted during the Yi Dynasty and associating personal identity closely with group identity forced the individual out of the limelight of public attention.[19] It was the continuing nondevelopment of the individual's personality that allowed *Rodong sinmun* to say in a poem about Kim Il Sung, in complete disregard of all of the realities that everybody confronted day to day, "your hands cleared the rubble of the war that the U.S. imperialists had instigated against our brilliant work of construction; and from this grew countless steel works, mechanical engineering plants, cooperative farms, schools, hospitals and theaters."[20] This tradition of the individual subordinating his interests to those of a group, combined with the aftermath of the war, allowed mass mobilization under the *Juche* banner to acquire a distinct military touch.

A strong sense of national identity presupposes a progress-oriented preservation of tradition. An extremely important element of any tradition is religion. Religion was not, however, permitted to play its proper role in the process of establishing and strengthening national identity. Instead, religion was dismissed as either pro-American (as in the case of Christianity) or medieval (as in the case of Buddhism). It was therefore hardly surprising that a kind of surrogate religion had to be found. This surrogate religion took the form of the Kim Il Sung personality cult from 1967 on. This was highlighted in *Rodong sinmun* where it was written, "You, our leader, you make flowers grow on desert islands and in the mountains, where even birds are scared to fly."[21]

After political independence had been won, it was no longer possible to define national identity as primarily boiling down to a rejection of foreign rule, as had been the case during the struggle against Japanese colonialism. As a result of the new political situation, the United States came to be considered the principle enemy of national identity, as was reflected in the statement, "we have a 5000 year history; and long before the United States of America had appeared on the scene, our people had created a brilliant nation."[22]

After the end of Japanese colonial rule, and especially after the end of the Korean War, North Korea began to look for a historical awareness of its own. Like in the case of other ex-colonial peoples, an attempt was made in North Korea to discover ways of deriving natural identity from history. National identity requires a certain amount of knowledge of, and a lot of pride in, national history. A large number of historians did exemplary work, investigating many aspects of Korean history and thus contributing to the strengthening of national identity. This is especially true of the research done into the affairs of the Kokuryo state.

Objectively, *Juche* had to give people new bearings so that what had not been accomplished in the colonial era could be accomplished now. However, since historians had concentrated their attention on the uprisings and other armed struggles of the Korean people, the Korean people's defense against foreign invaders and first and foremost the struggle waged by the partisans, they had to disregard many other research opportunities which presented themselves as a result of their general investigations into Korean history.

In the final analysis, *Juche*-based historical research, although producing some fine results, did not manage to deal with everything great and memorable in Korean history and, most importantly, ignored achievements made by bourgeois figures in the past. Historians were constantly forced to rewrite history, a job that not only used up much of their energy, but one that also forced them to play a less important role than they might otherwise have played in consolidating national identity.

Official propaganda presented a picture of history that was quite obviously suited to achieve a false intensification of national identity by exaggerating the importance of, and even creating, historical events in order to make certain developments appear more significant than they actually were. An example of this was when *Rodong sinmun* distorted historical facts and wrote, "Even in the age of primitive man, our ancestors had the most advanced culture and technology in the Far East, and exerted a not at all negligible influence on their neighboring countries."[23]

Yet, the Korean people are in no need of having their history aggrandized or embellished; for their history is, by any standards, great and long, and produced an independent culture of a very high standard. Judgments like those by *Rodong sinmun* did not in any way help raise the country's reputation abroad, something necessary for the encouragement of national identity. The paper wrote, "The appearance of Kim Il Sung, our people's true hero, was the best thing ever to happen in Korea's long and difficult 5000 year history."[24]

From the very beginning *Juche* proved to be valuable as an ideology capable of mobilizing people to contribute to the economic construction of the country, especially when the ideology began to materialize in the shape of a Chollima movement, launched in 1958.[25] Yet it became clear as early as the early 1960s that this would not be enough for running the economy successfully. For that reason, Kim Il Sung proclaimed the Chongsan-ri method for agriculture and the Taean method for industry.

The Party committees, whose members included not only Party officials, but also engineers, technical experts, and skilled workers, were put in charge of factories everywhere. But workers did not, of course, become good foremen by being declared so under the Taean method. This and many other factors, including a considerable increase in military expenditures in accordance with the 1962 economic policy calling for a parallel development of the economy and national defense, delayed the fulfillment of the 1961–1967 seven-year economic plan until 1970.

Nor should it be overlooked that the self-sufficient economy called for under *Juche* was beset by numerous problems. The establishment of a self-sufficient economy, especially in a small country and at a time when the global division of labor was deepening more than ever, was bound to sever the DPRK's links with the outside world and have far-reaching economic consequences.

Finally, the question arises whether the political socialization that was common in *Juche* and was not fully developed until the 1970s and 1980s was capable of providing the country with a new political culture required for carrying out urgently needed reforms. All foreign scholars working in the DPRK consider it a truism to say that many of the issues that they set out to clarify remain unclear even after they have stayed in the country for many years. Many issues remain unclear to an outsider even if he or she visits a large number of factories in all parts of the country and has numerous contacts with old friends and other members of the country's population. Yet, there is one thing that is very easy to recognize and deserves special emphasis and appreciation: The people have very close emotional ties with their country, ties which have been built through making a lot of sacrifices. And they consider their country to be the DPRK, and display justifiable pride in their achievements. If this is ignored when the two Korean states move closer together in the future, then the dignity of these people will be trampled underfoot and new festering wounds which will take generations to heal will be inflicted.

NOTES

1. Bibliographies show that the issue of national identity is at present being discussed more than ever.

2. *The Korean Central Yearbook*, Pyongyang: Foreign Language Publishing House, 1961.

3. Kim Il Sung, *Selected Writings*, Pyongyang: Foreign Language Publishing House, Vol. 4, 1960, Pyongyang, pp. 325–354.

4. Quoted from *History of Korea*, Vol. 2, Moscow, 1974, p. 162.

5. Kang Man-Kil, *Modern History of Korea*, Seoul, 1985, p. 55.

6. *Rodong sinmun*, November 3, 1960.

7. *Choson Gundae Hyongmong Undong Sa*, Pyongyang, 1961, p. 291.

8. Since I lived among North Korean students in a students' hostel in Leipzig for eight years, I know this problem only too well. Lack of space in this paper, however, does not permit detailed discussion.

9. Documents and materials of the Third Congress of the Korean Workers' Party (in Russian), Pyongyang, 1956.

10. Ibid, pp. 5–138.

11. Ibid., p. 397.

12. I have often witnessed such depressing scenes myself.

13. R.A. Scalapino and Jun-Yop Kim, eds., *North Korea Today: Strategic and Domestic Issues*. Berkeley, Calif., 1983, p. 233.

14. I. Göthel, *Geschichte Koreas (History of Korea)*, Berlin, 1978, p. 53.

15. *Rodong sinmun*, November 13, 1970.

16. *Rodong sinmun*, July 8, 1968.

17. *Rodong sinmun*, September 8, 1968.

18. Marx and Engels, *Werks*, Vol. 4. Berlin, 1968, p. 48.

19. *Choson Munhwa sa*, Pyongyang, 1977, p. 368.

20. *Rodong sinmun*, April 16, 1976.

21. Ibid.

22. *Ministeium fur Auswartige Angelegenheiten*, Archives, Berlin, Akte (Dossier) 1107, p. 67.

23. *Rodong sinmun*, April 16, 1976.

24. Ibid.

25. This production contest movement was launched at the Kangson Steel Works in 1958 and got its name from a fictional horse which, according to legend, was capable of making jumps of 1000 li (250 km).

3

EDUCATIONAL REFORMS

JIANGCHENG HE

Peking University, Beijing

REFORM IN THE SCHOOL SYSTEM

Before World War II, education in North Korea was very backward as a consequence of the obscurantist policy pursued by the Japanese colonialists. At the time of the proclamation of Korea's independence, there were only 1,000 primary schools, 50 junior middle schools, and three secondary vocational or specialized schools in the northern half of the Korean peninsula. There were no senior middle schools, let alone colleges or universities (The only university was located in Seoul). Sixty-five percent of school-age children were denied access to school education. Only a small fraction of the indigenous population were well educated, and the number of teachers of Korean descent was simply negligible.

During the last fifty years following independence, North Korea has implemented a succession of educational reforms, which culminated in the creation of a new education system centered on eleven-year universal compulsory education. The arduous efforts have proved highly rewarding. Nowadays, an average Korean citizen has a secondary school education. The 1988 statistics indicate that the number of North Korea's schools has increased by leaps and bounds over the decades. That year it boasted 4,700 primary schools, 4,400 middle schools, 230 colleges (the latest number is 270), 570 polytechnical or vocational schools, and 60,000 kindergartens.

Since the Communist takeover, North Korea has instituted a total of four major educational reforms. The reforms consisted of an overhaul of not only the structure but also the curricula of the school system. The year of 1946 witnessed the implementation of the first reform, which led to the establishment of the first independent education system in North Korean history. The second reform was carried out in 1959, resulting in the abolition of senior middle schools and secondary vocational or specialized schools, the expansion of technical schools, and the creation of college-level technical schools. The third reform, implemented in 1967, focused on the large-scale enforcement of nine-year compulsory technical education on an experimental basis. The quest for an ideal education system reached its height with the fourth reform, which paved the way for the introduction of the current eleven-year compulsory education system.

The ensuing sections will first address themselves to a discussion and evaluation of the four major reforms in North Korea's education system and then will proceed to an in-depth investigation of the contents and methods of education in North Korea.

THE REFORM OF 1946

On December 18, 1946, North Korea's Provisional People's Committee promulgated the "Decision Concerning the Education System in Korea," which authorized the establishment of a "people's democratic educational system," as well as the abolition of the fascist education system "imposed by the Japanese militarists to perpetuate the enslavement of the Korean people." The reform led to the creation of a multitrack school system. This system had the following components:

- *General Schools*: These schools included one-year kindergartens for children age six or older as preschool education; one-year academies for children age seven in preparation for attendance at people's schools (primary schools), four-year people's schools, three-year junior middle schools, and three-year senior middle schools.
- *Secondary Technical Schools*: Among these technical schools were three-year primary technical schools, which enrolled primary school graduates and prepared them for employment as skilled workers, and three- or four-year secondary vocational schools, which recruited junior middle school graduates and trained them as intermediate-level technicians.
- *Normal Schools*: This category included three-year normal schools in which eligible junior middle graduates would complete an intensive course in pedagogy and qualify themselves for careers as elementary school teachers; two-year teachers universities which offered training courses for senior school graduates and provided them with credentials as secondary school teachers.
- *Higher Education*: The three components of this system were five-year comprehensive or polytechnical universities, four- or five-year professional or specialized colleges or universities, and three-year graduate schools.
- *In-Service Training*: Under this designation were three-year spare-time junior middle schools and senior middle schools, three-year spare-time junior technical colleges and three- or four-year spare-time secondary vocational schools.

Later, the above-mentioned system underwent modifications and alterations. Starting from September 1, 1947, one-year academies in preparation for the people's schools were abolished and the duration of education in people's schools (primary schools) was extended to five years with students admitted at age seven. In July 1953, the length of attendance at the people's schools reverted to four years. At the same time, the required residency at some vocational schools was lengthened from three years to three and half up to four years. Moreover, the regime legislated for the institution of four-year compulsory primary education, effective August 1956, followed by that of universal free compulsory education, effective April 1959.

THE REFORM OF 1959

1959 was a hectic year in which a nationwide economic thrust metaphorically known as the Chollima Movement[1] was launched in North Korea and soon gained much momentum. As the movement was in full swing, that year registered an unprecedented high rate in economic growth. Rapid growth stimulated the demands in various economic sectors for well-qualified technical personnel. During that period, only a small fraction of senior middle school graduates were able to go on to higher education, while the majority of them would directly join the labor force. Those who sought employment after graduation were mostly ill-prepared for ready assimilation by industries since they were plagued by a deficiency in technical skills and practical experiences. These graduates had almost insuperable difficulty coping with the intricacies of modern science and technology. In this connection, in October 1959, at the behest of the Party, the sixth session of the Second Supreme People's Assembly issued the "Decree Concerning the Reorganization of the People's Education System," thus ushering in the second stage of educational reform. The reform resulted in the abrogation of senior middle schools and their replacement by secondary and tertiary technical institutions. A concomitant of the reform was a redefinition of the Party's educational policy. The theme which resonated throughout this educational reform was the integration of education with productive labor and general education with technical training. The regime made it mandatory for schools at all levels to abide by this principle underlying the new educational policy. The reform also laid emphasis upon the continuity and systemization at different levels.

The centerpiece of this educational reform was an expansion of two-year technical schools, accompanied by the suspension of senior middle schools and secondary vocational schools. The syllabi of the dual-level technical schools provided that time of instruction be evenly divided between the core (or general) curricula and technical curricula (including practices in production). By the time of graduation the students would have acquired a solid foundation in general fields equivalent to that of senior middle school graduates while outperforming their secondary technical school counterparts in specified technical fields. The innovations which emerged in this reform can be summed up as follows:

- *General Schools*: Children would be admitted to kindergarten at age three and to primary school at age seven. The length of attendance would be four years for primary school, three years for middle school, two years for technical school and senior institute of technology, four years for college and university (five years for science and technology and six years for medical school), four years for graduate school, and two years for the doctoral program.

- *Normal Schools*: Teachers' universities would accept technical school graduates to the three- or four-year programs oriented toward training kindergarten, primary, and secondary school teachers. Graduates from senior institutes of technology were eligible for admission to normal universities, where the residency requirement was four to six years. The students would complete an intensive study program designed to qualify them for employment as faculty members in technical schools and senior institutes of technology.
- *In-Service Education*: This system incorporated two-year workers' schools, three-year workers' middle schools, two-year technical schools and four- to six-year colleges affiliated with industrial plants. In addition, senior institutes of technology and regular full-time colleges and universities offered in-service training in evening or correspondence schools attached to them.

THE REFORM OF 1967

In November 1966, the sixth session of North Korea's Third Supreme People's Assembly adopted a resolution authorizing the introduction of nine-year compulsory technical education, effective April 1, 1967. The motivation behind this reform was the realization that students' premature adoption of specializations in accordance with the educational laws enacted during the previous reforms militated against their chances of receiving a complete general education or acquiring technical and practical skills. In other words, this type of education was flawed by its failure to provide the younger generation with a technical and cultural equipment to cope with the demands of the nation's modernization drive. Practical considerations were also an important element of the calculus of the advocates of reform. At that time the legal age for employment was seventeen, but most students were under seventeen when they graduated from technical school. This situation put them in limbo because they could neither seek employment nor pursue further studies. To redress the problems of the existing system, the North Korean government decided to embark on another round of educational reform. It led to the creation of a nine-year compulsory education system. Below is an overview of the overhauled education system:

First, there was a merger of two-year technical schools and three-year middle schools into five-year middle schools. A combination of four years of primary education and five years of secondary education constituted the so-called nine-year compulsory education available to all school-age students. This innovation was the key element of the educational reform of 1967.

The required residency at senior institutes of technology was lengthened from two years to three or four years. The objective of this change was to enhance the quality of performance of prospective intermediate-level technicians.

The newly created senior middle schools would recruit five-year middle school graduates and the gifted among their students would proceed directly to higher learning upon graduation.

Another type of school which emerged during this reform were three-year senior normal schools which focused on the enrollment of five-year middle school graduates and the training of kindergarten teachers. At teachers' university, which was geared to the needs for training primary school teachers, four years instead of three years of academic work was required of students for graduation. Four- or five-year normal colleges and universities remained unaffected but they were now entrusted with the task of training middle school as well as senior technical school and college teachers.

Technical and vocational schools were a new addition to the system, dedicated to enrolling middle school graduates and training them as skilled workers.

A moratorium was put on education in factory-affiliated technical schools. In lieu of these schools, senior institutes of technology and the in-service training and correspondence courses they offered provided three- to four-year programs of study.

The reinstatement of senior middle schools, technical schools, and secondary normal and vocational schools was the uppermost priority on the agenda of the architects of the educational reform of 1967. But these reincarnated schools differed from their predecessors in that they now all operated on the principle of integrating academic work with productive labor though with emphasis on different types of education. The emphasis of five-year middle schools was on general education, while secondary professional schools attached more importance to specialized technical training. In short, the reform of 1967 revolved around the integration of education with productive labor as well as of general education with basic technical training.

THE CURRENT EDUCATION SYSTEM

In April 1973, the second session of North Korea's Fifth Supreme People's Assembly legislated for another reform of the education system through the issuance of the "Decree Regarding the Introduction of Ten-Year Compulsory Senior Middle School Education and One-Year Compulsory Preschool Education." The major stipulation of the Decree was the authorization of the establishment during the 1972–1973 and 1976–1977 academic years of a system of eleven-year compulsory education for citizens age six to sixteen.

This reform was oriented toward providing secondary education for all citizens in the form of compulsory education. As an integral part of the reform, additional school time was allocated for instruction in political ideology and Marxist orthodoxy. In the meanwhile, priority was given to such natural science courses as mathematics, physics, and chemistry and foreign languages. This reform brought into existence the current school system which has since remained in place and unchanged in North Korea. The following section will be devoted to a description of this system.

General Education

It includes two years of kindergarten, which is divided into junior and senior classes, with the senior class for children age five serving the purpose of one-year preschool education. Children age six will be admitted to four-year primary schools. Attendance at middle schools will last six years, with the first four years in junior middle school and the last two years in senior middle school. A student will remain in school for a total of eleven years beginning with preschool academy up until graduation from senior middle school.

Higher Education

Two types of schools, universities and higher professional or specialized colleges, fall under the category of institutions of higher learning. With the exception of teachers' universities which offer a three-year study program, all universities require four to five years of residency. At the moment, the required length of attendance for higher professional or specialized colleges is three years, that for graduate schools three to four years, and that for doctoral programs two years. These institutions basically target for recruitment senior middle school graduates who are just out of school or as an alternative have experiences in productive labor, as well as demobilized or honorably discharged military personnel. Upon completion of their degree programs all college graduates will receive job assignments from the government. It is illegal and impossible for anyone to seek employment on his or her own.

Normal Education

Normal schools and colleges include three-year teachers' universities for training kindergarten and primary school teachers, and four- to five-year normal universities for training middle school teachers. In addition, North Korea has set up normal universities of technology and other institutes of technology for similar educational purposes.

Adult Education

The North Koreans refer to adult education as part-work and part-study training. At the present moment in North Korea there are three-year senior workers' schools, three-year factory-affiliated higher professional or specialized colleges and evening and correspondence schools appended to them, four- to five-year factory-, farm-, or fishery-affiliated universities, as well as evening and correspondence schools affiliated with regular full-time universities. Students are concurrently employees with industrial firms and agricultural or fishing establishments. Usually, academic pursuit does not exempt them from their routine duties in their work units. In other words, they have to study while working. Upon completion of their degree programs they will continue to work for their original employers and no transfer of work units will take place. Other than these schools, there are special schools for workshop managers and work team leaders and factory-affiliated vocational or technical schools.

THE CONTENTS AND METHODS
OF SOCIALIST EDUCATION

The motto of education in North Korea is that "Socialist education should inculcate in the young people revolutionary and working-class ideals and foster a generation of Communist new men who are developed in an all-around way—morally, intellectually, and physically. The curricula of socialist schools should be steeped in a revolutionary spirit so as to ensure their being scientific and realistic."[2]

Although the Communist regime in North Korea reaffirmed on various occasions its commitment to all-around development of students as an objective of socialist education, in practice it favors an educational policy ensuring the prevalence of ideological indoctrination over intellectual and physical development. It has unabashedly and unequivocally declared that "political and ideological education should occupy the most important place in socialist education."[3] In the North Korean political parlance, moral education is a synonym and euphemism for political indoctrination.

When it comes to the relationship among moral, intellectual, and physical education, the North Korean Communist leaders insist that to turn students into revolutionaries espousing a Communist ideology and observing a new revolutionary code of ethics is contingent on success in political and ideological indoctrination. They are convinced that such indoctrination is also of pivotal importance to the effort to induce them to fully develop their intellectual and physical potentials.

Even a cursory investigation of education in North Korea reveals that its leaders' words are really matched by their deeds. Both in rhetoric and practice they make a point of giving primacy to political education and ideological indoctrination. Below is a brief description of the contents and methods of North Korea's moral, intellectual, and physical education.

POLITICAL AND IDEOLOGICAL EDUCATION

The North Korean Communist regime is convinced that "the building of socialism and communism in the wake of the establishment of the socialist system entails continuous revolution. For this reason, it is imperative for us to strive for the capture of the Communist ideological and materialistic fortresses."[4] "Of the two tasks confronting us, the capture of the ideological fortress is the more important."[5]

In its opinion, the contemporary young men and young women have not experienced the trials and tribulations of their forefathers in old society and have not suffered from class exploitation and foreign oppression. Moreover, unlike veteran revolutionaries, they have not been baptized in the revolutionary wars. Therefore, it is indispensable for them to receive an intensive political education. The North Koreans have over the decades accumulated extensive experiences, and have synthesized them into a complete and effective teaching methodology.

The Contents of Political and Ideological Education

Education in the Juche *Idea:* The North Koreans maintain that "the most important approach to political and ideological education is to arm students steadfastly with the *Juche* idea,"[6] "because only by arming themselves with the *Juche* idea can students become genuine masters of themselves and independent and talented revolutionaries in both revolution and construction."[7]

To instill the *Juche* idea in students, the North Koreans emphasize education in the Party policies and the revolutionary tradition. Such education is intended to foster loyalty to the leaders and the Korean Workers' Party and to transform the students into faithful revolutionary fighters who will selflessly and unconditionally carry out the Party line and Party policies.

Revolutionary and Communist Education: North Korea's revolutionary education and communist education programs have many dimensions. They encompass education in such areas as the Communist credo, revolutionary optimism, patriotism, internationalism, observance of socialist discipline and laws, Communist morality, and socialist lifestyle.

The Methods of Political and Ideological Education

A positive approach figures prominently in political and ideological education. It puts a premium on persuasion with patience, elicitation, self-redemption, and voluntarism.

The North Koreans believe that only when the Communist ideology is sensed and possessed by the students can it become their firm faith. Therefore, ideological education should adopt a way of explanation and persuasion instead of coercion and imposition. To those who have backward thoughts and other shortcomings, patient persuasion is believed to be of particular necessity to let them realize and correct their mistakes.

Positive education through persuasion is a fundamental approach to ideological education in North Korea. As the young people are sensitive to new phenomena, have a high sense of justice, and are ready to emulate exemplary personalities, positive examples may have profound repercussions upon, and strong appeals to, the younger generation. Usually, the young people are first called upon to learn from the revolutionary martyrs who laid down their lives during the Anti-Japanese War. Then they will be urged to follow the shining examples of outstanding students among their peers.

Ways and Forms of Political and Ideological Education

Instruction in Politics: The North Korean Communist regime devotes much attention to political education through instruction in political courses as an integral part of school curricula. Schools of different types and levels offer courses in political education which are varied in subject matter and contents. These courses are meticulously designed and carefully tailored to the needs of students of different age groups and different levels of learning ability. In primary schools, 8.8 percent of the time of instruction is allotted to instruction in politics. In secondary schools 10 percent is portioned out for this purpose. In colleges and universities, the allotted time increases to 22 percent.

Primary schools (People's Schools) used to offer such political courses as The Childhood and Youth of Kim Il Sung, and Kim Il Sung's Revolutionary Activities and Communist Ethics, which take up about 10.8 percent of the total time of instruction. Since the new academic year of 1985, the course Kim Il Sung's Revolutionary Activities and Communist Ethics has been dropped and replaced by another course entitled The Childhood and Youth of Kim Jong Il. After this change political courses account for 8.8 percent of the time.

Political courses in middle school originally included Policy of the Korean Workers' Party, The Revolutionary Activities of Kim Il Sung, A History of Kim Il Sung's Revolution, and Communist Ethics, to which 9.8 percent of the total time of instruction was devoted. Since the new academic year of 1985, the course Communist Ethics has been canceled and replaced by the course Kim Jong Il's Revolutionary Activities and Their History. To these courses about 10.2 percent of the time is allotted.

Institutions of higher learning provide instruction in such courses as Works of Kim Il Sung, Works of Kim Jong Il, A History of Kim Il Sung's Revolutionary Activities, Philosophy, Political Economy, and The Current Policies of the Workers' Party. There are variations among different types of schools in the allocation of time for political courses. On average 20 percent of the time is set aside for them.

Membership and Activities in Political Organizations: A number of political organizations operate among children and youths of various age groups. Among them are the Young Pioneers in primary schools, the Socialist Labor Youth League in middle schools and colleges, and the Workers' Party exclusively in colleges. At regular intervals these political organizations sponsor or preside over extracurricular activities such as criticism and self-criticism, ideological indoctrination sessions, and lectures on organizational discipline. The North Koreans are convinced of the efficacy of students' membership in political organizations and participation in extracurricular activities sponsored by them in fostering revolutionary successors.

Social Activities: Academic institutions at all levels in North Korea often make arrangements for students to take part in off-campus social activities. Students could avail themselves of these social opportunities to contribute to the effort to give publicity to the Party policy and at the same time to acquire field experiences and additional training. The North Korean Communist authorities subscribe to the belief that such practical experiences are conducive to the elimination of a divorce of theory from practice as they enable students to apply their book learning to real life. Social activities cover a wide range of topics and areas. At the behest of the school authorities, students go to factories, mines, farms, and neighborhoods to explain and publicize the government policy or to disseminate scientific, technological, and hygienic information among the populace. In addition, students frequently launch "Good People" and "Good Deeds" campaigns on an extensive basis, in which they will vie with each other in performing laudable feats so as to win public recognition. For example, they will contribute to the reforestation effort by planting trees in the so-called Young Pioneer forests or Socialist Youth Labor League forests or by volunteering services to construction sites or agricultural farms.

   Positive Education in Other Forms: North Korea boasts a multitude of public facilities scattered across the land. The notable among them are the Young Pioneers' Palaces, the Young Students' Clubs, the Pioneers' Summer Camps, and public libraries. In these facilities the Communist authorities sponsor and organize a variety of activities with more or less relevance for political indoctrination, including reports on current affairs, scientific seminars, festival report meetings, revolutionary story-telling sessions, theatrical performances and art exhibitions. The schools also encourage students to see movies on revolutionary themes, visit industrial and agricultural establishments, and tour revolutionary and historic sites and scenic spots. In short, the regime explores all possible avenues for politically socializing the younger generation.

Organizational Guarantees of Political and Ideological Education

North Korea has a contingent of professionals specializing in ideological work. This group assembles in its midst instructors in political courses, teachers in charge of classes, Young Pioneers' counselors, and instructors of the Socialist Labor Youth League. These professionalized ideological workers are faithful and reliable executors of the Party policy and the mainstay of political indoctrination.

   The North Korean Communist leaders are also convinced that it is necessary to enlist the support and assistance of other segments of the population in the political socialization effort. In their opinion, schools, society, and families should work in concert with each other so as to achieve optimum results in the indoctrination process. Members of the trinity should strive to strengthen their mutual relationships, and to inform and help each other. The primary channel for communication is the contacts between schools and parents. Interactions between them take the forms of teachers' visit to the family, teacher-parent meetings, and two-way correspondence.

EDUCATION IN SCIENCE AND TECHNOLOGY

Education in science and technology is oriented toward imparting general and specialized knowledge. The North Koreans adhere to the belief that general knowledge is an asset which each and every member of the socialist society should possess. Eleven-year compulsory education just serves the purpose of acquainting students with the general facts, concepts, and principles embodied in a systematic secondary education. Specialized education represents an expansion and upgrading of secondary education and should be offered at the stage of higher learning.

As course offerings and curricula vary widely among institutions of higher learning, it does not behoove us to dwell on them as an exhaustive examination of their educational programs is beyond us. Therefore, we will concentrate on general education in this study.

The Contents of Education in Science and Technology

Primary school programs generally encompass three types of courses. Political courses such as Kim Il Sung's Childhood and Youth take up 8.8 percent of the total time of instruction. General knowledge courses include the Korean language, foreign languages, mathematics, and nature, accounting for 64.8 percent. Of all these courses, the Korean language and mathematics receive the greatest attention, and the time allotted for the two courses combined is 57.2 percent of the total. Technical skill courses include physical education, music, and fine arts and handicraft, and account for 26.4 percent of the time. At the fourth grade primary school students are required to study a foreign languages; but no more than a one-hour session a week is devoted to this study. Students will satisfy the requirements of the course with a mastery of only 200 to 250 words and the simplest sentence patterns. A course like that basically serves as a preparation for more advanced studies in foreign languages in middle school.

Political courses, including those in adulation of Kim Senior and Kim Junior and those expounding the Party line and policy, account for 10 percent of the total time of instruction. General knowledge courses, such as the Korean language and literature, Chinese, foreign languages, history, geography, mathematics, physics, chemistry, and biology, take up 74 percent of the time. Skill courses are offered in such areas as physical education, music, and fine arts and account for 7 to 8 percent of the time.

The middle school program of study also includes instruction in technical skills which prepare students for employment after graduation. Each student is expected to acquire at least one technical skill. Generally speaking, urban youths should learn to drive cars and trucks and to operate machine tools; rural youths should learn to operate tractors and to familiarize themselves with farming techniques. On the other hand, girl students should learn machine-sewing, tailoring, embroidery, and cooking. Urban girl students would also be required to learn telecommunication and the techniques of radio transmission.

Instruction in politics in colleges and universities include four to six courses and makes up 20 percent of the total time. A variety of specialized courses are offered, depending on the nature of disciplines and concentrations.

Methods of Education in Science and Technology

The teaching of science and technology courses also thrives on the elicitation methods. The elicitation methods are instrumental in improving students' ability to think critically and enhancing their initiative and creativity. They allow students to have a better and firmer grasp of their studies by stimulating active and independent thinking. The guiding educational principle favoring the integration of theory with practice and education with productive labor also finds reflection in science education.

PHYSICAL EDUCATION

The North Koreans argue that physical education plays a pivotal role in building up the health of young students and preparing them for participation in productive labor and national defense.[8] Physical training can not only improve the physique of adolescents and young adults but also boost their morale and fighting will. In addition to taking physical education as a mandatory course, students participate extensively in sports activities, such as physical exercise during breaks, group jogging, group gymnastics, and sports meets. Each student is supposed to be well versed in at least one sport.

THE SOCIALIST EDUCATION SYSTEM IN NORTH KOREA

After years of exploration, experimentation, and research, North Korea has developed a unique education system congruent with its national character and conditions. Below is an overview of the system.

A Universal Compulsory Education System

Comprehensive compulsory education is a key element of North Korea's socialist education system. "The Socialist Educational Program" has made it very clear that the socialist education system is in essence a system of universal compulsory education. It aims at converting members of the whole society rather than some particular strata to a Communist-minded new type

of people. In this society everybody is entitled as much as he or she is oblig-
ated to receive education.

Schools are the primary vehicle for universal compulsory education.
It is, therefore, incumbent upon the government as the purveyor of the needs
of the people to set up schools and finance their daily operation so as to guarantee every citizen an educational opportunity commensurate with his or her
abilities. The adoption of part-work, part-study training as a supplement to
full-time regular education provides educational opportunities for every
citizen, irrespective of his or her age or occupation. As a result, both school-
age children and youths and older citizens can pursue their educational goals.
The government has mapped out an overall plan, which makes allowances
for regional characteristics and balances and ensures a reasonable geographical distribution of educational facilities. A reasonable school network has
come into shape, covering the whole territory and ranging from cities to
villages and from industrial to agricultural areas.

A Universal Free Education System

Education in North Korea is financed by the government and totally free. By
universal free education we mean a package of educational benefits
including free use of state-owned educational facilities by all children and
students, waiver of tuition and miscellaneous fees, free textbooks and school
supplies, as well as free boarding in campus dormitories.

The North Koreans claim that universal free education is unique to
their compulsory education. Since the governments of socialist countries are
in possession and control of the means of production and educational facilities, only they are in a position to provide universal free education.

A Part-Work, Part-Study
Training System

The part-work, part-study training system is a system which enables both
manual and mental workers to pursue academic studies without having to
relinquish their current jobs.

The part-work, part-study training is practiced broadly in such
places as workers' schools, factory-affiliated senior specialized schools,
correspondence and evening schools attached to senior professional and
specialized schools, factory-affiliated universities and their correspondence
and evening schools, and farm-affiliated universities.

This system provides valuable educational opportunities for those
who have received little or limited formal education. It also allows employees
to refurbish their rusty knowledge and skills or to keep abreast of the latest
developments in their particular fields of interest. Another advantage

inherent in this system is that it will alleviate or eliminate a divorce of theory from practice and facilitate a close integration of work and study.

A System of State Support for Child Care and Child Rearing

The system of state support for child care and child rearing refers to the system under which all preschool children will lead a communal or collective life in nurseries and kindergartens, while the government is committed to defray all expenses incurred by the children. The establishment of this system reflects on the North Korean Communist regime's adherence to egalitarianism. The regime claims that the system will guarantee equality in living standards and educational opportunities for all children, irrespective of their parents' social status and income levels.

The North Koreans declare, "The socialist and communist societies are societies based on collectivism Communal or collective education is an essential form of fostering a new generation of Communist-minded people."[9] An objective assessment of the system indicates that it really assures women of the right to participate in production, employment, and social activities because they are no longer tied down by child care and child rearing.

TEACHERS IN NORTH KOREA

Since the Communist takeover, the development of education has been one of the top priorities on its agenda. For this reason, it has held school teachers and college professors in high esteem in recognition of their key role in this effort.

The Communist policy toward intellectuals has two dimensions. On the one hand, the regime makes strenuous efforts to train a new generation of scholars and experts. On the other hand, it makes conciliatory gestures to old intellectuals who were educated and worked in the old society. It does not balk at enlisting the assistance of the old intellectuals while at the same time subjecting them to reeducation and reform. The North Koreans believe that as a social stratum intellectuals have a dual character. They could serve either the exploiting class or the working class. Having lived through the ordeal of oppression and discrimination under the Japanese imperialist and colonial rule, the majority of the intellectuals have nurtured anti-imperialist sentiments and embraced democratic and revolutionary views and ideals. All this provides justification for the government policy in this regard.

There is no denying, however, that the main thrust has been directed at fostering a new contingent of intellectuals. Normal school education and teacher training programs are the major avenues for producing teachers for schools of all types and levels. Teacher training institutions and programs are endearingly called "breeding grounds" of the younger generations. Therefore, primacy is given to teacher training in the government educational plan. The teacher-training system has several components. Teachers' colleges require a residency of three years and recruit graduates from ten-year middle schools. First-level teachers' colleges train primary school teachers, whereas second-level teachers' colleges produce kindergarten teachers. Normal universities operate on a four-year system and enroll ten-year middle school graduates and ex-soldiers with a strong academic background. First-level normal universities train senior middle school teachers, and second-level normal universities train junior middle school teachers. The five-year Kim Hyong Jig Normal University is an exception and serves as a cradle of faculty for teachers' colleges and normal universities. Its graduates are also available for recruitment by senior middle schools and educational administrative agencies. The University is the only institution with a graduate school within North Korea's teacher-training system. Four-year technical teacher training universities accept ten-year senior middle school graduates and demobilized or discharged military men and women. Some universities of technology offer teaching training programs, to which graduates from these universities are admitted. After completing a one-year teacher-training course, they are expected to join the faculty of senior professional or specialized schools or ten-year senior middle schools and teach technical courses. Other universities occasionally have graduate schools or doctoral programs which train university professors or R & D personnel.

In order to enhance their professionalism and performance, the educational authorities encourage school teachers to undertake further studies through correspondence courses and allot time for their self-study. Those who have subsequently passed a teacher reevaluation examination will be awarded a "Qualified Teacher" certificate. They will be put on a par with teachers trained at the same level in regular universities and receive the same salaries and fringe benefits. Besides, short-term or crash training courses are offered. The course offerings and duration of these programs are usually dictated by the prevalent needs or circumstances of the time. During winter holidays and summer vacations seminars lasting half a month are often held. During these seminars, teachers will examine new teaching materials, exchange teaching experiences, and discuss major issues in education. Sometimes teachers are temporarily relieved of their teaching duties to take advanced studies at provincial teachers' or normal universities so as to obtain a "Qualified Teacher" certificate or an academic degree. All study expenses are covered by government grants. In recent years, it has been made a rule for teachers to receive a three- to six- month retraining at an interval of three to five years so as to alleviate technical obsolescence.

North Korea's close attention to boosting the quality of teachers' professional performance is only matched by its unrelenting efforts to improve their social status and financial situation. The authorities have honored teachers with the title of "career revolutionaries" or "anonymous men and women of action" in recognition of their contributions to the cultivation of revolutionary successors. Exemplary and outstanding teachers have been elected to the People's Committees at various levels, where they at least ceremoniously exercise power in the management of state affairs. Also, the government confers such honorary titles as "People's Teacher," and "Meritorious Teacher" upon those who have over the decades performed meritorious service as school teachers. Teachers who have won the title of "People's Teacher" will be granted an equivalent of a university professor or a government minister's social status and monetary compensation. "Meritorious Teachers" receive an equivalent of an associate professor or vice-minister's compensation. Normal college or university graduates' salary on average is 20 percent higher than that for those who have received the same level of education but are engaged in other professions. For instance, in 1988 the monthly pay for a graduate from a six-year medical college was 64 won, whereas a normal university graduate can earn 90 to a 100 won a month as a Grade Three teacher. It is evident from the monetary compensation for teachers that North Korea attaches great importance to basic education.

The society has high regard for teachers and frequently pays tribute to them. Teachers are invariably given preferential treatment when it comes to the distribution of housing, medical care and consumer goods. Respect and favorable treatment for teachers are rewarded by a flourish of education in North Korea.

NOTES

1. In December 1956 after a plenary session of the Korean Worker's Party, Kim Il Sung went on an inspection tour of the Steel Mill, where he issued the call upon the workers to do their utmost to boost productivity and reduce cost of production in emulation of Chollima, a personified mythological horse which allegedly covered a distance of one thousand li within a day. After that, a nationwide Chollima campaign was launched in North Korea.

2. See *The Socialist Education Program*. Pyongyang: Foreign Language Publishing House, 1986.

3. Ibid.

4. Ibid.

5. Ibid.

6. Ibid.

7. Ibid.

8. Ibid.

9. Ibid

4

THE IMPACT OF *JUCHE* UPON LITERATURE AND ARTS

VLADIMIR PUCEK

Charles University, Praha

The humanities and social sciences in North Korea have exibited positive, albeit limited, development over the past forty years. Yet, one can hardly overlook the obvious negative consequences of the influence of the *Juche* idea, the government-sanctioned official ideology of the state and the Korean Workers' Party (KWP) on literature and art. As with all other aspects of North Korean politcs and society, *Juche* has occupied a predominant position in literature and art.

In order for us to trace the development of literature and the arts in North Korea, it is essential for us to trace the origin and evolution of *Juche* , now the recurrent and central theme in North Korea. The avowed objective of the *Juche* idea is to provide viable solutions for the intractable problems encountered in the Korean revolution. Based on this, the Korean people can successfully implement and complete the revolution without having to adopt any development models of foreign origin. In its earliest stages, *Juche* was based on an adaptation of Marxist-Leninist theory to the concrete conditions in Korea. The doctrine also has a very strong element of nationalism, as is evidenced by the original meaning of *Juche*—subjectivity. In fact, it does not behoove Kim Il Sung and his cohorts to claim the credit for the coinage of the term *Juche* . It emerged and came into use long before the mid-1950s. During the first half of the twentieth century when Korea was still under Japanese colonial rule, patriotic Korean intellectuals used it as a slogan in their advocacy of Korea's nationhood. They called for the promotion of national consciousness and the invocation of the national power in the struggle against the enemies who threatened Korea's independence. From the outset, the idea of *Juche* was considered antithetical to *sadaejuui* (meaning flunkeyism). Used during the feudal times, the term specifically referred to a cult of China as promoted by Korea's Confucian scholars who admired the Chinese culture. Since the 1950s, however, the term has taken on added significance and has come to imply slavish subordination to strong neighboring countries or superpowers. As a result, there is a widespread rejection of the idea of *sadae-juui* as it is believed to be conducive to national nihilism and the forfeit of national sovereignty and even nationhood. In this context, the struggle against flunkeyism becomes synonymous with a fight against the order imposed by the superpowers and the unquestioning and slavish adoption of foreign models without regard for the country's objective conditions.

If the term *Juche* was still interpreted as the creative application of Marxism-Leninism to the concrete conditions of Korea toward the end of the 1950s, since the early 1960s there has been an innovative modification in the official interpretation of *Juche*. Party ideologues began to argue that under new, different historical conditions, the Communist philosophy as expounded by Marx, Lenin, and Stalin should not be applied in a rigid, inflexible way as a panacea of all problems in the present society and socialist construction. For this reason *Juche* was elevated to the position of Marxism-Leninism in the era of the ultimate defeat and doom of imperialism. It was also eulogized as the only correct and decisive ideology which advanced Marxism to a new height.

Currently, the *Juche* idea has all but become a law governing both individual and collective thinking and behavior in North Korea. It has been declared the "one leading ideology of the KWP," the almighty guidelines which have penetrated every sphere of social life. Loyalty to *Juche* was even incorporated into the statutes of the KWP and the Constitution of the Democratic People's Republic of Korea in 1972 (Article No. 4). Later in the adulation of Kim, even a bizarre and awkward term "*Juche*-ization of the whole society" (or *sahoeui Juche sasanghwa*) was coined only to test the mettle and ability of translators.

It is inevitable that the promotion of Kim Il Sung's *Juche* idea first as a unifying state ideology and then as "the revolutionary Weltanschauung of the present epoch" (Kim Il Sung, 1985) has left an indelible imprint upon the humanities and social sciences in North Korea. Many reference books in these fields such as *Chongji Sajon* (*Dictionary of Political Terms*), *Kyongje Sajon* (*Dictionary of Economics*), *Ryoksa Sajon* (*Dictionary of History*), and *Munhak Yesul Sajon* (*Dictionary of Literature and Art*) furnished evidence of the ubiquity and profound influence of the *Juche* idea.

According the *Juche* idea, a man stands in the center of all activities. A creative movement of the masses aware of their sovereignty is the motive force of history. For this reason, special attention should be paid to political work among the masses and to revolutionary education within the organizations. And there will have to be a leader who plays a pivotal role in guiding the masses.

The concept of *Juche* (as opposed to *sadaejuui*) emanates from a number of factors. Among them are the history of a small country exposed to the danger of foreign aggression and worried about the interference in its domestic politics and violation of its sovereignty by neighboring foreign powers. The traumatic and embittered experiences under decades of Japanese colonial rule still rankled in the minds of the Korean people. The Koreans were also very resentful of the arrogance of its Communist allies the Soviet Union and China which, as the liberator and protector, tried to dictate North Korea's domestic and foreign policy and to impose their development model upon North Korea with the help of their surrogates within the Party and government.

On the other hand, it is by no mean coincidence that the *Juche* idea was first made public in 1955. Its announcement came only after the death of

Joseph Stalin in 1953 and his denunciation at the Twentieth Congress of the Soviet Communist Party in 1956. This epoch-making Congress severely criticized Stalin and other Soviet leaders' errors, including their arrogant neglect of the rights of "fraternal" Communist parties and their flagrant infringement on the sovereignty of friendly socialist countries. The KWP leadership availed themselves of this opportunity to assert for the first time their autonomy, despite the fact they had serious reservations about other aspects of the campaign, to repudiate the Stalinist political excesses, as was launched in the Soviet Union and other Eastern European countries. They found it especially difficult to reconcile themselves with the severe criticism of the personality cult, totalitarianism, and the contempt for basic individual rights under Stalin's dictatorial regime.

The main thrust of North Korea's domestic and foreign policy was directed at strengthening the totalitarian regime and consolidating the monopoly of power by the Party, state, army, and police in all possible spheres as they affect the individual as well as society. The Kim regime's efforts seemed to be highly successful, and before long the Kim clan was at the height of its power.

At the same time the North Korean Communist regime became increasingly suspicious of new and what they viewed as "soft" positions on the issue of war and peace, and it became nervous and wary about indications of detente between the East and the West. In this context, Kim's regime began to ardently advocate self-reliance; it gradually receded into a cocoon of self-imposed isolation and became alienated from the rest of the world including the Communist and socialist-oriented countries.

Due to this concern with ideological impurity and extreme isolation, all research in North Korea is conducted strictly within the framework of *Juche*. In February 1964 the DPRK Academy of Sciences was split into two divisions, and a separate Academy of Social Sciences was established. But the new institution was not even authorized to sign agreements with any foreign partners including its counterparts in other Communist countries. Such a highly restrictive and extremely ludicrous policy made it all but impossible for the Academy to seek interaction and cooperation with any foreign countries even in the field of Korean studies.

The dire consequences of the dominance of the *Juche* idea and self-imposed isolation find revelations in North Korea's historiography. Blatant distortions of historical facts became rife. The most conspicuous examples include the myths that the Korean peninsula was the cradle of human civilization and that Korean culture, language, and literature developed in the absence of any foreign influences. The efforts for "Mal-tadumgi" (vocabulary readjustment) in language and purism in literature and culture emerged under Kim's tutelage in response to the needs for a rewriting of history. No less was the impact that *Juche* had on the development of literature and the arts in Korea. We will now turn our attention to this development.

GRADUAL ASCENDANCY
AND DOMINATION OF IDEOLOGY
IN LITERATURE AND PUBLISHING
AFTER THE KOREAN WAR

Several reforms implemented by the Communist regime have created favorable conditions for the execution of the social function of literature and the expansion of its positive influence on society. These reforms included the elimination of illiteracy, the abolition of the Chinese characters and their replacement by a Korean alphabet in the written language, establishment of the norms for a standard language, and technical and cultural revolution. All this has been conducive to a flourishing of democratic and popular art.

In spite of all this, under the dictatorship of the proletariat, a euphemism for Communist tyranny, literature and art are under constant Party and government guidance and surveillance. Literature has become an instrument for promoting and executing the Party's political and social policies. Literary workers are under obligation to assist in the efforts to attain the revolutionary goals set by the Party.

In this connection, Kim Il Sung and Kim Jong Il both paid close personal attention to this sensitive sphere. During the years following the Korean War, the North Korean Communist regime has repeatedly modified and revised its policies and strategies concerning central control over culture, the treatment of the intelligentsia, the national tradition, and the publishing policy in response to changes in both the domestic and international situations. But the basic guiding principle has remained unchanged.

A perusal of various North Korean documents including speeches by Kim Il Sung and Kim Jong Il, programs and declarations of literature and art associations, as well as the literary and art works themselves reveals that there have been several crucial themes developed by the Party which are meant to resonate throughout the literary and art arena in North Korea.

First and foremost, literature should be centered on contemporary man. It should serve the people. Literary workers should strictly abide by the principles of the Korean revolution in production. Literary works should in no way be divorced from the realities of the country and from the revolutionary sentiments of the working-class people. In addition to all this the Communist regime stressed the importance of complying with the revolutionary principles of the Marxist-Leninist theory of literature and art (later the *Juche* idea) and of endowing literary works with a socialist content and a national form. Special emphasis was placed upon such revolutionary attributes as uncompromising allegiance to the Party, class consciousness, and profound affection for the people. In the meanwhile, no efforts should be spared to prevent the penetration of the imperialist culture and ideology in North Korea's new literature.

All works should be evaluated and judged not only on the basis of their aesthetic value but also their educational effects and political impact, because there is a need for inculcating in the citizenry the socialist and communist moral principles, revolutionary optimism, socialist patriotism, and a deep hatred for class enemies. Literature is to describe in a spirit of revolutionary realism all the successes achieved by the Korean people in national liberation and socialist construction. Literature should make contributions to the cause of reunifying the divided fatherland. It is also supposed to assist in the efforts to expunge all kinds of old-fashioned, anachronistic, and unsound customs, norms, and conventions from people's minds.

As for cultural heritage, it is necessary to adopt a rather critical attitude toward it and preserve and promote those elements which are truly progressive and people-oriented. On the other hand, anything that is reminiscent of feudalism, offensive to the feeling of the people, or full of vulgarities should be forbidden. Folk art should also be subject to scrutiny and critical examination. Blind faith and unquestioning acceptance of all kinds of tractional art forms, methods and contents are reprehensible. Some of the classic works praised in the 1950s as sources of folk art were later criticized and repudiated because they dealt with Buddhism, Confucianism, or Shamanism. The ideological watchdogs made it very clear that they would tolerate neither of the two extremes—traditionalism (uncritical acceptance of the whole cultural heritage) and national nihilism (absolute rejection of all ancient cultural values).

It is obvious from all the above that there has been a subordination of culture to ideology and politics in North Korea. By analyzing the history of literature, contemporary art creation, literary criticism, and publication policy in North Korea during the period from 1953 to the late 1980s, we can identify three periods:

1. The first period: from 1953 to the mid-1960s;
2. The second period: from the mid-1960s to the late 1970s;
3. The third period: from the early 1980s to the early 1990s.

THE FIRST PERIOD:
FROM 1953 TO THE MID-1960s

The beginning of this period will live in infamy because of the political trials of the Pak Hon-yong and Yi Sung-yop factions within the Party. The kangaroo court trials were followed by the purge of a group of dissident writers such as Yim Hwa, Yi Tae-jun, and Kim Nam-chon for political and ideological reasons. The victims were charged with sabotage in the arena of literature and art.

During the same period, the history of Korean literature was rewritten to conform to Party orthodoxy. The various segments of the new history were first published by installment. Then it came out in its entirety in book form under the title of *Choson Munhak Tongsa* (*A Brief History of Korean Literature*), with the new-fangled revisionist literary theory incorporated into it.

The reevaluation of Korean literature from 1910 to 1945 is a classic example illustrating how party policy influenced research on literature. The history of Korean literature compiled during this period clearly bears the mark of the time and mirrors the then official policy of the Party and government. In other words, in this official history of modern Korean literature no mention was made of any literary trends other than realism. Information about anything related to nationalism or labeled as "bourgeois" was withheld. Under the designation of "bourgeois" trends were naturalism, symbolism, l'art-pour-l'artisme, decadence, formalism, Dadaism, mysticism, eroticism, and so on. All authors who remained in South Korea after the Liberation of 1945 became anonymous no matter how great the merit of their creative work might be. Political and ideological criteria were used as a yardstick for assessing the literary and art works, while at the same time aesthetic and artistic standards were put into abeyance.

Another prominent and influential school known as "Sin-sosol" literature (New Novels) was all but consigned to oblivion. Only one member of this School, Yi Hae-jo, and his *Chayu chong* (*Bell of Freedom*) were mentioned in passing and discussed very briefly in the History. Other preeminent writers belonging to this school such as Choe Nam-son, Yi Kwang-su, Kim Tong-in, and Hyon Chin-gon seemed never to have existed. Such an approach to the history of Korean literature virtually amounted to canceling a greater portion of the literature of this period. By contrast, *Choson Munhak Tongsa* eulogized the so-called proletarian literature as the most progressive and greatly exaggerated its social and artistic significance and influence. After all, many authors and literary critics associated with the KAPF at the time held important positions in North Korea's political and cultural life. It is natural that they would attempt to continue the tradition of proletarian literature. The official history betrayed its political bias by addressing itself extensively and one-sidedly to the works by such proletarian writers as Cho Myong-Hui, Choe So-hae, Yi Sang-hwa, Yi Ki-yong, Han Sor-ya, and some authors of literature for children. Out of a great number of other writers only a small fraction were fortunate enough to be exempted from this. Notable among them were Na To-hyang and Kim So-wol, whose works were declared to belong to the school of critical realism.

Works by other authors received no critical attention at all. In most instances, even their names were suppressed. The authors of this history of literature had no scruples about making a sweeping condemnation of "naturalist" authors such as Yi Kwang-su, Kim Tong-lin, Yom Sang-sop, Hyon Chin-gon, Hwang Sog-u, and O Sang-sun. They were explicit about their disgust for the "reactionary" literary groups and their publications such as *Si Munhak, Munye Wolgan, Haeoe Munhak,* and *Kuinhoe,* as well as their representatives, namely, Pak Yong-hui, Choe Jae-so, Paek Chol, Yim Hwa, Yi Tae-jun, and others. Highly biased official literary critics would make sweeping generalizations about their artistic activities by using such stereotyped political jargon as "Their bourgeois reactionary literature only preaches cosmopolitanism, individualism, and other erroneous ideas, which stand just on the opposite side of the people and the nation." From this we can clearly see the subordination of literature to the Party's political objectives and the gradual ascendancy and dominance of the *Juche* idea.

A concomitant practice of tampering with the history of literature is a new policy governing publishing and school education. Textbooks and anthologies of literature intended for various types of schools as well as literary works published also bore testimony to the North Korean Communist regime's historical revisionism inspired by political expediency. A typical example was *Hyondae Choson Munhak Sonjip* (*Anthology of Modern Korean Literature*).

Another blatant misrepresentation of the history of literature is made apparent in the myth that literature and art of high quality emerged from among the ranks of the guerrillas during the Anti-Japanese Movement. Many songs and dramas, which were accredited to guerrilla fighters and acclaimed as masterpieces of socialist realism, had actually existed under different titles for a long time. Later these works were simply attributed to Kim Il Sung. A typical example was *Pi pada* (*Sea of Blood*), an opera extolled to the skies by Kim's sycophantic followers as an immortal work, was originally a theater play known under the Sino-Korean title *Hyorhae*. It probably had existed in several different versions.

In spite of the gross misinformation and misrepresentations concerning modern Korean literature, we have to acknowledge that this was a period of relative prosperity and high productivity in literary creation, literary criticism and publishing, especially when compared with the later years and considering the prevalent political, economic, and social conditions of the time.

There was relatively more freedom of expression during the period before the early 1960s. During that period, seminars and symposia on literary studies and criticism were frequently held and realism and other literary trends were extensively discussed. Literary workers and critics were allowed to comment on problems ranging from aesthetics, literary forms, and genres to poetry. Careful and meticulous work was done to analyze the styles and achievement of both classic and contemporary writers. This period was also remarkable for a vast number of publications, translations, and adaptations of classic works. From 1955 until 1965 an extensive edition of *Choson Kojon Munhak Sonjip* (*Selected Works of Korean Classic Literature*) was published. The edition was originally planned to contain thirty-three volumes, but for some unknown reasons some of the volumes never came off the press.

That period also witnessed a gradual rise in the number of literary and science magazines. In addition to the monthly reviews *Choson Munhak*

(*Korean Literature*), which has been in existence since 1953 up to now, and *Adong Munhak* (*Children's Literature*), a new monthly review *Chongnyon Munhak* (*Youth Literature*) also appeared. The journal *Choson Omun* (*Korean Philosophy*) was divided into two separate periodicals, namely, *Choson Ohak* (*Korean Linguistics*) and *Munhak Yongu* (*Literary Studies*). Moreover, in the first half of the 1960s, the Writer's Union published its own quarterly literary reviews *Si Munhak* (*Poetry*) and *Kuk Munhak* (*Drama*).

These changes provided a forum for lively and extensive discussions on literature. Many exponents touched upon the foreign influence, which later became a taboo topic. They were allowed to examine the close relationship between Korean literature and traditional Chinese writings and the impact of the Far Eastern culture as a whole in the earlier times. They also inquired into the European and Japanese influences in modern times. During this period of relative freedom of expression, they were not required to overload their writing with quotations from Kim Il Sung or the various Party documents. Such practices later on became the order of the day.

During that period North Korea had not yet been turned into a hermetically sealed, xenophobic, Communist enclave. Literary circles and the reading public had not yet been completely isolated from the outside world, and they were still allowed to have some useful, albeit limited, contacts with foreign countries. Although there were no periodical publications for translated works, North Korea embarked on a program for translating world-renowned classic and modern works into the Korean language with emphasis, naturally, upon Russian and Soviet writers.

At the same time authors of university textbooks began to explore the possibility of an objective assessment of the history of literature even though they were still not allowed to overstep the official ideological boundaries set by the regime. However, the downside was that more writers, including Chong Chi-yong and Kim Ki-rim, fell into disfavor with the regime and came under official attack.

Even during this period the totalitarian regime never loosened its grip over literary circles and imposed a series of restrictions on artistic creation. Nevertheless, many valuable works were produced. This is largely because their authors were mostly leftovers from the past whose pre-Liberation links with cultural and scientific circles in Seoul had provided them with a broader outlook and more rigorous professional training.

THE PERIOD FROM THE LATE 1960s
TO THE LATE 1970s

During this period the North Korean Communist regime mounted a gigantic campaign to infuse the *Juche* idea into both the theory and the practice of literature, art, and history as well as its publishing policy. Kim Il Sung and his son Kim Jong Il inundated the nation with an avalanche of directives, commentaries, and essays regarding the approaches to apply the *Juche* idea to literary and art work. Step by step, the *Juche* theory of literature and art took shape and replaced the Marxist-Leninist theory of literature and art. With the help of their political power Kim Senior and Kim Junior established themselves as unchallenged theoretical authorities in this field. These theories are embodied and expounded in the book *Studies on the* Juche *Theory of Literature and Art*. Its basic tenets can be summarized as follows:

- The *Juche* theory of literature and art is a new, superior, and original theory of socialist realism, valid in the present era and based on the *Juche* idea;
- The methods of socialist realism represent the only creative methods in our era;
- Socialist realism must develop from the *Juche* Weltanschauung or world outlook, which should be completely accepted and thoroughly understood by the authors and artists;
- The basic criteria for evaluating literature and art should, in addition to artistic standards, include loyalty to the Party, proletarian class consciousness (nodong kyegupsong), a right attitude toward the masses of the people, ideological content (sasangsong), and political consciousness (chongchisong);
- Works must have a socialist content and a national form;
- Art must correctly reflect the Party's political guidelines and create a new type of hero—a real revolutionary engaged in socialist construction;
- Choice of the basic themes and ideological schemes of a piece of work (in Kim Jong Il's terminology scheme is called "chongja"—core) should be made on the basis of its political significance;
- *Juche* literature and art should be an integral part of the irreconcilable struggle against all manifestations of the bourgeois ideology. Bourgeois literature finds expression in such trends as formalism, positivism, social Darwinism, naturalism, traditionalism, and so on. *Juche* art should reject all theories in favor of "pure art," "art which rises above class consciousness," "art for mankind," and so on;
- Literature and art constitute the primary medium for educating the broad masses of the people to accept revolutionary thoughts and to adopt the *Juche* idea;
- Party control over this sphere is an important condition and a key element of the *Juche* theory of literature and art. As the vanguard of the working class, the Party serves as a guarantor of a fruitful development of literature and art as it provides the only correct guidance in all stages of its development.

The key points of the *Juche* theory cogently demonstrate that literature and art are interpreted in a very narrow sense as merely instruments for disseminating the *Juche* idea, defending and glorifying the Party's policies, and promoting Kim Il Sung and Kim Jong Il's personality cults. Judged by the universally accepted literary standards, the literary and art works created under the auspices of the Party were generally unconvincing, insincere, and contrived, and lacking in artistic value and mass appeal. Increasingly tightened Party supervision turned out to be a disaster. Development of literary theory was impeded and literary criticism became stagnant as literary workers had to proceed with utmost precaution within the limits set by the regime in their artistic pursuit. Classic literary studies and evaluation of contemporary works have virtually been reduced to a game of citing or paraphrasing Kim Il Sung and Kim Jong Il's works. The newly compiled history of literature devoted still less attention and space to classical literature. Research on classical, sometimes even contemporary writers, had virtually ground to a halt, and the studies were all but withheld from publication. Strict restrictions were imposed upon the publication of pre-Liberation modern literature. For a total of twenty years not a single novel or poem, not even those considered as masterpieces, was published if it was written before 1945. The ban also applied to the commentaries on these works. The only exception was the guerrilla literature during the Anti-Japanese movement period. But the proletarian literature was not exempt from prohibition.

Most literary and scientific journals had ceased publication. In their place the presses affiliated with the Association of Social Scientists (ASS) and Kim Il Sung University (KISU) started publishing miscellanies of essays and other items, with literary works accounting for only a minimal part of these publications.

In the name of combating the "bourgeois literature," a prolonged moratorium had been put on the publication of translated works, including those from other Communist countries. In this context, inevitably no studies on the history of world literature or the literature of any particular countries were conducted or published.

The new, officially approved histories of Korean literature were two five-volume editions both entitled *Choson Munhak* but published by the ASS and KISU, respectively. Compared with their predecessor *Choson Munhak Tonga* published in 1959, the two new editions discussed in much greater detail "Sin-sosol" (more specifically referring to the works of Y Hae-jo and Kim Kyo-je, Choe Chan-sik and An Kuk-son). In the new editions short stories written at the turn of the twentieth century were identified as pioneering critical realism. The previously disgraced author Hyon Chin-gon was rehabilitated and portrayed as a master of critical realism tinged with a strong element of naturalism. The authors analyzed Sin Chae-ho in much greater detail and depth, characterizing him as representative of romanticism. Folklore and especially folk songs received more appreciation than before. Other noticeable changes in the history included the reevaluation of the proletarian literature. The name of Han Sor-ya, a prominent figure of this literary movement, was deleted from the new histories. He had fallen into disfavor and vanished from both the political and literary scenes because of his political and ideological rift with the Kim faction. To fill in the gaps left by these purged and decimated writers, the authors of the new histories evoked the names of some lesser known novelists, poets, and literary critics such as Y Ik-sang, Kim Yong-pal, and Song Sun-il who had hitherto remained in obscurity or even anonymity. Poets like Pak Par-yang and Pak Se-yong and novelist Song Yong, who were previously held in high esteem, were relegated to a much less visible position. In the 1950s, several of the works which were considered as the best specimens of proletarian literature were hailed as masterpieces of socialist realism. Now such an assessment was recanted. Their authors were found guilty of failure to espouse revolutionary views as reflected by the ideological immaturity of their works.

The importance of proletarian literature as a whole was also downplayed as compared with its previous assessment. It was no longer viewed as representing the acme of literary creation. In its place, a few songs allegedly composed by Kim Il Sung's parents were described as the crowning achievements of socialist realism.

Such willful tampering with the history of literature was intended to reinforce the myth that the best literature and art originated with the guerrillas during the 1930s. The guerrilla writings were eulogized as the zenith of pre-Liberation literature. Many of such writings, mostly by anonymous guerrilla authors, only had their titles and a few fragments preserved. Now they miraculously reappeared as completed works with their titles and the names of authors changed. These works were credited to Kim Il Sung as immortal masterpieces and had different genres (songs, operas, drama, and music). They were declared to be the earliest works of socialist realism created in line with the *Juche* idea in Korea. With such great achievements the Great Fatherly Leader now became the inventor of creative methods in Korean literature.

The authors of the new histories also strived to convince the readers of the immense influence of Kim's literary works not only upon the Korean writers including those of proletarian literature but also upon the subsequent literary creation and cultural activities in Northeast China.

Such a highly innovative approach to literary history entails a major revision of the time sequence of important events in modern Korean history. The authors now used different stages of the guerrilla movement before Liberation and important political events or the Korean Workers' Party resolutions after Liberation as demarcation lines between different stages of the development of Korean literature and art. In many instances, the year of 1919 was no longer considered as an important turning point. As for Kim Il Sung's parents, Kim Hyong-jik and Kang Pan-sok, the works ascribed to them were subsumed under the category of literature during the period of the Independence Movement.

In this way new literary criteria based on *Juche* dictated the chronological division of the history and the evaluation of Korean literature, especially when post-Liberation literature was concerned. Several writers, such as Han Sor-ya and Pak Ung-gol, had vanished and many others were downgraded, more often than not for political reasons rather than for artistic reasons.

A pantheon of young writers were swept onto the scene almost overnight and experienced meteoric rise. They had been rewarded for their obsequious and strict observance of Kimist literary prescriptions based on *Juche*. Their works were not judged on their artistic merit but according to the political significance and ideological orientation. They would be subsumed under a certain category primarily because of their themes. These works consistently and invariably followed a set pattern and the choice of themes were extremely limited. The officially sanctioned themes included the epoch-making achievement of the Great Leader, the revolutionary tradition as created by the Great Leader, the martyrdom of stereotypical revolutionary fighters against the Japanese, the legendary efforts of the people to achieve democratic reform in society, the heroism of the army and the people during the Korean War, the viciousness of class exploitation in the pre-Liberation era, the meritorious service of the people in socialist construction, education in class consciousness, the reunification of the divided fatherland, the South Korean people's struggle against U.S. imperialism, and the fight of the ethnic Koreans residing in Japan against oppression and discrimination.

North Korea's cinematic art flourished. Screenplays came out in profusion and film literature attained a status as a separate genre of literature. This was due partly to the official perception of cinematography as an art for the masses and partly to the personal intervention and patronage of Kim Jong Il, who allegedly is infatuated with movies and movie actresses.

Adaptation for movies of the works attributed to Kim Il Sung and his parents as well as those made under his guidance were undertaken on a massive scale. Most of them glorified the supermanlike contributions of the Great Leader and members of his family. Some of them paid homage to those who had boundless love and loyalty for the Leader. The prosperity of the movie industry brought with it a boom in movie review.

In the 1960s and 1970s a novel phenomenon known as "chipchejak" (collective works) occurred in the sphere of literature and art. The personality of the individual writer or artist was suppressed in favor of group work. Under collective authorship (the names of the members of the groups should be held in confidence) large numbers of novels, operas, movie plays, music, dramas, and paintings were produced. The best known of these groups was the "April 15th Writing Staff of the Central Committee of the Korean Writer's

Union." These writers were entrusted with the task of glorifying the life and revolutionary achievements of Kim Il Sung and members of his family. Their brainchildren were later described as the masterpieces of the 1960s and the 1970s and believed to embody realism.

The most publicized of them formed a series of novels collectively known as the *Immortal History* (*Pilmyurui Ryoksa*) which took the form of biographical novels and depicted the revolutionary guerrilla activities of Kim Il Sung during the period from 1932 to 1940. In these novels Kim assumed the pseudonym "Kumsong." By 1980 five volumes had been published. The same writing group "April the 15th" produced novels describing Kim Il Sung's childhood and his way to the career as a revolutionary.

Even a cursory examination of the contents of these novels reveals that they were nothing more than fabricated stories, myths, and legends about the revolutionary career of Kim Il Sung, which were disguised as literature. They were too devoid of historical authenticity to be considered literary biographies. They described and interpreted the history of the Korean national liberation movement the same way as *Choson Chonsa* (*Complete History of Korea*) did. All these publications were designed to serve the same purpose—the promotion of Kim's personality cult.

Our conclusion is true of other works produced by the writing group. This basically fictitious stuff portrayed Kim Il Sung's father Kim Hyong-jik (*Ryokasaui Saebyok Kil, Dawn of History*, Vol. 1, 1972) as a dedicated revolutionary and educator and his mother Kang Pang-sok (*Chosonui Omoni, Mother of Korea*, 1970) as a paragon of virtue. Even Kim Il Sung's first wife Kim Chong-suk became a beneficiary of the adulation drive. She was posthumously canonized as a *Juche*-type revolutionary in the very lengthy novel *Chungsongui Han Kireso* (*On the Way of Loyalty*, 5 vols., 1975–1985).

The histories of literature compiled and published by ASS and KISU also devoted much space and attention to similar works produced by groups or individuals in different styles and genres during the entire period. The one published by KISU even subsumed Kim Jong Il's writings during his childhood under this category despite the fact that these writings were no more than a few short poems composed by an immature and naive child. These sycophantic literary historians even had the effrontery to call them "immortal classics and masterpieces."

The discriminatory and prejudiced publishing policy favored the investment of a disproportionately large part of the available resources in political propaganda. They seemed to have aroused widespread interest in historical novels. But only a small number of them came off the press.

The domination of the *Juche* theory over creative work in literature and art and the imposition of socialist realism as the only acceptable approach to literary creation produced an adverse and degrading effect upon North Korea's literature and art. The writers and artists in isolation can hardly expand their knowledge or improve their techniques by keeping abreast of the developments in the outside world. In addition, their reputation abroad has been seriously compromised since their foreign counterparts have dismissed them as soulless puppets and their productions as worthless rubbish. The fact that few scholars or researchers abroad have ever indicated any interest in translating post-Liberation North Korean literature testifies to the validity of this conclusion. Even in other Communist countries where the Stalinist concept of socialist realism has been totally repudiated since the debates held in the 1950s and 1960s, only a minimal amount of postwar North Korean literature was translated into their languages. Besides, the translators preferred classic and pre-Liberation contemporary literature, including prole-tarian literature which had been discredited in North Korea itself.

THE PERIOD OF THE 1980s

During the decade of the 1980s the *Juche* theory of literature and art still held sway in North Korea, as was evident from the fact that the above mentioned series *Immortal History* and short stories depicting the achievements and character of Kim Jong Il continued to be published and distributed.

On the other hand, there began to appear some signs of a reversion to the policy of the second half of the 1950s concerning literary creation and cultural activities. Under the influence of major changes in both the interna-tional and domestic situations (improvement in the international climate and the resumption of North-South dialogues), there seemed to be some loosening in North Korea's rigorous policy. Moreover, a less restrictive policy governing literature and art seemed to be in order as the reading public became increasingly surfeited with rigid and stereotyped writings and political moralizing in literature. A segment of writers and readers deplored the sorry state of North Korea's culture and literature and the contempt for national heritage. Even some ideologues within the ruling Party became aware of the problems of stagnation and distortion in literature and raised an alarm. However, only sporadic and insignificant changes have taken place and North Korea remains a tightly closed society impervious to change.

Although all changes made up to this point have been cosmetic, there have been some positive developments with regard to policies concerning publishing and research in the social sciences. As a rule, any shift in policy orientation was justified by a quotation from the Great Leader.

A more recent anthology of literature has provided some clues to the possible shift in the direction literature and art will follow in the foreseeable future. This collection of literary works, entitled *Selected Modern Literary Works of Korea*, is an extremely voluminous one (approximately 100 volumes) and includes the authors and works which had been passed over in the previous editions as well as those which had recently emerged from obscurity. The section on modern literature even reintroduced *Sin-sosol* (Vols. 1–3, 1987, by Kim Ha-myong), which had been banned for many years. However, Y In-jik's *Hyorui nu* (*Tears of Blood*), a landmark work, was still missing from the anthology as the ban on it had not been lifted.

During this period special attention was paid to children's literature. Although the overwhelming majority of books for children still have an overtone of political indoctrination, the more recent publications have shown some diversity in topics. Allegedly at Kim Jong Il's behest, the Munye Publishing House published a children's literature series entitled *Segye Adong Munhak Sonjip* (*A Collection of Children's Literature of the World*), thus lifting the unwritten injunctions against foreign literature which had for a long time been maligned as decadent and harmful. This series was followed by another reader for children in paperback edition *Choson Minhwa Chip* (*A Collection of Korean Folk Tales*), published by Kumsong Chongnyon Publishing House in 1986.

Earlier in 1983 there was another breakthrough in the publishing policy. That year a publication program got under way, which resulted in the release of an anthology of classical literature entitled *Choson Kojon Munhak Sonjip* (*Selected Readings of Korean Classical Literature*, Munye Publishing House).

The compilers of *Choson Munhak Kaegwan* obviously adopted a new approach to the history of modern literature, which was suggestive of a possible reversal of the regime's policy of hostility toward some nonconformist writer. There was obviously a better balance between medieval and modern literature. Besides, more objective standards were applied in the selection of authors up to 1945. For example, in the chapter on "enlightened bourgeois writers (sin-munhak)," Choe Nam-son, his works, literary career, and the magazine he edited–(*Sin-si*), Kim Ok and his translations of the French symbolist masters, Y Kwang-su and his theory of national reformism (Minjok Kaeron), and many other authors received renewed albeit still reluctant, and scant, attention. Previously, these writers were under suspicion and all information about their literary careers was suppressed.

Other writers also received more favorable treatment. Han Yongun was actually rehabilitated. Hyon Chin-gon and his critical realism were no longer viewed as at odds with the *Juche* theory. Compared with the previous far less flattering comments on him, the new anthology gave him a more balanced, factual, and fair evaluation. Other authors like Chae Man-sik and Y Hyo-sok were first-time entries; while the previously purged Han Sor-ya was reintroduced. On the other hand, for the first time ever in the history of Korean literature, a separate section was devoted to reverence for Kim Jong Il, under the title "Prose Portraying the Dear Leader Kim Jong Il."

There was a renewed interest in research on classic literature and social sciences including archeology, ethnography, philosophy, art, and especially linguistics. Many of the published research reports were still couched in the jargon of *Juche* politics and there is a strong streak of ideological continuity in all of them as their authors strived to preserve as much of the previous two decades' research work under Communist surveillance as possible. But the difference was that these research papers became more truthful and factual when it came to the nation's tradition and cultural heritage. Besides, they refrained from being deliberately sketchy or negligent when commenting on some controversial literary figures.

After a hiatus of many years, the publication of foreign literature was resumed, but the majority of them were just reprints of the translations published in the 1950s. To this day there is not a single comprehensive library of the world's masterpieces. In this respect, North Korea lags far behind the rest of the world. Even the professional literary journal *Choson Munhak* paid very little attention to foreign literature.

INFLUENCES OF *JUCHE*
UPON OTHER FORMS OF ART

From the 1960s to the 1980s, contemporary themes dominated the movies and the theater. A vast number of literary works, those attributed to Kim Il Sung in particular, were revised for ready adaptation to all artistic and theatrical forms. In 1971 an anonymous writing group adapted the drama *A Sea of Blood* to a title opera on a revolutionary theme under the auspices of the Great Leader. In such adaptations classic European opera was rejected as historically outmoded and incompatible with the present time and aesthetic values of the Korean people. Arguably, classical European operas were only the preserve of the ruling elite. Aria, duet, and choir singing were considered too difficult for the common people to understand or digest, and too remote from their feelings and sentiments. The official North Korean theatrical theory, which the Communist regime hailed as an original North Korean contribution to the development of opera in the world, encompassed the following principles:

- The content must be revolutionary and must reflect the present time and the sentiments of the people;
- Outdated operatic cliches will be removed and the deeply rooted *sadaejuui* will not be wiped out unless new forms are adopted;
- The *Juche* idea must resonate throughout these works and find reflection in their revolutionary ways of persuasion, ideological orientations, characterization of popular heroes, discussion of the national mentality, communication of ideas;
- Songs should be divided into stanzas as they are important vehicles for the expression of feelings and sentiments;

- Accompanying choirs (Panchang) singing by the side of the stage, a North Korean innovation, and orchestras combining Korean and European musical instruments are effective in intensifying the stage atmosphere;
- Ballet dancing (a la coreene) should be an integral part of an opera;
- Use of audio and video equipment such as stereo amplifiers, light, slides, and Korean-style paintings (Chosonhwa) will aid in the performing arts;
- Simultaneous projection of scripts on side screens will facilitate the understanding of the contents of the opera.

As a result, operas on the revolutionary themes actually integrated the elements of various types of performing arts and subsequently served as a norm and model for all contemporary operas (officially known as Pipada-style revolutionary operas). Rumor had it that Kim Jong Il was personally involved in their creation. He provided many instructions in this regard.

In the sphere of drama Kim Il Sung's "immortal revolutionary masterpieces" (*Songhwang dang*) were defined as models in this newly elaborated genre by contemporary professional playwrights who wanted to ingratiate themselves into the favor of the regime. These plays were invariably indictments of class oppression and exploitation in pre-Liberation North Korea, the malicious influence of religions and superstition (Shamanism, Buddhism, and Christianity).

Adherents to the *Juche* theory of drama contend that a theatrical play should integrate the elements of music, songs, choir singing (Pangchang), and dancing. For this reason, in the 1970s and the 1980s, only "*Songhwang-dang*-style revolutionary dramas" were allowed to be staged. The official repertoire teemed with plays purportedly authored by Kim Il Sung and set in the 1920s and 1930s, such as *A Letter from the Daughter* and *An Chung-gun Shoots Ito Hirobumi*. Even a cursory reading of literary journals and manuals of literary history might reveal that many of these titles were actually preexistent. But they were very rarely staged probably because European-style drama had very limited appeal to the Korean people and could attract only very small audiences.

The *Juche* idea found striking resonance especially in movies, which were under Kim Jong Il's personal control and supervision. Though a constellation of outstanding actors and actresses appeared on the screen, their image was marred by an obsession with class consciousness and subservience to the Party, as was the case with literature. The most prominent and best-known productions released during this period were mainly adapted from other genres such as opera. Notable among them were the cinematic versions of revolutionary operas like *Sea of Blood* (1969), *The Flower Girl*, and theatrical plays like *Yi Chun Mission at the Hage Conference in 1907*. Others worthy of mentioning were a nine-episode *Star of Korea*, depicting the activities of Kim Il Sung in the 1920s and 1930s, and the twenty-episode *Anonymous Heroes*. All of these movies, as well as *Wolmido Isle*, were on the theme of the Korean War. Movies based on classical literary works reappeared albeit in a limited number again in the early 1980s.

To sum up, North Korea's achievements in theatrics and other performing arts in the last twenty years have been simply abysmal. Only a pathetically small number of plays have been created and staged. Foreign dramas, operas, and ballets were the first casualties to the government's highly restrictive and xenophobic policy. Cultural exchanges with foreign countries were reduced to a minimum, with only a small number of foreign folk song and dance ensembles, variety show groups, and chamber music orchestras invited to visit North Korea.

In the field of music, adherents to the *Juche* theory of art strongly advocated tapping the rich resources of traditional music with special attention on the rhythms, melodies (Minyo and Kayo in particular) and national musical instruments employed in the traditional folk music. However, some types of Korean traditional music and singing methods were abandoned because they were hardly understandable or sounded strange to the Korean people. The same principle applied to Western instrumental music. In the field of fine arts, traditionalism prevailed over modernism. Traditional Korea painting (Chosonhwa) was preferred to Western-style oil paintings and other types of brushwork, but they were predominantly on contemporary themes. In sculpture and architecture, oversized pompous and grandiose statues and skyscrapers were the favorites, suggestive of the narcissism and megalomania of Kim Senior and Kim Junior. However, the greatest irony was that for all protestations of national pride and patriotism, not a single statue or bust was erected to honor the nation's countless folk heroes, political and military leaders, and outstanding scientific and cultural figures. Only Kim Il Sung's statues dominate the horizon of North Korea. All this cogently demonstrates that the *Juche* idea has been as much an impediment to the development of fine arts as it was to that of literature in North Korea. The corollary is an ever-deepening isolation of its cultural life from the rest of the world.

COMMENTS ON THE DEVELOPMENT OF CULTURE AND ART

In the past forty years North Korea has devoted enormous attention and resources to the development of literature and art. There is no denying that the level of overall literary and artistic attainments has shown a major improvement over the pre-Liberation period. Achievements included educational reform, progress in science and technology, construction of cultural institutions, and expansion of mass involvement in cultural and art activities. All these remarkable achievements contributed to an elevation of the cultural and educational level of the citizenry. A spinoff of this government-sponsored gigantic undertaking was the emergence of a large number of gifted and skilled professional and amateur authors and literary and art groups.

On the other hand, the dominant official ideology of *Juche* interfered with literature and art in a very serious way and with devastating consequences. Under the Kim regime, literature and art became an instrument for implementing Party policy, for strengthening the totalitarian regime, and for promoting Kim Il Sung's personality cult. The only period of respite from such rigorous ideological domination was the 1950s.

Deplorably, the rigid and unrelenting central control over literature and art virtually stifled creative activities and thwarted genuine artistic endeavors and deterred fruitful and free debate. From the dominance of the *Juche* idea ensured through heavy censorship and other administrative measures arose insuperable difficulties in the free pursuit of literature and art. Diversity and pluralism in art were completely eliminated. Both the outside world and history were examined and analyzed strictly within the ideological parameters of *Juche*. *Juche* has been the sole legitimate world outlook and political philosophy. Only one approach—socialist realism in its extreme form—received official approval. It was devoted first to the adulation of the Kim dynasty and then to the glorification of the Party for its leading role in society.

As for contemporary South Korean literature and art, the North Korean people were kept in total ignorance about them and allowed absolutely no access to them. All they could have was misinformation provided by the Pyongyang purveyors of lies. The situation was further exacerbated by its isolation not only from South Korea but also from the rest of the world. Minimal interaction with writers, artists, and scientists abroad results in an insular mentality and parochialism and makes it difficult for its people to comprehend problems related not only to the rest of the world but also to Korea itself. Given the obduracy of the Kim Il Sung regime, the transformation of the deeply ingrained system is a long-term process. North Korea's literature and art will still stagnate, much like the process of reunification.

5

IDEOLOGY AND WOMEN IN NORTH KOREA

KYUNG AE PARK

University of British Columbia

Studies on the position of women in society have shown considerable disagreement regarding the type of social system that may be conducive to the emancipation of women. The Western liberal modernization perspective expects that the process of industrialization will remove traditional constraints on women, change the traditional pattern of sexual division, and thereby foster the liberation of women. Women are supposed to be one of the most favored beneficiaries of the fruits of modernization. The subordination or marginalization of women in capitalist society is regarded as a "deviation" from the Western social norms of equality, freedom, and justice. It results from the fact that fruits of modernization have benefited primarily men as only men were working in the public sphere while women were confined to the domestic sphere. Yet, the problem of sexual inequality can be corrected within the capitalist system through technical reforms such as legal and attitudinal changes. It is assumed that women can be liberated by being well integrated into the public sphere of the capitalist structures and into the process of modernization.

The Marxist perspective, on the other hand, sees the roots of sexual inequality, like other forms of social inequality including class hierarchy, lying in private property. Private property required the family institution in order to preserve wealth through inheritance within the paternal line. In the bourgeois family, woman became the property of her husband, whose responsibilities included unpaid domestic production and reproduction. Hence, according to this perspective, wives are proletariats exploited by their bourgeois husbands. Accordingly, oppression of women is a structural problem that cannot be solved within the capitalist structure. The subordination of women can only be solved by a socialist revolution of class struggle, which will eventually free women from unpaid domestic labor, and integrate them into social production.

North Korea has closely adhered to the Marxist perspective on the "woman question." Today, it claims that North Korean women have already achieved a liberation in the country of a women's paradise. Although there has been a remarkable improvement in the women's position after the establishment of the socialist regime in North Korea, this extreme optimism seems to have some loopholes. This paper attempts to examine North Korea's policies on the "woman question" and the status of women in order to analyze how the socialist system has contributed to improving the women's lot in that political system.

As North Korea is an extremely closed system, a dearth of data and information severely limits any study on that country. Up to the present, a very limited number of studies touched the subject of women, most of which are short accounts of fact-finding trips to North Korea. As one scholar notices, information on North Korean women is "conspicuous by its absence in most studies on women in post-revolutionary societies."[1] The present study is mainly based on North Korean sources including a woman's magazine, speeches of President Kim Il Sung, newspapers, and other government publications. But, in an effort to balance the reliability of these materials, South Korean government sources were also consulted.

MAJOR POLICIES ON WOMEN

Since the Communist revolution aimed at changing the traditional social structure and liberating the oppressed under the traditional society, such as women and peasants, the North Korean leaders incorporated this task into the regime formation process. Since as early as 1946, North Korea has instituted various policies regarding women's emancipation. These policies seem to aim at three basic goals: liberation of women from the patriarchal family and social systems; liberation through social labor; and creation of a socialist woman.

Liberation from the Patriarchal Family and Social Systems

Immediately following liberation from Japanese colonialism, the North Korean leaders launched a series of campaigns and reforms, including family and land reforms and nationalization of all enterprises that had been owned by Japanese capitalists or Korean collaborators, as an integral part of the socialist regime formation effort. Concurrently, various laws for social change were promulgated by the Provisional People's Committee, such as the Law on Land Reform, the Law on Sex Equality, the Labor Law, and the Law on Nationalization of Essential Industries.

In March 1946, an agrarian reform was instituted with some one million *chongbo* of land confiscated for redistribution gratis among about 724,000 poor and landless peasants. It granted women equal allotments of land as Kim Il Sung mentioned: "At the time of the agrarian reform women in the countryside received their share of land on a par with men and became the owners of lands like all the rest of the peasants."[2] The most progressive law that brought a sweeping change to the traditional position of women was the Law on Sex Equality announced on July 30, 1946. The purpose of the law was to "transform the old feudal relations of the sexes" and to encourage women to "participate fully in cultural, social, and political life." It emphasized equal rights in all spheres of State, the right to a free marriage and divorce, and equal rights to inherit property and to share property in case of divorce. It ended arranged marriages, polygamy, concubinage, buying and selling of women, prostitution, and the professional entertainer system. Thus, for the first time in history, women were placed on an equal footing with men in all areas. The Labor Law was also an important legislation with regard to women's rights at work. In Articles 14 through 17, it stipulates the rights of mothers and pregnant women, including seventy-seven days of maternity leave with full pay, baby-feeding break during work with pay, prohibition of assigning pregnant or nursing women on overtime or night work, and transferring of a pregnant woman to easier work with equal pay. In addition, the Law on Nationalization of Essential Industries, which was the beginning of an elimination of private property, contributed to a weakening of the economic power of a patriarch.

Along with these laws, North Korea abolished the family registry system based on male lineage in 1947, replacing it with the new citizen registry system. Considering that South Korean women's organizations have failed, up to present, to abolish the system in spite of their arduous struggle against it for almost three decades, leaders of North Korea appear to have had a strong commitment to the abolition of the feudal family system. At the same time, in 1946, the mass organization for women, the Democratic Women's Union of North Korea, was established to unite the women's movement under the Korean Workers' Party (KWP).

These sweeping changes brought a profound impact on the traditional patriarchal systems, especially on the family system: Kinship clans eventually disappeared, the family lineage-book system was completely destroyed, and thus, the nuclear family system began to emerge. Without doubt, these policies announced as early as 1946 and 1947 laid a basis for the emancipation of women from the feudalistic patriarchy of the family and social systems. These legal guarantees were reinforced later by the Constitution of the Democratic People's Republic of Korea of 1949, the Socialist Constitution of 1972, and other statutes of North Korea.

However, the legal granting of equal rights was not enough to liberate women from patriarchy. These rights were given to women from above almost overnight. In view of the authoritarian culture of the nation, the concept of "equality" was alien to both men and women, and it soon received tremendous resistance. On the eve of the historic first democratic election, men openly opposed women's right to vote and the election of women candidates on the People's Committee, mobilizing every means including abstentions to prevent them from being elected. Kim Il Sung soon felt the immediate need for awakening and educating the people to his equal rights campaign. He delivered numerous speeches, stepped up the education of the women through the organizational enlargement of the Women's Union, and launched an extensive campaign to wipe out illiteracy among the women to awaken them to their rights. On the occasion of the democratic elections, he pointed out:

> Still others maintain that women should not be elected to the people's committees and even that they should not be allowed to take part in the elections. This is also wrong thinking. Women account for half of the population. If half of the people do not take part in electing the organ of power or in its work, such power can hardly be called a genuine people's power. Women constitute a great force, and large numbers of them are sharing in the work of rehabilitating our country no less creditably than men. In our country women are guaranteed by law equal rights with men in all fields. The Law on Sex Equality, therefore, should be fully enforced in the elections, for only then can they be truly democratic elections.[3]

As such, emancipation of women from the patriarchal family and social systems was one of the basic goals of North Korea's policy on the "woman question."

Liberation through Social Labor

In the tradition of classical Marxist theory, particularly in the theory of Friedrich Engels, sexual equality will result from economic liberation, and women's participation in economic production outside the home will lead to their full emancipation. Engels argues: "The first requisite for the emancipation of women is that all women participate again in social labor; to achieve this, individual families are required to be no longer the units of the social economy."[4] Kim Il Sung embraced this idea when he said: "The women. . . can achieve complete emancipation only if they strive with no less devotion and awareness than men to solve the problems arising on the productive fronts of the factories and countryside. . . "[5] Based on this basic tenet of Marxist theory, North Korea initiated "working-classization" of women, which was to enhance their economic independence.

It was not until the late 1950s when North Korea embarked on a program to instill in the populace the socialist values, norms, and ideals. In fact, Kim Il Sung himself admitted in 1955 that the party did not propagandize very actively for socialism prior to this period:

> If we had advocated building socialism in Korea immediately after the liberation, who would have listened to us? People would never

have come near us, because the Japanese imperialists had conducted malignant propaganda, even alleging that under socialism many share one bed and eat meals from one common pot.[6]

In order for a socialist construction, North Korea initiated the mass mobilization campaign, the *Chollima* (Flying Horse) movement. It aimed at reaching a "revolutionary high tide of socialist construction" and realizing industrialization through the mobilization of the masses. With this mass mobilization campaign, the focus of women's policy shifted from achieving equality and liberation from traditional oppression to Engels' "liberation through labor." The purpose was to inject socialist ideas that women's emancipation would be achieved only through loyalty to the regime's task of building a socialist Korea. Accordingly, it was claimed that women had already achieved liberation since the groundwork for equality had been laid in the law, and thus, they now should turn their energies into productive work to help build socialist Korea. Kim Il Sung made this point clear in his speech:

> An important question in Women's Union activities in the past was to wipe out illiteracy and eliminate the feudalistic ideas that oppressed the women. But this work no longer seems to be of major importance in our society. Today, the Women's Union should actively campaign for women's participation in socialist construction and bend its efforts to provide conditions that will allow them to work well.[7]

As such, women were encouraged to play a role "as one wheel of a wagon in the work of nation-building."

In order to mobilize women outside the family the regime pushed for socialization of housework. According to Lenin, although participation in labor is a necessary condition of female emancipation, the real emancipation will begin "only where and when an all-out struggle begins against this petty housekeeping. . ."[8] Engels is in accord with Lenin when he said that true equality comes only when "private housekeeping is transformed into a social industry, [and] the care and education of children becomes a public affair."[9] In North Korea, as early as 1946, Kim Il Sung pointed out that the state should take steps to bring up the children under public care in order to encourage women to take part in public life.[10] Later, the Fifth Congress of the KWP in 1970 announced freeing women from the heavy burden to household as one of the major goals of the party, which was reflected later in Article 62 of the Socialist Constitution of 1972. The article stipulates some benefits of women in order to provide every possible condition for them to participate in public life, including maternity leave with pay, maternity hospitals, free nurseries and kindergartens, and reduced working hours for mothers of large families. At the same time, the Law on the Nursing and Upbringing of Children of 1976, and the Socialist Labor Law of 1978 stipulated a progressive provision that women with three or more children under 13 receive eight-hours pay for six-hours work. Through these measures, the point was made clear that it was the responsibility of the state and society to bring up children and to protect working mothers.

With the launching of the *Chollima* movement, North Korean women's housework began to be socialized through nurseries, kindergartens, laundries, and an efficient food industry. In 1949, North Korea started with only 12 nurseries and 116 kindergartens, which increased to 7600 and 4500, respectively, in 1961, admitting 700,000 children. It was reported in 1976 that almost 100 percent of the 3.5 million children could enter more than 60,000 nurseries and kindergartens.[11] In addition, there is reportedly an extensive network of food "take out" services for busy working women. One Women's Union member summarizes the socialization of housework in North Korea:

> Children are brought up at state expense. If there is pressing and ironing [to be done] it goes to the laundries. The foodstuffs industry has been developed, so food can be bought at any time. So what is there left to do in the family?[12]

At the same time, women were urged to participate vigorously in the technical revolution by acquiring at least one technique in order to free themselves from their arduous labor. The technical revolution is one of the programs of the "triple revolution" of technology, culture, and ideology, which begun under the slogan, "Let's meet the requirement of *Juche* (self-reliance) in ideology, technology, and culture."[13] It is regarded as the prerequisite for successful construction of socialism via the *Chollima* movement.

All these measures and the *Chollima* mass mobilization campaign greatly expanded women's participation in the labor force. The female labor force, which was only 20 percent in 1956, has steadily increased, and women now constitute about 48 percent of the total labor force. The 1980 data showed that women occupied 56 percent of the labor force in the agricultural sector, 45 percent in the industrial sector, 20 percent in mining, 30 percent in forestry, 15 percent in heavy industry, and 70 percent in light industry.[14] In the educational area, women accounted for 80 percent of the elementary school teachers, while the figures for the middle and high school, technical school, and college levels were 35 percent, 30 percent, and 15 percent, respectively. Women are playing a particularly prominent part in agriculture, light industry, and education.

At the same time, women's participation in public and political affairs was also encouraged. In 1961, Kim Il Sung emphasized that there should be many women with master's degrees and with doctorates, pointing out that no woman had yet received a doctorate. He also pointed out that there was a very small number of women cadres, in view of women's making up half the population of the country, and that even those women cadres were in the areas of secondary importance.[15] By 1972, women accounted for more than 20 percent of the Supreme People's Assembly (SPA) (see Table 1), and at the local levels of people's assemblies in provinces, cities, and counties, women have occupied between 20 and 26 percent since 1956. It was also reported in 1976 that a third of all deputies to representative government organizations, ranging from the Supreme People's Assembly (SPA) to local people's assemblies, were women.[16]

In the early 1950s, the North Korean leadership, which had been fairly tolerant of private enterprise, began to accelerate the process of nationalizing the remaining private industry as well as trade and transportation, and collectivizing agriculture through cooperatives. This goal, the socialist transformation of ownership of the production means, became reality by the end of the 1950s. As Engels argued, efforts were made to replace individual families with collectives as the units of the social economy. The total collectivization of agriculture and industry, which was accompanied by the *Chollima* movement, greatly contributed to the weakening of the patriarchal power. Elimination of private property led to the demolition of inheritance, which destroyed the material basis of traditional patriarchy. At the same time, the collectivization efforts accelerated the mobilization of women outside the family for their productive labor. In sum, women were encouraged to take more economic, social, and political roles for socialist construction. They could acquire economic independence through paid labor,

TABLE 1

PERCENTAGE OF FEMALE SUPREME PEOPLE'S ASSEMBLY (SPA) MEMBERS

SPA	Date	%
First	August 1948	12.1
Second	August 1957	12.6
Third	October 1962	9.1
Fourth	November 1967	16.0
Fifth	December 1972	21.0
Sixth	December 1977	20.8
Seventh	February 1982	NA
Eighth	December 1986	21.1
Ninth	May 1990	NA

SOURCES: The First through the Sixth: Dae-Sook Suh, *Korean Communism: 1945–1980* (Honolulu: The University Press of Hawaii, 1981), p. 442. The Eighth: *Choson Yosong*, April 1989, p. 29.

became socially active, and held responsible positions. They were provided with non-traditional new roles.

Creation of a Socialist Woman

Another goal of North Korea's women's policy is to create a socialist woman. Since the early 1960s, this goal has been pursued along with the cultural and ideological revolutions of the "triple revolution." The cultural revolution was meant to dispose of remnants of traditional ideas and political culture of Confucianism, and replace them with a new socialist culture. In order to bring about new socialist culture, intellectualization of the whole society through education was an important goal to be achieved: "To intellectualize the whole society means training all members of society following their working classization, to be fully developed communist-type men with the cultural and technical standards of the university graduate."[17] A new eleven-year compulsory educational program got under way to produce fully developed men and women of the *Juche* type, and the whole country was required to study under the revolutionary slogan, "Let the entire Party, the entire people and the entire army study!" It was claimed that all the working people, without exception, were enrolled in the study networks of Party and working people's organizations and the system of adult education. Closely related to the cultural revolution are the regime's efforts to remold people through political indoctrination. Close attention was paid to the ideological education of the masses, so as to arouse enthusiasm of the masses, and to model the society on the *Juche* idea. Through all these measures, North Korea attempted to increase the political consciousness of the masses so that they work selflessly for collective objectives, which the new socialist men and women should embrace.

The women's task here is to revolutionize and work-classizing themselves first before undertaking the role of upbringing their children. The Fourth Congress of the Party in 1961 proposed as its important function the task of educating and rearing children along communist lines. Mothers were charged with this "honorable revolutionary duty" as first the educator of children, and were urged to become excellent communists to assume the duty. Kim Il Sung singled out as an important responsibility of the Women's Union the task of "making all women communist mothers and fine communist educators for the new generation. . ."[18] He added that in order to become a communist mother, she should participate in public life because it would help her keep abreast of realities and quickly acquire communist ideology. Along this line, the Chairwoman of the Women's Union Kim Song Ae (Kim Il Sung's wife) announced that the basic task of the organization is to correct the tendency to perceive the organization as a culturally enlightening group, and to educate and indoctrinate women with communist ideology. In order to achieve this task, the Union formed nation-wide study groups named the

"Mother Kang Ban Suk Study Groups" to allow women to "Learn from Mother Kang Ban Suk" and from other women members of the Anti-Japanese Guerrilla Army. It also reorganized the adult education system, "Mothers' School," and shifted its emphasis from the enlightenment of women to ideological education. In addition, in 1961, "Mothers' Exhibition Gallery" was open to educate women through showing them the achievements of communist mothers and communist women. Very recently, this task of the Union was reaffirmed during the tenth plenary meeting of the Central Committee, held in May 1990. All women, including mothers and nurses at the day-care centers were urged to become "true communists" equipped with the *Juche* idea so that they can assume the role of communist mothers and teachers to raise children as socialist revolutionaries.

Prospects

As examined above, North Korean women experienced radical changes after the socialist revolution. The leaders were committed to change the traditional family, economic, and social systems, which brought the North Korean women various legal and institutional arrangements for equal rights. As mentioned earlier, these rights were given to them almost overnight from above. Throughout the post-revolutionary period, opportunities for women in public life have been greatly expanded through many affirmative measures such as the quota system in various political positions. Furthermore, women's status in a family has largely been enhanced as a result of gaining economic power through work. Thus, North Korea's legal provisions and institutional mechanisms for improving women's lot in the society appear to be impressive, especially when they are compared with other developing countries.

Nevertheless, North Korean women cannot be said to have achieved a level of socioeconomic status as admirable as claimed by the North Koreans themselves. In his theory of social inequality, Gerhard Lenski identifies a set of three sources of power influencing inequality in society as the "power of property" (economic power), the "power of position," and the "power of force."[19] As alluded to earlier, the most remarkable improvement for the North Korean women was made in the economic arena due to the regime's emphasis on liberation through labor and to the abolition of private property that led to the decline of economic power of the patriarch. However, it is evident that male and female wages are not equal in North Korea, although no specific information is available concerning a pay scale.[20] The wage difference can be attributed to the unequal representation of women in various occupational structures, indicating a sexual division of labor. As shown earlier, women are well represented in such areas as light industry, agriculture, public health, and education. However, sexual parity is obvious in the several male-dominant arenas, including heavy industry, mining, and high technology. This suggests that the North Korean women do not seem to share the "power of property" completely, although they have shown a major advance in this area.

Women do not seem to have achieved the "power of position" in North Korea. Although women occupy about one-third of the representative positions in the lower echelons of power, they are greatly underrepresented in the upper levels of power structure, perhaps with the exception of the SPA which is not considered the real decision-making center (see Table 1). As one examines the more powerful organizations such as the Central Committee (CC), the Politburo of the KWP, and the Administrative Council (the Cabinet), it becomes apparent that very few women have been in positions of power. As shown in Table 2, the proportion of women members in the CC has fluctuated between 2.4 percent to 5.1 percent for full members, and 4.9

TABLE 2

FEMALE CENTRAL COMMITTEE MEMBERS

Congress	Date	Full Members	%	Candidate Members	%
First	August 1946	Ho Chong Suk[a] Pak Chong Ae[a]	4.7	—	—
Second	March 1948	Pak Chong Ae Ho Chong Suk	3.0	—	—
Third	April 1956	Pak Chong Ae Ho Chong Suk	2.8	—	—
Fourth	September 1961	Pak Chong Ae Kim Ok Sun	2.4	Yi Yang Suk[b] Hwang Sun Hui Pak Hyong Suk Yi Yong Sun Han Kyong Suk	10.0
Fifth	November 1961	Chong Kyong Hui[a] Hwang Sun Hui[a] O Suk Hui Yi Son Hwa Yu Sun Hui Chon Yong Hui	5.1	Ho Chang Suk[b] Wang Ok Hwan[b] Kim Kum Ok Ho Yon Suk Chon Yong Hui	7.3
Sixth	October 1980	Chong Kyong Hui Ho Chong Suk Hwang Sun Hui Kim Song Ae Yu Chong Suk	3.4	Yi Yang Suk Yun Ki Jong Ho Chang Suk Wang Ok Hwan Pak Sol Hui	4.9

[a]. Reelected to full membership.
[b]. Reelected to candidate membership.
SOURCE: Compiled by the author from Dae-Sook Suh, *Korean Communism: 1945–1980* (Honolulu: The University Press of Hawaii, 1981).

percent to 10 percent for candidate members. Up to the Sixth Party Congress, only eleven different women have served the CC as full members, among whom four were reelected. In the highest decision-making body of the KWP, the Politburo (Political Committee), only Pak Chong Ae has served, in the Fourth Congress, as a member. Chong Kyong Hui was appointed alternate member of the Politburo in the Sixth Congress, and was later joined by Kim Bok Shin. Thus far, only three women could climb to the highest level of the power structure. In the Administrative Council, women have filled only two positions on the average in each cabinet (see Table 3). Currently, Kim Bok Sin serves as deputy premier of the Administrative Council.

This manifest low representation in the ruling bodies is exacerbated by women's low representation in the military. Women's participation in the military, which has been one of the most significant sources of power and leadership in the KWP,[21] especially during the early years of the regime formation, has virtually been insignificant. When asked what was the highest rank held by a woman in the military, a representative of the Women's Union did not know except that some women held the rank of Colonel as heads of military hospitals.[21] This suggests that there is no prominent female figure in the armed forces. During the revolutionary period, there were independence heroines and fighters, but they never gained *control* of the means of coercion. North Korean women do not seem to share the "power of force."

In short, it seems that women showed a major advance in obtaining part of the "power of property," yet, the "power of position" and the "power of force" have been monopolized by men. A handful of women played a part in the political leadership hierarchy. However, since women were not organized as *women*, this lack of power bloc resulted, to use Salaff and Merkle's term, in the "star system." Individual women are promoted as "symbols of the fulfillment of revolutionary promises rather than a substantial commitment to end the oppression of women *as a category.*"[23]

In North Korea, the problem of organizing women as *women* is largely based on the basic tenet of Marxist theory that women would not be fully liberated until communism came into a full swing. As the "woman question" should be subsumed under the "class question," a communist revolution is needed to free women. Therefore, any attempt to organize the masses around women's issues is seen as selfish and divisive to class solidarity. In fact, those who confine themselves to the "woman question" are considered bourgeois women, and it is maintained that women should pursue the equality of men and women together rather than focusing on their status as women. Kim Il Sung once made this point clear by labeling a women's organization that claims emancipation "apart from economic and productive activities and all other social activities" as a "rich women's club."[24] Accordingly, feminism, which places women's concerns first, is evil and counterrevolutionary. Many leftist women as well as men would oppose

TABLE 3

Some Female Members of the Administrative Council

Cabinet	Appointment	Ministry	Name	Tenure
First:	1948	Minister of Culture and Propaganda	Ho Chong Suk	9 years
	1957	Minister of Justice	Ho Chong Suk	1 month
Second	1957	Minister of Justice	Ho Chong Suk	2 years
	1961	Minister of Agriculture	Pak Chong Ae	1 year
	1962	Minister of Commerce	Yi Yang Suk	1 month
Third	1966	Minister of Culture	Pak Yong Sin	1 year
	1967	Minister of Foodstuff and Daily Necessities Industries	Yi Ho Hyok	1 year
	1967	Minister of Textile and Paper Industries	Yi Yang Suk	1 year
Fourth	1967	Minister of Foodstuff and Daily Necessities Industries	Yi Ho Hyok	5 years
	1967	Minister of Culture	Pak Yong Sin	5 years
	1967	Minister of Textile and Paper Industries	Yi Yang Suk	5 years
Fifth	1972	None		
Sixth	NA	Minister of Finance	Yun Gi Jong	NA
Seventh	1982	NA		
Eighth	1986	Chair of External Economic Commission	Kim Bok Sin	NA
	1986	Minister of Finance	Yun Gi Jong	NA
Ninth	1990	Chair of the Light Industry Commission	Kim Bok Sin	present
	1990	Minister of Finance	Yun Gi Jong	present

First–Sixth: Both original and interim appointees.
Seventh–Ninth: Only original appointees.

SOURCE: Compiled by the author from various sources.

feminism as being too selfish and bourgeois, and view women's problems as peripheral to the proletarian struggle. This ideological tenet discouraged the women's movement in North Korea, and it may help explain why the campaign to liberate women from traditional oppression has been left to the KWP and that its goals and strategies have been defined by the men who dominate the KWP.

In sum, although the position of women in North Korea has been much improved from that of pre-revolutionary days, especially in the economic arena, women still lack the powers of position and force. North Korea's adherence to the Marxist perspective that undermine feminists' struggle for liberation, coupled with the tradition of male superiority of Neo-Confucianism that is still very much alive in the people's belief system, seems to be a major hurdle to overcome.

NOTES

1. An earlier and extended version of this chapter was published in *Pacific Affairs* (Vol. 65, No. 4, Winter 1992-93, pp. 527-545). Jon Halliday, "Women in North Korea: An Interview with the Korean Democratic Women's Union," *Bulletin of Concerned Asian Scholars*, 17 (3), 1985, p. 50.

2. Kim Il Sung addressed the Communist Worker's of Women's Union, who were scheduled to attend First Conference of Democratic Women's Union of North Korea. See his speech, "On the Future Tasks of the Women's Union," May 9, 1946, *Kim Il Sung Works*, Vol. 2 (Pyongyang: F.L.P.H., 1980), p. 185.

3. "On the Eve of the Historic Democratic Elections," speech at a Pyongyang Celebration of the Democratic Elections, November 1, 1946, *Kim Il Sung Works*, p. 463.

4. Quoted in Phyllis Andors, "Social Revolution and Woman's Emancipation: China During the Great Leap Forward," *Concerned Asian Scholars*, Vol. 7, January-March 1969, p. 35.

5. Kim Il Sung's speech "Congratulations on the Founding of the Magazine, *Korean Women.*" See *Kim Il Sung Works*, September 6, 1946, p. 354.

6. "Some Questions Concerning Party and State Work," April 14, 1955, *Kim Il Sung Selected Works* (Pyongyang, Korea: Foreign Language Publishing House, 1976), Vol. I, p. 291.

7. "The Duty of Mothers in the Education of Children," speech at the National Meeting of Mothers, November 16, 1961, *Kim Selected Works*, Vol. III, p. 227.

8. V. Lenin, "A Great Beginning," in *The Emancipation of Women: Selections From the Writings of V.I. Lenin* (New York: International Publishers, 1966), pp. 63–64, quoted in Phyllis Andors, "A Look at the Present Socio-Economic and Political Context of the Changing Role of Women and the Family in China," *The Australian and New Zealand Journal of Sociology*, 12(1), 1976, p. 23.

9. Quoted in Jane Jaquette, "Women and Modernization Theory: A Decade of Feminist Criticism," *World Politics*, 34(2), 1982, p. 274.

10. "On the Future Tasks," p. 194.

11. Kim Il Sung, "On Further Developing the Nursing and Upbringing of Children," speech delivered at the sixth session of the Fifth Supreme People's Assembly, April 29, 1976.

12. Halliday, p. 53.

13. For a detailed discussion of the triple revolution and *Juche* ideology, see Kyung Ae Park and Han S. Park, *China and North Korea: Politics of Integration and Modernization* (Hong Kong: Asian Research Service, 1990), Chapter III.

14. Tae Young Lee, *Bukhan Yosong* [*North Korean Women*] (Seoul, Korea: Silchon Moonhak Sa, 1988), p. 194.

15. "On Revolutionizing and 'Working-Classizing' Women," speech at the fourth congress of the Democratic Women's Union of Korea, October 7, 1971, *Kim Selected Works*, Vol. VI, pp. 105–126.

16. *Rodong sinmun*, July 3, 1976.

17. Muhammad Missuri, *Kimilsungism* (Pyongyang, Korea: Foreign Language Publishing House, 1978), p. 228.

18. "The Duty of Mothers," p. 225.

19. Gerhard Lenski, *Power and Privilege: A Theory of Social Stratification* (New York: McGraw-Hill Book Co., 1966).

20. Halliday, p. 48.

21. Military representation in the CC has fluctuated between 12 and 20 percent: 12 in the Second Congress; 13 in the Third; 20 in the Fourth; 16 in the Fifth; and 17 in the Sixth Congress. See Kyung Ae Park, "A Comparison of Political Involvement of the Military in China and North Korea," paper delivered at the Annual Convention of the International Studies Association, Washington, D.C., March 5–9, 1985.

22. Halliday, p. 54

23. Janet Salaff and Judith Merkel, "Women in Revolution: The Lessons of the Soviet Union and China," *Berkeley Journal of Sociology*, Vol. 15 (1970), p. 182.

24. "On Founding of the Magazine," p. 354.

6

POLITICS AND IDEOLOGY IN THE POST-COLD WAR ERA

VASILY MIKHEEV

The Academy of Sciences, Moscow

Tight control of the public institutions over the life of its citizens is a main characteristic of the internal situation in the Democratic People's Republic of Korea (DPRK). Slogans like "not to know any ideas but those of *Juche*" and "to live without feeling envy towards anybody" as well as showing up "the advantages of our system of socialism" reflect a pattern of social order which is desired by the North Korean regime. In such a situation the spiritual and social stability is guaranteed through the isolation of the people from the world processes and with the help of the repressive institutions which leave almost no chance for the belief in, much less the expression of dissenting views.

However, in our contemporary, interdependent world the isolation cannot be absolute and the qualitative changes in the international environment which took place at the beginning of the current decade could not help but affect the internal situation in the country. The world socialist system has disintegrated. The ideas of socialist totalitarianism have been defeated in Eastern Europe and have been gradually falling down in the Soviet Union. Those changes have also affected the Asian countries of China, Vietnam, and Mongolia. Due to these changes, the old autocratic and ideological links between North Korea and the USSR and Eastern Europe, as well as its Asian partners, have been dismantled. For that reason the Pyongyang administration was forced to look for ways to adapt itself to a new situation.

In addition, a drastic worsening of the economic situation is pushing the country to seek new approaches. An imbalance in the domestic economy, a long-lasting deficit, and technological backwardness have combined with the aggravation of the food situation and the USSR's nearly complete cancellation of shipments of oil and other valuable goods since the beginning of 1991 to create a threat of hunger and social unrest.

In this situation, as always happens in the moments of crisis, the activities of two main mechanisms of the North Korean totalitarianism, propaganda and repression, have been intensified. The trend of the ideological propaganda has changed; attempts are being made to modify theoretical conceptions of the building of socialism and new details are appearing in political life. A new situation requires a new analysis and a new evaluation of the ideological climate in North Korea.

JUCHE AS AN IDEOLOGICAL BASIS
OF THE KOREAN SOCIETY

The ideas of *Juche* are recognized as the ideological basis of the Korean society. In the 1960s and 1990s an increase of its influence on the country's

life was observed. At the same time, it was turning from the method of ideological warfare and an object of discussion within the party to a political line
and then into an ideology. Due to these circumstances, it seems wrong to
qualify the *Juche* only as an ideological system formed in 1950s and 1960s
and not to take into account its dynamics and its growing influence upon an
increasing number of aspects of life.

In the 1950s *Juche* was used as a method of political activities of the
Korean Workers' Party (KWP). It was supposed to formalize and dogmatize
"the thoughtless extrapolation of the methods of work used in other countries on the Korean present-day reality".[1]

During the Fourth KWP Congress (1961) the establishment of *Juche*
was related to the ideological and political struggle between different
factions. During the same Congress a wide interpretation of *Juche* as an anti-
dogmatic principle to guide an approach toward the different problems of
public life was presented. Nevertheless, nothing was said yet about *Juche* as
an ideological platform. According to the Congress, "Marxism-Leninism and
scientific knowledge are a powerful weapon of revolution."[2]

By the middle of the 1960s, *Juche* affected every element of the
KWP's domestic and foreign political activities. The task of establishing *Juche*
in that period was interpreted as a step toward becoming independent in
policy, economy, and adequate self-defense.[3]

By the beginning of the 1970s *Juche* had already had a strong influence on ideology. In that period Korean leaders understood that they had to
give their own interpretation of the social processes, rescind from Soviet-
Chinese ideological disagreements and from the Eastern European anti-
totalitarian events of the second half of the 1960s. In the KWP Congress
(1970), *Juche*, as well as Marxism-Leninism, was proclaimed an ideological
basis of the party: "Today in our country a single ideological system has been
established, a monolithic unity has been achieved on the ground of
Marxism-Leninism and the ideas of *Juche*".[4]

By the middle of the 1970s, *Juche* was consolidated as the ideological
basis of North Korean society. It was stated "the ideas of *Juche* are a scientific
and revolutionary philosophy which every man of communist stamp must
take as an armament."[5] In 1970, when the six-year economic plan was
adopted, the necessity of uniting on the ground of Marxism-Leninism and
Juche was stressed. When the results of the same plan were presented in 1977
they told only about the special role of *Juche*: "Fulfilling the six-year plan
every worker adopted the ideals of *Juche* and on this basis their cohesion has
consolidated even more."[6] In his speech on the occasion of the thirtieth
anniversary of the DPRK, Kim Il Sung put forward the task that "every
member of society should be armed with the ideas of *Juche*." Nobody spoke
about the rule of Marxism-Leninism.[7]

During the Sixth KWP Congress (1980) the reorganization of the
whole society on the basis of the ideas of *Juche* was presented as a "general

goal revolution" which meant "the building of the communist society" that has a priority over all other political and economical tasks.[8]

In the 1970s and 1980s, the leaders of the KWP tried to internationalize the ideas of *Juche*, placing them in opposition to Marxism. From the beginning of 1971, international conferences on *Juche* were held, groups and research institutes which study the propaganda of *Juche* were organized.

In the 1980s, the leaders tried to turn *Juche* into a theory of universal historical importance, including it as a main element in Kimilsungism which is declared a "solely correct revolutionary theory" that "in present-day conditions has substituted Marxism-Leninism." At the same time, they proclaimed Marxism-Leninism obsolete because it was "unable to define the ways of solving current problems."[9] Said Kim Jong Il: "Kimilsungism cannot be explained in terms of Marxism."[10] Contrasting Kimilsungism to Marxism, he underlined the differences in their content and structure. There are three basic elements of Kimilsungism, namely, the ideas of *Juche*, a revolutionary method, and an administrative method. In contrast to Marxism, which is based on materialist dialectics on the postulate that matter is primary and consciousness is secondary, Kimilsungism "solves the main question of philosophy in a different way," affirming that "the man who rules over the world instead of being its parties is the basis of everything." Continued Kim: "This philosophical principle cannot be explained from the point of view of Marxist dialectics."[11] These explanations given by Kim at a time when his position inside the country was being strengthened, are qualified as a new stage of development of the theory, as a formation of Kimilsungism-Kimjongilism. In other words, on the one hand, it is a plagiarism of Marxist terminology, but on the other hand, it is an effort to shut Kim off from the ideological research being carried on within the world communist movement under the banners of Eurocommunism or communism with a human face, Maoism, or developed socialism.

In the 1980s, the ideological stock of the KWP was widened by the ideas about leadership and power inheritance. Revolutionary practice was presented as solely the activities of the leader, activities which require an adequate continuation after his demise. This argument was based on the following factors: A leader is needed for the victory of a revolution and every new generation of revolutionaries is coming to replace the previous one. This circumstance poses a question about a new leader; only Kim Jong Il can be a leader because "he was together with the leader from childhood and inherited his methods of leadership."[12] In fact, these conclusions can be explained by the fear of Kim Il Sung due to the social and political instability which comes while the superleadership is changing. In his private talks during his visit to Moscow in 1984, the North Korean leader said that "a depreciation towards the problem of successor to power" was a mistake of Stalin and Kruschev that cost them defamation of their names.

Hence, in four decades of the DPRK existence, *Juche* has shifted from a principle of political work into the ideological basis of the North Korean society. By the 1990s, the *Juche* philosophy, from an exponent of the North Korean leadership's reaction to the inner-party struggle and the struggle within the world communist movement, has become a self-sufficing ideological theory whose purpose consists of glorifying the leader's image and in founding the legality of his son's claims on the power.

CONCEPTION OF SOCIALISM IN THE DPRK

Nominally, the ideas of *Juche* are the basis of the North Korean conception of socialism, but in fact they were originally copied from the Stalin strategy followed by the USSR in the 1940s and 1950s.

The KWP regards socialism as reflecting a transitional society in which some remnants of the old society remain. In order to overcome them, a continuous class struggle and uninterrupted revolution are needed. While defining the purposes of the socialist society, the growth of the economic and cultural standard of people's life (Eastern European formula) and the free and all encompassing development of an individual (demagogic formula of the Soviet propaganda under Brezhnev) are replaced by the ideological tasks to "reform the whole society on the *Juche* ideas" and "to achieve a full self-dependence of the people." It is believed that "self-dependence is a criterion of the progress upon the whole."

The building of socialism in the DPRK is subdivided into two stages: a transitional period and a "full victory of the socialism," which opens a way a "towards an ideal communist society." The KWP upholds the view that class struggle should continue within the whole period of socialist building (Stalin's thesis). The dictatorship of the proletariat (in fact, an unlimited partocracy's power) is recognized as the only form of State power.

According to the principle of self-reliance, the KWP divides the transitional period into substages. At the stage of "biding up the basis of the self-dependent national economy" (1956–1960) "victory of the socialist system was gained" which is related to the strengthening of the "socialist relations of production," in other words, with the general nationalization of every aspect of the economic and public life. After the completion of that stage, the next substage consisted of "strengthening the self-dependent national economy." In the 1980s, the problem of subdividing the socialist building in North Korea into substages was not discussed in theoretical publications of the Labor Party and the current period of the development of the Korean society is considered to be a "struggle for the definitive victory of the socialism" through three revolutions. Perhaps such an incomprehensible formula suits the present leaders and will help them keep the basis of the system intact for a prolonged period. This system can be qualified as a system that minimizes objective factors of development. In other words, the system is subjective and pseudorevolutionary.

Pseudorevolutionism prevails in the KWP's views on international relations as well. It upholds a view that the world is an arena of a relentless struggle between socialism and capitalism. "To beat off a furious attack of the enemy" is a main political task of the KWP in its ideological activities among its people. Ideas of new political thinking and an interdependence of the world are refuted definitively as "revisionist."

The *Juche* theory of socialism pays great attention to the problem of educating a subject of revolution through "revolutionizing working people and educating them, taking as a pattern the working class." The refusal of personal welfare, absolute devotion to the leader and the party, and a selfless work ethic in order to fulfill their tasks are announced as the purpose of the life of every individual. As for labor relations, the role of material incentive is minimized. It is said that the growth of welfare decreases the revolutionary enthusiasm of the working masses. The equalization of wage and consumption as well as the regulation of the cultural and personal life of the working people are being popularized. The development of democracy is viewed only as an approximation of the party functionaries to the masses, as a task to know their thoughts and needs.

One of the most important elements of Korean socialism consists of the conception of a "self-dependent national economy." This term is interpreted as a formation of the whole economic complex which produces all the goods the country needs. Priority is placed on the military and heavy industry. Foreign economic relations should play a passive role to fill the gaps that appeared due to the failure of the planning and distributing system. The North Korean leadership needs protection from the outer world and from the world market because it wants to demonstrate to its own people that it is independent and not vulnerable to any outside pressure.

The interpretation of the relations of property and the market-monetary relationships reveals a subjective approach held by the KWP toward the problems of development. After having recognized the existence of two forms of property under socialism, State and cooperative, in the DPRK, the latter is considered less desirable and a strong effort is made to convert it into state property. The difficulty for the DPRK lies in finding a proper method of carrying this out. Perhaps it can be accomplished through raising the awareness of the working people. Today, in fact, the difference between the administration of state property in industry and the cooperative property in agriculture has been lost. But the fact is that agricultural production cooperatives are administered by district party committees on the State plan of distribution of equipment and fuel and removal of produced foods for distribution afterwards through a rationing system.

Commodity money relations under socialism are explained by the existence of two forms of property (once more it's Stalin's model) and by the low level of working people's consciousness. Besides, it's underlined that within the single state property and due to a high consciousness of masses the commodity money, relations can be replaced by a detailed planning in kind indices. The economic activities of enterprises are being carried on according to a detailed plan delivered by the central state institutions which leaves no room for the price mechanism. An "economic independence" of enterprises is viewed as "a right to make heroic efforts to fulfil the Party's resolutions."

A so-called "tehan system" which abolishes the personal management of the director and which provides a decisive part of the plant's Party committee in the administration of production was developed, although, of course, a Party propagandist must yield to a professional manager's viewpoint.

At the close of the 1980s with economic problems as a background the Labor Party returned, from time to time, to declare economic tasks, namely, to develop foreign economic relations and to accelerate the scientific and technological revolution in subordination to the goals of the *Juche* of the society. Self-financing (a Soviet version of self-financing within the command administrative system) is viewed as "a principle of administrating based on the political labor with the people." The measures to attract foreign capital are expressed in setting up a court branch of economy which is to find convertible currency to satisfy the needs of the governing establishment and which is not taken into account by the economic plan.

All in all, the ideological platform of the KWP remains stable. Its purpose to satisfy the interests of Kim Il Sung and his retinue makes it immune to the changes which took place in formerly socialist countries that were similar to the DPRK. That's why the varnishing measures are unable to change the essence of Korean socialism which cannot be reformed internally.

SOCIAL AND POLITICAL PANORAMA

The reason the socialist ideology (although reformed) and the practice of the socialist totalitarianism were accepted in the DPRK is the same as that in all other socialist countries of Asia. In contrast with Eastern Europe, the Asian socialist systems don't stand due to the Soviet military and partocratic presence but rather due to their own basis of a traditional etatism, Confucian hierarchical thinking, and organization of the society. To be a part of the whole, to be an element of a machine, to know its place in life and to attempt to change it, to have a servile attitude toward power and its bearers, the officials, to defend the monopoly of the State system in economy are not new concepts for North Korea.

Let us compare the current North Korean conceptions with the ideas of Chinese politicians who developed the conceptions of the State economy as far back as two thousand years ago.

> In the Seventy-Third chapter of *Yangeluhn* it is stated that if the whole people's profit comes through a single channel, this State is invincible, but if it comes through four channels, this State will inevitably disappear. The old tsar knew it very well. That is why they limited people's consumption of food and did everything they could in order to cut private profits. The sovereign decided to give or not to give. The people believed that the sovereign was like a sun or a moon and loved him like people loved their mother and father. . . . If people are rich, it's impossible to make them work for salary, but if they are poor, even a punishment cannot terrify them.[13]

An "inner disposal" of the North Korean society to accept the socialist state structures predetermined a comparatively easy formation of the modern totalitarian political structures without any opposition on the part of the traditional structures. The leader and his plan are on the top of the political pyramid. The party administrative staff, which took under its control the ideological and political life of the country, is the following element of this system. Order and loyalty are guaranteed with the help of the widened duties of the repressive institutions. The legal proceedings in fact do not leave any chance for the accused to be defended by law. Penal and civil codes are published with the stamp "for inner use" and are practically confidential. The bar as an institution practically doesn't exist. High party officials administer justice by means of punitive bodies. Show-trials and public executions are in vogue.

In such a situation, fear and ignorance are the main guarantee of the system's stability. This ignorance is twofold. First of all, people must not know what is going on in other countries in order to prevent the infiltration of "alien ideas." Second, the people must not know what is happening in their own country. People cannot move freely within the country, nor can they be in correspondence without special permission. These restrictions create obstacles, including rumors spreading. Frequently, inhabitants of one district or city receive information about some negative events which took place in other side of the country only after a long day.

"Groups of three revolutions" and so-called "inmihnbans" play an important role in political life. The first ones should guarantee the party control of the labor, social, and personal life of the citizens. These groups are composed of young students and high school graduates. To be a member of the above mentioned groups gives them an opportunity to obtain quick promotion. The groups are subordinated directly to a Labor Party Central Committee department headed by Kim Jong Il, leaving out district and province party committees. In recent years, the role of those groups isn't so important. Perhaps, it's due to the fact that, on the one hand, those groups had a negative influence upon production leaders, irritating them and complicating economic activities. On the other hand, we can suppose that Kim Jong Il's position was strengthened and his control of the upper bureaucratic staff increased. That is why it is not necessary to create a parallel staff.

Inmihnbans are a traditional form of control of people's lives in their residences. As a rule, it is exercised by a life-long headman who maintains a general atmosphere in the inmihnban. His role does not consist of intimidating or delating neighbors, but his task consists of creating a climate in which citizens cannot behave in a way that differs from the commonly accepted. Everything and everybody is in the public eye. From the everyday ethics' viewpoint, everything which is generally adopted is decent but if it doesn't agree with the established rules and traditions, it is not. Neighbors can be accused of buying goods that are too expensive or modern. In this connection, one shop manager's confession that he was listening under the pillow to broadcasts from abroad because he was afraid of being surprised and denounced by his own wife is very significant.

On the whole, we have many reasons to affirm that there are information, ideological, and organization factors to hold the people in submission. If we want to analyze the probability of anti-government actions, we must underline two circumstances. First of all, in North Korea there is no ideological basis for insurrection because the people have no access to information about how other people live and they are not really aware of any alternatives. The powers that be, who have an access to the information from abroad, do nothing to make it available to the masses, because their own lives are acceptable enough. For that reason, in comparison to Romania, for instance, where the people as a whole had an idea what they were fighting for, in North Korea people have no such idea. Even if they gain victory in the insurrection provoked by an emotional discontent of the citizens, these actions will not have a constructive component and will have only a destructive component. Therefore, even a theoretically successful insurrection doesn't mean that the victors will have an exact idea about what to do the day after their triumph. Furthermore, the conditions for the spread of protest or unrest do not exist in North Korea. The restriction of movement, communication, and connections allow the ruling bodies to easily localize every form of discontent. Besides, the system of control of the labor and the personal life of the working people makes it unlikely that somebody can form an opposition organization. However, if we even suppose that the repressive bodies can make mistakes, the restrictions of movement and communication as well as the "inmihnbans" themselves, can hardly allow the opposition to bring a wide struggle. Nevertheless, there are some preconditions which are able to provoke discontent among the North Korean people. In 1990, the daily food ration was reduced once more to some 300–400 grams of rice or its substitutes. Manufactured goods deliveries were limited, too. Commercial restaurants wanted rationing cards and checks as well as payment. Due to the shortage of fuel, the transportation and municipal services situation has worsened. Long lines waiting for buses and cold apartments in the winter don't increase labor enthusiasm. Many Koreans say the situation in their country is worse than in the USSR.

Step by step the *Juche* ideology is losing its mobilizing role which is indirectly proved by the intensifying calls "to improve the labour to unite the people on the ground of *Juche*." Although the majority feel a deep respect toward the leader, some dissatisfaction with him can be seen. The system of cramming quotations from the leader's speeches two hours each day produces an inner rejection of that which was studied. Despite the fact that the masses don't know any other ideas or concepts, they believe instinctively in the leader. This is a symptom known as an element of the totalitarian socialism practiced in the USSR and China. That is why the masses become victims of traditional socialist double thinking: Those ideas are for others and these are for my personal use. But only youth can fight against the double thinking because the people who give priority to personal security and the security of their families, rather than to the problems with social reorganization, will not run risks for the sake of an unknown and inaccessible "other world" and will go on accepting or pretending to accept the leader's ideology.

Hence, we cannot see conditions for the opposition movement proceeding from the bottom, although there are some preconditions for such a phenomenon. Reforms of the society can start only from the top and in this connection, a problem of stability inside the ruling elite is very important.

The fact of the power descent to Kim Il Sung's son was a subject of much speculation. Early in the 1990s this process had entered its decisive stage. In fact, Kim Jong Il put under his control all aspects of the internal life and a great part of foreign policy although Kim Il Sung was still playing the main role. Kim Jong Il's people had key positions: prime minister, foreign minister, Central Committee secretary for reunifying, heads of police, and so on.

Of course, it was not all smooth sailing, but by the beginning of the 1970s Kim Il Sung had already finished the personal power consolidation stage and moved on to the question of a successor. At first, Kim Jong Il seemed to have a rival in the person of Kim Young Ju, the leader's younger brother, but already in the middle of the 1970s, he "left the stage." In the 1980s Kim Pyong Il, a young brother of Kim Jong Il and the first son of Kim Song Ae, the second wife of Kim Il Sung, appeared for a moment on the political stage. Nevertheless, he quickly resigned himself to the role of a second person. At any rate, only analysts who are seeking sensationalism can seriously place Pyong Il in opposition to Kim Jong Il; there is no proof of such a struggle.

The old staff, which surrounds mainly the War Minister O Jin-U, is another potential opposition group, but their reasons are not ideological ones. They are irritated by Kim Jong Il's effort to guarantee cushy jobs for his people in the armed forces and displace old servicemen from their usual lives. Let us remember a recent episode when the former chief of the Armed Forces Staff, Oh Geuk Ryol, making use of O Jin-U's illness, tried to concentrate the command of the army in his own hands, but the old guard complained to the leader and the unlucky serviceman was moved aside.

Of course, we can suppose theoretically that without his father's aid Kim Jong Il could withstand some difficulties in his relationships with the old guard of the armed forces, but we can immediately deduce two opposite arguments. First of all, the generals' claims to power require activity and health which are diminishing. Then the heir keeps under his full control the national security institutions or, more precisely, the security of the leaders. None of those competing institutions can give an ear to such a sensational information.

The problem of the opposition can be viewed from a traditional position: pragmatists-technocrats against leftist-ideologists. In certain conditions we can accept such considerations. As confirmation we can remember the economic reform which was being prepared to be put into practice according the Chinese pattern in the middle of the 1980s. The reform we are talking about consisted of allowing the activities of small non-State producers in agriculture and services, as well as of the foreign capital in special export zones. At the same time, there are some rational propositions to modernize industrial technology and to develop the scientific and technological progress. In modern branches of science and production the opportunities of *Chonryon* were used. Innovations were associated with the activities of the former prime minister Kan Song San, but at the last stage high Korean leaders rejected the plans. We can suppose that the final decision was adopted due not only to the traditional faithlessness toward the market mechanism, but also due to great economic assistance which the Soviet Union granted to North Korea after Kim Il Sung's visits to Moscow in 1984 and 1986. Perhaps, the Korean leader decided not to begin putting into practice the reform projects because the Soviet-Korean cooperation has never been based on the market mechanism, but on the mechanisms of administration and distribution. Then, some personnel changes took place.

We should underline that Kim Il Sung always made use of this Stalinist method to shake up ruling bodies in order to keep them in awe and obedience and disunite the rivals in the struggle for power.

Of course, the plans for reform in the DPRK, as well as the other facts, provide that in this country there are many well-educated and clever people who are skillful and active managers, scientists, and inventors, but their energy is not used effectively. It is not a revolt of technocrats that is the main danger for the system but a dominance of ignorance and mediocrity, which is ready, as in other countries of totalitarian socialism, to devour those who are disposed to search and experiments. A clever and active people are not a potential opposition because the work under the Party and punitive bodies' control leaves no chance for an organized resistance. But it is difficult to say that they will be reformers, adherents of market economy and democracy. They provide a potential basis of the movement for reform if it is initiated by the leaders. They must still show their worth. It is not impossible that at the first stage they will be reformers of the socialist type whose aim is "to change without changing," to eliminate defects without destroying the basis of Korean socialism. At the end of our analysis we must say that the inner-Party processes in the DPRK cannot be observed directly and we make our conclusions based on data which cannot be verified easily. Therefore, we must take into account personal ambitions which are thoroughly concealed and which can, in a critical situation, stimulate unknown persons to try to seize power. In this case the political analysis will be wrong. However, proceeding from rational arguments and disposable knowledge about Korean society, we can say that despite the existence in North Korea of a section which is able to provoke an explosion, there are no real conditions to make this explosion a "directed" one. High Korean leaders are not interested in changing their pleasant life. The simple people have no opportunities to do something serious. We must remember, too, that reform policy in the USSR or in China to a great extent was predetermined by the existence of the professional or political opposition. The Soviet leader Gorbachev, for instance, needed new ideas for pretending highest power and had to withstand a great resistance of the conservative "grown-over" Politburo. It was exactly these considerations which provided impetus to the machine of changes.

In North Korea such a situation does not currently exist. Besides, the European experience shows that the dismantling of socialism can be very hard for its former leaders. The execution of Ceausescu, trials against Zhivkov and Honecker, persons with whom Kim Il Sung has met not long ago, perhaps exerted a great influence upon the North Korean leaders. They seem to be ready to do their best in order to avoid every sign of dissidence, every attempt against the order of things determined for years. In this sense, a real power is in the hands of Kim Jong Il. Hence, the North Korean society lasts due to the slave labor of its members and the help of Chonryon, China, and the USSR. Perhaps a change of the international situation around North Korea will be required to bring about internal change. In such a situation the previous course of Pyongyang should be both ideologically and practically impossible to continue.

NEW MOMENTS AT THE BEGINNING
OF NEW DECADE

At the close of the 1980s, major changes in the socialist world and in the relations of the DPRK with its allies have essential influence over the ideological and political situation inside the DPRK. The breaking-off of the ideological cooperation and dismantling of the partocratic basis on which the links with the Soviet Union were placed have had a very serious effect on the North Korea. First of all, the economic aid based on the command administrative methods lost its support when the Soviet Union passed to the market economy. When in January 1991, bilateral trade moved to payments in convertible currency at world market prices, it shocked North Korea. Although the economic crisis in the DPRK is caused by socialist totalitarianism and inefficiency of the administrative structures, the leaders of the country associate the troubles of their people with the Soviet rebuilding process called perestroika.

From the political point of view, the DPRK was quite shocked by the fact that the USSR and some Eastern European countries established diplomatic relations with South Korea. This measure may bring about international isolation for Pyongyang and therefore it has to seek some alternatives, declaring its readiness to normalize its relations with Japan and to begin contacts with the United States, but in this way the North Korean system puts an end to its own anti-imperialist song. It has to look for explanations for its own people to explain why the former brother betrays the KWP's struggle for the unity of the country and why they negotiate with aggressors and enemies.

The only way out of the situation is to prove that the leader is impeccable, revealing the political degeneration of the allies. The strengthening of the orthodox elements in the public and political life of North Korea was the first answer to the reform undertaken in Eastern Europe. Beginning at the end of 1989, a wide propaganda campaign aimed at blaming the market economy, democracy, pluralism, and Western aid was started. At the same time, the line to strengthen the class struggle and the priority of the ideological goals in the development was confirmed. The scope of that campaign can be proved by the fact that instead of half-secret propaganda measures which were traditional for this country, the mass media of the entire nation took part in it. "After establishing the socialist system," the Korean press wrote, "the economic and cultural living standard is improving, as the revolutionary enthusiasm of the working people is decreasing, one or more negative phenomena which discredit socialism are observed. . . The main reason for what is happening consists in disregarding the ideological revolution." The same press qualifies Western aid to the socialist countries as "an attempt to undermine socialism from inside" and the market reforms as "an ideological concession to the capitalism."[14] A new period of the anti-perestroika and anti-Soviet campaign began at the end of 1990 when Moscow agreed to the recognition of South Korea. Not long thereafter the closed and then the open propaganda qualified this step as a "betrayal" of the cause of socialism. The Soviet Union was charged with forming "an aggressive alliance between Washington-Seoul-Moscow" and was blamed for "aggravating the situation in Asia." Some other actions took place. They began to explain to the people that the worsening situation in the country is due to the actions of the USSR. Ideological, inter-party, and scientific (humanitarian branches) links were interrupted. Now the cooperation is continued only in the branches in which North Korea extracts direct profits and where the ideological aspect is absolutely absent, namely; military, technology, and mutually beneficial commercial and economic projects.

Among the propagandistic means of the KWP new ideas are appearing. Pluralism, for instance, is called "a bourgeois form of social system," because in a single monolithic socialist state there is no room for considerations which differ from the leader's.[15] The topic of "cohesion around the leader," of love and fidelity to the leader, is being discussed actively. Ethic and moral relationships are being looked at from a new point of view. A man is regarded as a little part of the State and only the characteristics which don't distinguish him among other human beings must be developed. Creative activities are permitted only within the fulfillment of the leader's instructions.[16] With a renewed energy Kim Jong Il confirmed the present day ideological credo that makes the local party staff responsible for all difficulties and mistakes. Says Kim: ". . . in the socialist society it's impossible to refuse the party ruling role as a governing party or to attempt to weaken the State power on the plea of fighting against bureaucratism and administrative methods".[17]

A violent ideological attack of the KWP is accompanied by tough organizational and political measures. The decision adopted one year ago to allow free citizens across the country has been canceled. All Korean students studying abroad were returned to the country and had to sign a document promising not to spread information about positive experiences of the reform in the Eastern Europe. Propaganda about the negative aspects in the current Soviet situation is being intensified. Instead of victorious information about buildings and new satellites, the Korean press publishes only the news about an increasing criminality, moral degeneration, and degradation of the Soviet society. Criticism against the USSR is completed with the thesis: "We remain alone and must learn to suffer deprivations."

In provinces punitive measures have been strengthened. People are arrested for singing banned songs or for criticizing the leader. Citizens are more responsible for their neighbors' loyalty. If some time ago *inmihnbans* only revealed discontented people and informed on them to the correspondent bodies, in many places the *inmihnban* today is responsible for its members' behavior. In some cases entire families were moved to almost inaccessible regions because they were suspected of disloyalty. Nonetheless, ideological brainwashing cannot have a simple explanation. It seems that under slogans of following *Juche*ization of the society a strictly pragmatic approach toward the achievement of immediate aims is observed, especially among high-ranking persons. In order to stimulate Western tourism there are luxurious shops and restaurants which accept convertible currency, the black market of goods and currency widens its activities, and North Korean citizens who work abroad have a right to pay for goods with their own earned currency. All of the above intensify the stratification of the Korean society and the contrast between poverty and the ideology of aestheticism for lower classes and the standard of living of the upper classes, especially in Pyongyang. A growth of the tension combined with the double-thinking situation objectivity is going toward the point beyond which it can remain controlled. Once more, repressive bodies are acting and brainwashing is intensified. Once more, the people must resign themselves to the inevitable and continue living with double morality. The segment of the people who are loyal to the leader is a passive basis of the system and a section which keeps good feelings towards the "old" Soviet Union, its political leaders, and its culture.

Additional difficulties are related to the necessity to find ideological support for the statements that they are ready to normalize relationships with Japan and carry on a North-South dialogue. Pyongyang is obliged to make changes in order to keep up a balance between the inner (to create a pacific image of North Korea) and outer (negative influence of the South's successes upon the North Korean people) aftereffects of such steps. The North Korean propaganda is spreading the thesis that the South is a "colony" of the United States and the dialogue with it is presented as a "victory of the DPRK," because Japan cannot already disregard successes and a growing international prestige of the North. Talks about Japanese compensation for the period of its colonial domination are interpreted as "Tokyo's defeat" of the DPRK.

In the 1990s, perhaps, we may expect new ideological and political maneuvers of North Korean leaders between the two vectors. The first one is to imitate an openness for international cooperation and the second one is to go on keeping the people in full ignorance about not only what is happening in the world, but about themselves as well. In this connection, the question of whether international influences can urge on internal political struggle is very significant. In the DPRK domestic difficulties are increasing, hopes for receiving help from the USSR and East European countries are diminishing, and although China is more flexible about providing assistance, the Chinese leadership still has reservations. Due to all these factors, it would be logical to create policy to respond to the many changes around the DPRK. But the continuity of ideology in the post-Kim Il Sung era will prevent drastic changes which might destabalize the leadership.

Changes will be aimed at adaption to the international situation through a double policy: intensifying repression inside the country and trying to make the system attractive to the international community. Changes inside the country are possible only if ideological and informative obstacles which separate North Korea from the outer world are destroyed. Pyongyang understands this and does its best to avoid it.

SOVIET APPROACH

Perhaps it will seem a paradox, but the current Soviet-Korean relationships can be beneficial to the USSR. Before the beginning of perestroika Moscow kept under its strict supervision the ideological pureness and the socialist immaculacy of Pyongyang. Attempts to step aside from an "authentic Marxism-Leninism," replacing it with the ideas of *Juche*, greatly irritated the Soviet leaders. For example, the fact that at one time the DPRK tried to present *Juche* as a "creative application of the Marxist ideas in the DPRK" seemed to be very acceptable for Moscow in contrast with the Eurocommunist currents or the ideas about a "socialism with a human face." However, the direct opposition of *Juche* to Marxism produced a drastically negative reaction on the part of Brezhnev's people. The Kremlin's reaction to some signs of the cult of Kim Il Sung was not so tough. The term "cult of personality" itself was banned from use, including in secret reports.

Despite its unattractiveness, the dismantling of former relations helps solve a variety of significant problems. First of all, the factor of political pressure upon Soviet economic institutions which have business contacts with the DPRK disappears. In the second place, the USSR is now given more freedom on the Korean peninsula to develop official relations with both Korean states. Furthermore, Moscow gets a real opportunity to build its relationship with Pyongyang based on a pragmatic coordination of the interests without any losses of the "fraternal friendship." In this way some prospects are offered to bring North Korea to some form of compromise in international relations. The potential for the DPRK to act in a confrontational fashion is reduced due to the diminishing level of Soviet political and military aid.

Intensified anti-Soviet propaganda inside North Korea can hardly be regarded as an extraordinarily negative fact that cancels out any positive moments in a new stage of the development of the Soviet-North relations. First of all, the propaganda does not in any way disturb its cooperation with the USSR where it is profitable. In addition, the anti-Sovietism is not something new. In fact it has existed for a long time in less intensive forms. Furthermore, the inertness of the public awareness in the DPRK allows for the hope that the attitude of different sections of people toward this propaganda will vary. In any case, high-ranking people and those who are near them do understand what the propaganda means.

However, there are not many reasons to be optimistic for the present for the prospects of the Moscow-Pyongyang links. Of course, the downfall of the partocratic basis opens a way toward a pragmatic cooperation, but only theoretically. Time will be a required pretext for continuing Soviet aid to the DPRK. In fact, political and economic interests of the DPRK were sacrificed to the ideological and political principles of Soviet-Korean cooperation. The USSR didn't want to undermine its friendship with socialist Korea and for that reason it abstained with obstinacy from natural and mutually beneficial relations with South Korea. By fulfilling friends' requests, Moscow was incurring direct economic losses, helping an inefficient centralized North Korean economy, and losing profitable offers from South Korea. Under Chernenko as Secretary General, the anti-imperialist and socialist rhetoric of the DPRK was transformed into new large credits granted to this country and some dangerous agreements such as the building of an atomic power station in North Korea and a dramatic growth of military hardware deliveries.

In fact, the advantages of the "fraternal Soviet-Korean friendship" were nominal. The DPRK supported global Soviet pacific proposals which didn't affect its direct interests, but as for the questions of vital importance there was no constructive cooperation. On the other side, ideological cooperation is rather two-faced. Outside the country Pyongyang used socialist language, while inside the country its propaganda was aimed at minimizing the role of the USSR in the life of DPRK, at separating the Korean socialism from the socialism of Soviet pattern and, finally, at glorifying its own leader in contrast with the Soviet ones.

Meanwhile an effort to blame the USSR for all mistakes prevails, although this is not an easy task because the Soviet Union tried to impose its pattern of socialism on the DPRK and is partly responsible for North Korean socialism.

Today the Soviet Union confronts the difficult question of how to cooperate with North Korea. It is obvious that there is no room for the Brezhnev doctrine and a compulsory imposing of the ideas of *perestroika* on the DPRK. The USSR is not ready politically or economically to exert an effective and direct influence upon Pyongyang. Besides, this problem (democratization of the totalitarian structures from without) cannot be solved outside the global context, in other words, when the whole world is not ready for global regulation.

Neither can the Soviet Union feel offended by Pyongyang and for that reason cancel all links with it. Because of the importance of maintaining good neighborhood cooperation as well as the important political reason of avoiding the narrowing of Soviet relations with Korea, the total cancellation of relations would not be wise. This policy could have a rather dramatic negative impact on the region.

Actions based on a real analysis of the current state of the North Korean society and which don't make a direct effort to stimulate economic and political reforms in the DPRK are the most rational. We have to normalize and develop Soviet–North Korean links on a pragmatic basis, drawing Pyongyang in to discuss the variety of regional economic, ecological, and political problems. The aim of such an approach is to make easier a gradual transition of the DPRK to compromise and civilize forms of international intercourse.

Pragmatism screened by *Jucheization*, double thinking, intolerance toward those who are not like-minded, democracy, and pluralism put the DPRK out of the civilized process of developing the world and make any dialogue with this country difficult. Nonetheless, there is no other way but a dialogue with Pyongyang. Multilateral contracts between scientists, politicians, and businessmen to discuss the Korean situation and to coordinate countries' efforts to draw the former "outpost of socialism" in the Far East into a constructive exchange of opinions and in the cooperation are of great importance. In essence, only a political and ideological world climate of this kind, which in the end the North Korean closed society must accept, will be able to drive the country to change. If we can open, even if only slightly, the country and show it the advantages of a civilized life, progress will be made.

NOTES

1. Kim Il Sung. *Selected Works*, Pyongyang: Foreign Language Publishing House, 1970, V. 1., p. 626.
2. IV KWP Congress. *Documents and materials*. Pyongyang: Foreign Language Publishing House, 1961, p. 5.
3. Kim Il Sung. *Selected Works*, Pyongyang: Foreign Language Publishing House, 1970, V. II, p. 324.
4. V KWP Congress. Documents and materials. Pyongyang: Foreign Language Publishing House, 1970, p. 19.
5. Kim Il Sung. "On Socialist Education" (thesis), Pyongyang, 1970, p. 19.
6. *Rodong sinmun*, January 1, 1977.
7. *Rodong sinmun*, September 9, 1978.
8. *Rodong sinmun*, October 11, 1980.
9. Kim Jong Il. "On correct comprehension of the origin of the Kimilsungism," Pyongyang, 1984, p. 60.
10. Ibid., p. 4.
11. Ibid., p. 2.
12. *Kulloja*, 1979, No. 4, p. 60.
13. Quotations from Shtein V. Guan-dji. *Studies and translation*. Moscow, 1959, p. 355.
14. *Rodong sinmun*, December 12, 1989.
15. *Kulloja*, 1990, No. 10, pp. 5–6.
16. *Communist Ethics of Public Life*, Pyongyang: Foreign Language Publishing House, 1990, pp. 6–7.
17. *Kulloja*, 1990, No. 10, p. 10.

7

THE POWER BASE OF KIM JONG IL: FOCUSING ON ITS FORMATION PROCESS

TAKASHI SAKAI

Ministry of Justice, Japan

INTRODUCTION

The death of The leader of the Democratic People's Republic of Korea (North Korea), Chairman Kim Il Sung, has posed the most critical political issue for North Korea, that is, how successful a transfer of power to Kim Il Sung's political successor and son, the Party's General Secretary Kim Jong Il, can we expect? Given the significance of North Korea in regional and global political concerns, this issue has naturally drawn most attention from abroad.

In order to determine the answer to this question, it is important for us to examine a variety of domestic and international conditions. Included in these must be Kim Jong Il's character and ability, his present power base, the situation of politics and ideology, the situation of the society and the economy, which are the basis for politics and ideology, and the international environment surrounding North Korea. This research will focus on a structural and historical examination of Kim Jong Il's power base. Most work on North Korea's political power has so far focused on the aspect of human relations among the significant individuals comprising the highest political leadership. In examining Kim Il Jong's power base such a focus does carry certain effectiveness and significance, but it has often encountered serious difficulty due to lack of information. In order to cope with the difficulty and to prepare a framework for our analysis, I shall try to explicate structural characteristics of his power base through examination of its functional aspects, or more specifically, processes of Kim Jong Il's leadership formation in different divisions where those functions are performed.

An answer to the question of Kim Jong Il's power base cannot be provided without answering one of the core questions in political science: "What is power?" In this research, I shall employ a rather conventional model of power. E.H. Carr indicates military power, economic power, and the power to control public opinion as three functions of political power in the international arena.[1] Toffler, in his recent work, named violence, wealth, and knowledge as basic powers to control a society.[2] Although these definitions were given in the context of international politics, they are thought basically valid in the context of domestic politics. Keeping those three components of power in mind, I define a person's power base as a part of an organization performing one of those functions over which he establishes his leadership or as a particular group of members of an organization over whom his power is established.

What organizations can be named as those capable of exercising those components of power in North Korea today? Major organizations can be grouped under the three components as follows:

1. *Military power*: National Defense Committee, People's Arms Department, People's Army of Korea, People's Guards, Soviet Red Army, Department of Social Safety, Public Prosecutor's Office, Law-Abiding Life Guidance Committee, National Security Department,and so on;

2. *Economic Power*: Party's departments in charge of economic affairs, Parliament's departments and committees in charge of economic affairs, local administrative and economic guidance committees of every level and their secretariats, industry cooperative associations, banks, Party's committee of each production site, Three Great Revolutions Teams, and so on;

3. *Power to Control Public Opinion and Ideology*: Party's Department of Campaign, Parliament's Department of Culture and Arts, Education Boards and schools at every level, research institutes, Artist Union, publishing companies, broadcasting organs, theatrical companies, producers' group, and so on.

Hereinafter I shall refer to these organizations by the divisions of power to which they belong: the division of military affairs, the division of economic affairs, and the division of ideology. This research will discuss how strong Kim Jong Il's leadership is in these three divisions.

Obviously, one's leadership in a certain organization can never be established simply by acquiring an institutional position. In order for him to have leadership, in addition to the institutional position there are various necessary conditions such as close connections with executive members of the organizations, strengthening of authority over all the members of the organizations concerned, and accumulation of positive achievements in exercising influential power over the organizations concerned.

In Japan, we have not yet had any notable work in examining the real condition of Kim Jong Il's leadership in these three divisions.[3] As a result, his leadership in them has often been misunderstood as nothing more than power inherited by virtue of being the son of Kim Il Sung, or as a result of his ideas being forced onto the political agenda through the pressure of Three Great Revolutions' teams, consisting of students with no administrative experience and unconstrained by law.[4] These misunderstandings have caused the omission of the examination of his leadership. This research will correct the existent, misperceived image of Kim Jong Il's power base by focusing on the conditions required to establish his leadership and presenting an examination of the process of his leadership formation in the three divisions.

LEADERSHIP IN THE DIVISION OF IDEOLOGY

Upon his graduation from Kim Il Sung University, Kim Jong Il began to work for the Party's Central Committee in April 1964. Within a mere eight months, using Kim Il Sung's authoritative influence, he strengthened his influence over the division of movie making. Using his own influence, he held an enlarged conference of the Political Committee of the Party's Central Committee with the presence of Kim Il Sung at the Korea Theatrical Movie Studio on December 8, 1964. (The contents of the conference have been kept secret.) In the background of this conference, there were two significant events held in advance: Kim Jong Il visited the studio on November 8 of the same year to deliver Kim Il Sung's speech, "On the Creation of Revolutionary Literature and Arts," which was delivered two days before; and he visited the studio again on December 7 to check the condition of the preparation for Kim Il Sung's visit.[5] The decision to hold this conference was made by Kim Il Sung after he had received a report on the real conditions of movie arts in the country. At the conference Chairman Kim delivered a speech entitled "Let's Create Many More Revolutionary Movies Contributing to Revolutionary Education and Class Education." This meaningful conference of the political committee was thought to be the starting point for Kim Jong Il's active involvement in the division of movie arts with his energetic and impressive leadership.[6] However, this event was nothing more than a prologue in the process of Kim Jong Il's leadership formation in the division of ideology.

Kim Jong Il started to actively influence the division of the campaign using the purge of Kapsanpa at the Party's Central Committee's Fourth Term Fifteenth General Assembly as momentum. This can be confirmed in the following statement found in a North Korean Document:

> The Glorious Center of the Party (meaning Kim Jong Il) strengthened our cultural project in order to drastically establish the one and only ideology system of the Party by rendering all the Party members to correctly recognize the crimes which were committed by anti-Party, anti-revolutionary elements and exposed at the Party's Central Committee's Fourth Term Fifteenth General Assembly, and by firmly equipping the Party members with the revolutionary ideology of the Great Leader.[7]

At that time, the Korean Workers' Party, in order to arrange the study system for its executive members, took steps such as the implementation of Wednesday lecture meetings, Sunday study meetings, and daily two-hour study and the establishment of the "One-Month Study Center" aiming at a one-month-a-year study system both in central and local areas (in which several hundreds of thousands of executive members participated every year). Of these the first step was thought to be brought into effect under Kim Jong Il's initiative.[8]

At that time, however, Kim Jong Il concentrated his effort in the division of ideology to the promotion of the "Revolutionary Tradition Education Project" described as follows:

> The Glorious Center of the Party has made it possible to promote revolutionary tradition education by carefully maintaining "Comrade Kim Il Sung's Revolution Evidence Museum" and "Comrade Kim Il Sung's Revolution Ideology Research Center" which were bases of the Party's one and only ideological education and also known as the old battle division of the revolution war and the evidence of the revolution respectively.[9]

In addition Kim Jong Il ordered the compilation of "The Pictorial Record of Comrade Kim Il Sung's Revolution History Research Center," prepared Kim Il Sung's handwritten manuscripts to be used in the record in March 1968, and ordered the production of a Kim Il Sung's statue which was to be placed in the research center.[10]

Maintenance of Historic Sites

In June 1967 in Haesan, Kim Jong Il built the Memorial Tower of the Victory in the Battle of Bochunbo celebrating the thirtieth anniversary of the victory.[11] The celebration on June 4 was attended by 50,000 people including executive members who were anti-Japan partisans.[12] In June 1972 Kim Jong Il took leadership in organizing the thirty-fifth anniversary of the victory at the same location. At that time, several ceremonies took place including a ceremony celebrating the erection of a memorial tower, a People's Army and Mass Demonstration, and a celebration banquet. A number of significant military and government officials attended each of these and at the celebration banquet, Oh Jin Wu, the Chief of the General Staff, delivered a speech.[13]

It is said that Kim Jong Il also ordered the careful display of documents and evidence when the Hon Won Museum of Revolution and the Li Won Museum of Revolution were built in September and October 1967 to commemorate his uncle Kim Hyong Kwan's achievement in the revolution.[14] In addition to these acts, Kim Jong Il is said to have had some influence when a bronze statue of his grandfather was built in 1968.[15]

In another strong symbolic gesture, it is said that in July 1968 he, together with a female anti-Japan revolution fighter, inspected the old battle field of the revolutionary war in Yangkang-do to create its maintenance plan and to initiate the project of "A Thousand Mile Road of Exploration March."[16]

Emphasis on "Revolutionary Tradition" in the Division of Culture and Arts

In order to embody the image of Chairman Kim Il Sung, Kim Jong Il organized special creative artists' groups such as the Pakdusan Creation Group, the April 15 Literature Creation Group, and the Mansudae Creation Group with eminent creative artists.[17] It is believed that all of these groups were created in the late 1960s For example, the Mansudae Creative Group, which is said to have made the opera *The Flower Selling Girl*, was established in 1969.[18] This development tells us that Kim Jong Il promoted a grand scale reform of the organizations of culture and arts around that time.

Kim Jong Il also aggressively promoted the enhancement of the authority of Kim Il Sung in the division of movie making. First, although the year is not known, he severely criticized the Art General Conference which had been held annually in the division of movie making and ordered that it be changed to the Research Meeting of Comrade Kim Il Sung's Ideology on Literature and Arts.[19] This research meeting is thought to have become a prototype of the "Party's Life Total System" that later prevailed among all Party members.

After promoting a change of the general atmosphere of the movie world as stated above, Kim Jong Il proposed to make a movie out of the theatrical drama *The Sea of Blood*, which is said to have been written by Kim Il Sung during the war against Japan, as the first step for the start of revolutionary tradition in the movies. He completed the movie in early September 1969.[20] Following that, he arranged to make a movie based on another drama by Kim Il Sung, *Destiny of a Member of the Self-Defense Group*, written during the war against Japan. In making the movie, Kim Jong Il visited the movie location by helicopter with the directing staff in February 1970, and proposed "speed-up tactics," thanks to which the movie was completed within forty days.[21] Reflecting upon the successfully rapid movie making, Kim Jong Il asserted at the Strategic General Session, the necessity of applying the speed-up tactics to other movies and thus made dozens of movies in 1970.[22]

During those days, there were many other examples of his directing movie making. One episode is that when Kim Il Sung highly evaluated a new movie *The Working Place of Wife*, on May 23, 1970, Kim Jong Il rushed the five-hour driving distance to tell the production group about the evaluation in person.[23] Judging from the date, it may be considered that Kim Jong Il started those activities right after Kim Il Sung's speech delivered to movie makers on November 1, 1968, entitled "A Few Problems Concerning Revolutionary Movie Making," in which he indicated problems in movie making in view of revolutionary tradition and ordered its improvement.

Another activity in which Kim Jong Il was involved during the late 1960s was the leadership of the Mobile Youth Campaign Force. Responding to Kim Il Sung's statement in the Second National Youth Mobile Campaign Force General Performance Contest, "Let's broadly develop the activity of Youth Mobile Campaign Force, and powerfully recall the importance of accomplishing Party's Policies," Kim Jong Il powerfully reminded the general public of the importance of accomplishing Party policies by correctly organizing the guidance system of the activities of the mobile campaign forces in each division including the Youth Mobil Campaign Force.[24]

During the 1970s, Kim Jong Il maintained his leadership in the division of arts and drove home the idea of revolutionary tradition. First, in February 1971, he gave intensive instructions to the division of movie making. In other words, he reported "Some Problems in Movie Making," on February 12, and "On Bringing a New Enhancement in Movie Making," on February 15.[25] In the latter report he asserted, "We have to solve all the problems posed in the movie making by setting the Great Leader's *Juche* ideology in literature and the Party's ideology in literature as the one and only standard."[26] Then Kim Jong Il is said to have established a new production guidance system, based on a scientific analysis of the reality in movie making and literature, and to have created the producer's committee in the Korean Movie Literature Production Company and the Literature and Arts Quarter aiming at promoting the level of political practice and production ability of writers.[27]

As to the division of opera, he felt the necessity of reform after watching an old fashioned opera titled *Under the Sunlight*, in the late 1960s. He worked on the opera revolution through making an opera out of *Sea of Blood* in whose production process at Pyongyang Great Theater in July 1971 he was directly involved. The opera's premiere performance was on July 17 with the presence of Kim Il Sung.[28] Within the following couple of years, he produced several original revolution operas such as *A Real Daughter of the Party*, *Jungles, Speak Up*, and *Song of the Diamond Mountains*, and made operas based on some literature such as *A Flower Selling Girl*, and *Destiny of a Member of the Self Defense Group*.[29] Kim Jong Il also showed his leadership in the division of theatrical drama by making a revolution drama titled *Song Hwang Dang* when he visited the National Theatrical Drama Association in November 1972. In addition, Kim Jong Il had numerous other publications and presented a great number of additional speeches during the late 1960s and early 1970s, each relating to the significance of art in the revolution.

Strengthening Leadership
between 1973 and 1974

As is generally known, between 1973 and 1974 the opposition to Kim Jong Il in the Party increased dramatically. Concretely speaking, Kim Jong Il was selected the secretary in charge of organization and campaign at the Party's Central Committee's Fifth Term Seventh Conference held from September 4 through 17, 1974, and was elected a member of the Political Committee in the Fifth Term Eighth Conference held from February 11 to 13 in 1974. In the Eighth Conference, it is reported that despite the fact that the issue of selecting a Political Committee member was not on the original agenda of the conference, a senior executive member who was a faithful follower of Kim Il Sung since the war against Japan recommended Kim Jong Il as a member of the Party's Central Committee's Political Committee.[30] It is said that the senior executive might have been Vice Prime Minister Kim Il.[31]

While working as the Secretary in charge of organization and ideology, Kim Jong Il succeeded in establishing his leadership. Furthermore, as soon as he was selected as a Political Committee member, he started exercising his influence over the division of ideology with more boldness and energy. One such influence was observed in his proposal for the policy of "the whole society thoroughly under Kim-Il-Sung-ism." On February 19, 1974, at the Lecture Class for the National Party's Campaign Relations Activists, he delivered a speech titled "Some Pressing Problems in the Party's Ideology Education Activity Aiming at the Permeation of Kim-Il-Sung-ism through the Whole Society" and insisted on (1) exhaustive education of the one and only ideology, revolution, and class; (2) promotion of the ideological dispute; (3) development of the economic campaign, and (4) improvement of the Party's operation system. Then Kim Jong Il presented a talk entitled "Some Possible Problems in Understanding *Juche* Philosophy" to activists specializing in the campaign on April 2, and published two essays titled "Let's More Firmly Establish the System of the One and Only Ideology in the Whole Party and the Whole Society," and "Our Party's Media and Publications Are the Powerful Ideological Weapons Contributing to the Permeation of Kim-Il-Sung-ism through the Whole Society," on April 14 and May 7 respectively. The Lecture Class for the Party's campaign activists as well as those for the organization's executive members is thought to have been organized and developed by the Party's Center.[32] In addition, in July and August he directed a Lecture Class for the National Party's Executive Members for several days with almost no sleep.[33] At the conclusion of the class on August 2, he delivered a speech titled "Let's Powerfully Promote the Movement to Hold the Whole Society under Kim-Il-Sung-ism by Improving and Strengthening the Party's Activities Fundamentally." It is said that Kim Il Sung sent the Lecture Class a note titled "On Further Strengthening Party's

Activities" which taught the class about establishing str∩ng organizational disciplines for the whole party to work only under the leadership of the Party's Center.[34] Later, on October 2, 1976, Kim Jong Il publicized an informal talk with the Party's campaign activists titled, "To Understand the Uniqueness of Kim-Il-Sung-ism."

It is thought that Kim Jong Il strengthened his leadership in the division of publishing and broadcasting using his inauguration as a Political Committee member as momentum. A North Korean document stated: "In 1974, as to the activities in publishing and broadcasting, the fire of the newspaper revolution, broadcast revolution and publication revolution gained headway under the energetic leadership of the Party's Center."[35] This movement started at the Fifth Term Eighth General Assembly in the form of the editorial revolution in the *Rodong sinmun*. Every day from February 14 to 22, the Labor newspaper serialized editorials concerning methods to implement decisions made in the Assembly. This editorial revolution in the *Rodong sinmun* was regarded as a model for a newspaper revolution which boldly destroyed old frameworks in the field of publishing and broadcasting.[36]

After inauguration as a Political Committee member, Kim Jong Il worked again on the reinforcement of the activities of Comrade Kim Il Sung s Revolution Ideology Research Center Network which he, himself, created in all parts of the country in the 1960s. Kim Jong Il promoted the establishment of the only ideological system, a system which faithfully reflects the loyalty toward the Great Leader by using a national network of research centers whose pinnacle is the Korean Revolution Museum built in Pyongyang in April 1972. As a result, all unhealthy elements like localism and familyism were overcome.[37]

The Present Condition of His Leadership

As stated above, the Fourth Term Fifteenth Central Committee Assembly in May 1967 was a turning point in Kim Jong Il's leadership in the division of ideology. The major steps in that process were the reform of Comrade Kim Il Sung's revolution History Research Center Network, the maintenance of the revolutionary war's battlefields and artifacts, and the establishment of consistency in the expression of "revolutionary tradition" in the division of arts, especially in that of movie making. These steps were targeted at powerful development of deification of Kim Il Sung based on his achievements in the struggle against Japan. Furthermore, Kim Jong Il vitalized the activities in the division of ideology by focusing on "the permeation of Kim-Il-Sung-ism" as soon as he was given the position of Political Committee member. Using such activities as leverage, he was able to take almost full control of the division of campaign.

Since then there have been many instances concerning Kim Jong Il's leadership in the division of ideology. As to the aspect of ideology, there is no doubt that his achievement in enriching and formalizing *Juche* has already been officially recognized. It should be noted here, in addition, that in the fall of 1990 members of the Korean Central News Service and Changjak Sa Korean Literature, organizations belonging to the division of ideology, proposed a movement to praise Kim Jong Il which adopted a new style of sending letters of oath to him. If we recall that changes in North Korean Society have often been started in the division of ideology, the future development of this movement is worthy of special attention.

LEADERSHIP IN THE DIVISION OF ECONOMIC AFFAIRS

Although Kim Jong Il has never assumed a leading official position in the economic sector, his role in policy making on economic affairs is crucial. In this section, I offer a very brief examination of the process of Kim Jong Il's power formation in the economic area since 1973 when he assumed the secretarial position in charge of propaganda in the Korea Workers' Party.

The Formation of Leadership

The "Small Team Campaign" (sojo undong) for Three Revolutions was officially created by Kim Il Sung in February 1973. In the fall of 1972, Kim Il Sung decided to organize and dispatch young cadres to light industrial production sites for guidance and leadership. In the following spring, the practice was expanded to all other areas of Three Revolutions with the epoch-making speech "Thought, Technology, and Culture for the Industrial Sector." Immediately after that, Kim Il Sung delivered another speech spelling out the same three principles for the Agricultural sector. In this way, the grassroots campaign penetrated into the economic life of the entire people of the country. The "Small Team Campaign" was designed to mobilize and dispatch a group of twenty to thirty youthful workers for the average-sized factory and up to fifty for larger enterprises.

Although there is evidence that Kim Jong Il was involved in these campaigns, it was not until 1975 that he was involved deeply in them when he spearheaded integrating campaigns by separate sectors into a centralized movement. Kim Jong Il was not only responsible for reorganizing the campaign but initiated educational programs for the Small Team members by requiring them to attend a variety of meetings and conferences within the government and Korean Workers' Party. In several major speeches during

1976, Kim Jong Il made the observation that members of the Small Teams were inadequately prepared for ideological and technical requirements for carrying out Three Revolutions and often instructed them to participate in educational programs. In this way, he exercised influence in decision-making processes of both the industrial and agricultural sectors.

Through the cadres assigned by the Party Center, Kim Jong Il pursued a pervasive leadership position. At first, he had to combat government bureaucrats and Party administrators but gradually his Small Teams were able to pave the way to institutionalization of all programs under the banners of Production Expansion and Technological Reforms. Throughout these efforts, Kim Jong Il made personal interaction with members of the Small Teams, personally handing out membership certificates and praising their contribution to the Three Revolutions campaign. In doing this, he was able to develop a "personal army" of sorts with active people who are dedicated to him. The number of members of Small Teams reached 170,000 of whom 20,000 earned membership of the Party. Kim Jong Il's leadership influence was not limited to the members of the teams; the members themselves, being leading figures in their workplaces, had a significant role in solidifying Kim's leadership at the grassroots level.

Kim Jong Il's influence in the economic sector did not begin with the Small Team campaign. In fact, even prior to that, he exercised a significant role as the framer and founder of the campaign known as "The Speedy War." When he was elected as a member of the Political Committee of the Korean Workers' Party's Central Committee in February 1974, he proclaimed "a new revolutionary principle of a 'Speedy War' which has provided the impetus for a nationwide movement under the same banner since then." Although the concept of "Speedy War" was originally designed to facilitate economic productivity, the campaign was developed as a comprehensive political and ideological, as well as economic, movement. The concept was presented as the realization of *Juche* ideology in a most comprehensive sense. In short, the leadership of Kim Jong Il in general economic policies and practices has been quite significant and effective and this leadership has carried over to other facets of his leadership.

LEADERSHIP IN THE DIVISION OF MILITARY AFFAIRS

Process of Leadership Formation

It is thought that Kim Jong Il already had a certain influence over the division when he mobilized the army for the parade on the Battle of Bochunbo memorial day in June 1972. It was in 1973 and 1974, however, when public documents started suggesting the existence of such influence. First, in October 1973 right after his inauguration as the Party's secretary, the Korean People's Army Commanders and Political Activists Conference was held gathering 20,000 army leaders. In the conference, Kim Il Sung presented a guideline for the struggle to further strengthen the People's Army, followed by O Jin U's report focusing on the reinforcement of all army units with Comrade Kim Il Sung's great revolutionary ideology and the Party's army policies. In response, in a discussion session, participants stressed the significance of promoting three great revolutions within the army, especially that of advancing an ideology revolution more than anything else.[38] This conference, judging from when it occurred and its contents, is considered to have been the most significant turning point for Kim Jong Il to strengthen his influence over the army. However, in the official conference report, we cannot sense the presence of Kim Jong Il. In addition, reports or comments on the Korean People's Army Establishment Memorial Day on February 8, 1974, did not mention "the Party's Center," a reference to Kim Jong Il.

It was on the Korean People's Revolutionary Army Establishment Memorial Day on April 25, 1974, right after Kim Jong Il's promotion to a Political Committee member, when the phrase of "the Party's Center" began to be used officially concerning the division of military affairs. The Party's newspaper, the *Rodong sinmun*, published an editorial titled "Beyond Generations Let's Gloriously Succeed and Develop the Flourishing Revolutionary Tradition Achieved by the Great Leader Comrade Kim Il Sung." The editorials called for loyalty toward Kim Il Sung by using the term "the Party's Center" as in "All the Party's organizations and activists must complete the great work of revolution beyond generations by praising the program of the Party's Center to color the whole society with Comrade Kim Il Sung's revolutionary ideology," and "On the roads to complete the Great Leader's teachings and the Party's Center's program, it is honorable regardless of living or dying."

Other signals of Kim Jong Il's rise can be noted. For example, on April 24, Kim Il Sung, together with the executive members of the Party's government, observed the revolutionary opera "Destiny of a Member of Self-Defense Group" which, as stated before, was produced under the leadership of Kim Jong Il. At the Glorious Korean People's Revolutionary Army's Establishment Forty-Second Memorial Central Lecture Meeting held on the same day, it was reported that all the participants of the meeting firmly decided to promote great construction of socialism like a lightning under the revolutionary flag of 'the speed-up tactics' proposed by the Party's Center." This kind of meeting was held at many places, such as every province, city, county, organization, office, collective farm, and unit of the Korean People's Army and Korean People's Guards.[39]

In 1975, such a trend became stronger. At the Twenty-Seventh Anniversary of the Establishment of the Korean People's Army on February 7, the Chief of General Staff, General Oh Jin Wu asserted in his report, "We, the people who are forever loyal to the Great Leader and the Party's Center, must show the whole country again our heroic spirit and inexhaustible creative power," and "We must drastically establish revolutionary spirit to produce, learn and live completely in the Anti-Japan partisan manner which the Party's Center proposed. In the February issue of *Kunroja Workers Magazine*, Lee Young Mu emphasized the necessity of holding up the policy of the permeation of *Juche* ideology through the whole society and the revolutionary policy of "speed-up tactics" presented by the Party's Center.[40]

In addition, in the October issue of *Kulloja*,O Jin U, So Chol, and Han Ik Su presented their papers in celebration of the thirtieth anniversary of the establishment of the Party, in which each of them called for subjugation to Kim Jong Il by using the expressions "the Party's Center" or "the Party's revolutionary leadership." O Jin U emphasized the penetration of Kim Jong Il's Leadership by stating, "we have to develop an unyielding and fierce struggle against any small phenomena or elements which oppose the Party's revolutionary leadership, by unconditionally receiving and thoroughly achieving all the policies proposed by the Party's Center in which he most accurately embodied the revolutionary ideology and intention of the Great Leader."[41]

Positive acceptance of the leadership of Kim Jong Il, however, was not necessarily shared by all the army leaders at that time. Public documents from 1975 through 1978, especially those around 1977, show that the army leaders tried to avoid direct reference to Kim Jong Il's leadership over the army. Of course, today we can hardly know how such changes in expression were relevant to the degree of army leaders' practical support for Kim Jong Il.

In any event, the leadership of Kim Jong Il over the army during this period was strengthened from the bottom through the movement of The Three Revolutions started in the end of 1975. It can be argued that Kim Jong Il increased his direct tie with the bottom ranks of the army by developing and leading this movement in the army. Several documents support this argument. The *Rodong sinmun* of February 9, 1976, reported that on February 7, memorial briefing sessions on the anniversary of the establishment of the army were held in all the units of the Korean People's Army and the Korean People's Guards. The article said, "In the briefing session of Comrade Choi Eung Chung's unit of the Korean People's Army, the reporter gave the Great Leader Comrade Kim Il Sung and the Party's Center the highest honor and appreciation with ever-lasting loyalty, and declared to prepare themselves as bodyguards, suicide corps, or storming corps, to protect, even at the risk of their lives, the political ideology of the Great Leader and the Party's Center." The article also reported that the briefing session of Comrade Kim Young Su's unit of the Korean People's Army declared their resolution to struggle to serve the Great Leader and the Party's Canter by dedicating their youthful time and energy and their lives.

The intermittent development of the movement of The Three Revolutions in the army, together with Kim Jong Il's movement toward the establishment of his leadership, was indicated in a paper in the November 1976 issue of *Kulloja* which called for the promotion of the movement and emphasized the necessity of thoroughly establishing strong revolutionary disciplines which breathe and move as one by following the Great Leader and the Party's Center.

In view of the establishment of Kim Jong Il's leadership over the army concerning the movement of The Three Revolutions, it is significant to note that the movement provided him with a turning point to directly influence the bottom stratum of the army through the political organ in the army and that it emphasized the anti-Japan revolutionary tradition as the ideological contents of the movement or more significantly as the spiritual base of the army. Such a trend was seen most apparently in the decision made in 1978 to change the date of the Korean People's Army Establishment Memorial Day from February 8 to April 25. The reason of the change, it was claimed, was that although the Korean People's Army was established in 1948, it was when the Great Leader Comrade Kim Il Sung established the Korean People's Revolutionary Army that the people came to possess their own real revolutionary power and that the Great Leader Comrade Kim Il Sung established the Korean People's Revolutionary Army on April 25, 1932.[42]

The emphasis on the anti-Japan revolutionary tradition, as stated above, played an important role in strengthening Kim Jong Il's leadership, especially in the division of military affairs. That is, such an emphasis is thought not only to have stabilized the support for Kim Jong Il among the participants of the anti-Japan combat who occupied the majority of army leaders but also to have expanded the support for him among the children of the participants of the anti-Japan combat, so-called "the children of the revolution heroes," many of whom are thought to have been in the middle stratum of the army.

Kim Jong Il started a new mass movement which involved army leaders in the end of 1979 when the Sixth Assembly of the Korean Labor Party decided to open the following year. It was the movement to follow and learn from Comrade Oh Jung Heum who served Kim Il Sung during the anti-Japan combat and died in battle that Kim Jong Il authorized. He instructed the Party's organization and the political organ to understand this movement as the Party's activity and promote it powerfully.[43] There were numerous articles in the party and military papers endorsing the strengthening of the movement and of *Juche*. Judging from the context, it is obvious that in each of these articles the term "the Party," frequently referred to, was used as a synonym for "the Party's Center." Furthermore, the *Rodong sinmun* of April 25 carried an article titled, "Visiting the Army Unit of Comrade Lee Ju O Who Acquired the Red Flag of the Three Great Revolutions," reporting that the unit started its recreation meeting with the chorus of the song, "Let's Desperately Defend the Great Leader and the Party's Center with Our Lives!" In this period, the movement in the bottom stratum of the army to give authority to Kim Jong Il is thought to have been promoted far more than the military leaders' careful expressions about the movement in the public documents.

The characteristics of the movement for the establishment of Kim Jong Il's leadership over the army during the 1970s were: (a) The movement came to surface around 1974 using the Party's organization, the division of ideology, and that of culture and arts in which Kim Jong Il had already established his leadership; (b) it was developed by using as a leverage the mass movement centering around the political organ in the army; (c) it was promoted by receiving the positive support from the anti-Japan combat participants; and (d) Kim Il Sung exerted positive influence in the important events which marked the stages of Kim Jong Il's leadership formation in the army.

Kim Jong Il was elected a member of the Military Affairs Committee of the Central Committee at the Sixth General Assembly in October 1980. It may be too obvious to indicate that during the following decade until May 1990, when he was elected the First Vice Chairman of the National Defense Committee at the Ninth Term of the First Assembly of the Supreme People's Council, Kim Jong Il developed his activities to establish his leadership in the division of military affairs more clearly and powerfully than during the 1970s.

Use and Present Condition of Kim Jong Il's Leadership

I would like to briefly refer to the achievements in Kim Jong Il's leadership over the military units. During the 1970s, such action was not known outside of the military at all. This, however, does not mean that Kim Jong Il was not active during this period. In 1980, Kim Jong Il's vsits to and leadership in the military units during the 1960s and 1970s were gradually introduced by the articles about the events on the Anniversary of the Establishment of the Army including the Artillery Anniversary on June 20, the Air Forces Anniversary on August 20, and Navy Anniversary on August 23. Of course, these are nothing more than the tip of an iceberg. Contrary to the propagandist attitude concerning the matters in the other divisions, North Korea, at least until today, has not always been positive in publicly announcing the relationship between Kim Jong Il and the division of military affairs.

By 1992, Kim Jong Il assumed the position of Chairman of the National Defense Committee of the Democratic People's Republic of Korea and was appointed as the Supreme Commander of the entire military. Although the accurate status of the National Defense Committee in the constitution is not clear, there is no doubt that, judging from the lineup of its members including Chairman Kim Il Sung as its Chairman, and Defense Minister O Jin U and the Chief of General Staff Koi Jurang as its Vice Chairmen, the committee is the *de facto* top authority over all the military organizations. We may safely conclude that Kim Jong Il, has effectively succeeded the position of the top leader over all the military organizations in North Korea including the Korean People's Army which is the regular army, the People's Guards which is under the department of social safety, and the Soviet Red Army which is the militia organization. The total personnel of the organizations is estimated to amount to 5 million, which is tantamount to a quarter of North Korea's total population.

We may be able to say that today Kim Jong Il's leadership over the division of military affairs is firmly established through not only his institutionalized position but also his human relations with the executive members of the military, and the establishment of his authority in the military.

CONCLUSION: THE CHARACTERISTICS OF KIM JONG IL'S POWER BASE AND ITS STABILITY

Based on this study of Kim Jong Il's power base, we may be able to indicate the following points as the characteristics in the process of its formation. The first characteristic is that the range of Kim Jong Il's leadership has expanded from the division of campaign to that of economic affairs and eventually to that of military affairs. It is important to note here, however, that the direction of the expansion of his leadership was not genuinely one-way but that it was synergistic, that is, the formation of leadership in each division has helped each other.

The second characteristic is that the three activities, that is acquiring the institutional authority and position which are the source of his leadership, arranging organizations to support the leadership by establishing necessary organizations, and initiating and leading various movements, have among them strengthened and established Kim Jong Il's leadership. It should be noted here, however, that the mass movement developed by him was not the one voluntarily started among the masses but the one which mobilized the masses.

The third is that Kim Il Sung, himself, played important roles in the significant events which could promote Kim Jong Il's leadership to a higher level. In addition, there were notable activities by Kim Il Sung's comrades-in-arms in the anti-Japan combat. The fourth characteristic, which is reversely related to the third one, is that the establishment of the absolute authority of Kim Il Sung and the emphasis on the anti-Japan revolutionary tradition were promoted in connection with the expansion of Kim Jong Il's leadership.

Next, I would like to point out a structural characteristic of Kim Jong Il's power base formed in the above mentioned manner. If expressed in a word, it means that Kim Jong Il's power base holds a "comprehensive" character in various ways. First of all, Kim Jong Il's power base, in view of its organization and structure, not only horizontally includes all the three divisions that support the three elements of the power, that is, those of ideology, economic affairs, and military affairs, but also vertically includes the bottom stratum to the top stratum in each of these divisions. As a result of that, a majority of North Korean people are controlled and mobilized inescapably by the meshes of the net of Kim Jong Il's power base. Also in view of personnel affairs, Kim Jong Il's power base horizontally involves alumni of each division from artists to scientists, the Party's executive members, and the members of the army and vertically comprehends three generations, that is, the seniors (the generation of the anti-Japan combat), the juniors (the generation of the leaders of the Three Great Revolutions teams), and the youths (the generation of students participating in the Three Great Revolutions teams).

As a conclusion of this study, I may be able to evaluate Kim Jong Il's power base as a stable one in the sense that it is hard to imagine "any opposition group" among the existent political powers in North Korea. Of course this conclusion does not completely exclude a possibility that some particular people or groups opposing Kim Jong Il may exist in North Korea. What this means is that even if there exists some anti-Kim Jong Il group in North Korea, such a group may not have any common political and social base in the existent institutions. Such a baseless group tends to be limited in its capability of increasing its members and in carrying out a long-lasting movement. After all, such a group is hardly expected to become capable of effectively confronting the comprehensive power base held by Kim Jong Il, defeating it, and forming an alternative political order to replace it.

However, saying that one can hardly imagine any opposition power to Kim Jong Il's power base and that the possibility of Kim Jong Il's losing his position to someone else in the country is low does not necessarily guarantee that Kim Jong Il's regime will stay as firm as a rock in the future. We might say that the worst crisis which Kim Jong Il's regime will face or has already faced, if any, could be the one not from the outside but from the inside. Such a crisis may be caused by competition among the divisions over loyalty toward Kim Jong Il, the spread of bureaucratism or nihilism, or the lack of objective evaluations of or function to reform policies already adopted. A scenario that, in the event of aggravation of such organizational problems common in any authoritarian political regime, Kim Jong Il's regime would actually stop functioning should be considered valid despite the stability of his power base.

NOTES

1. E.H. Carr, *Twenty Years' Crisis 1919–1939*.
2. Alvin Toffler, *Power Shift*.
3. Masao Onogi, "Ideology and Political Leadership of Kim Jong Il," in *North Korea at the Cross-roads* (in Japanese).

4. As an example, one may cite *Bukhan chongram* (Seoul, 1983) in which the nature of the Three Revolutions and Small Teams is described.

5. See *The Star of Leadership in the Self-Reliance Era* (in Japanese). Published and distributed by the Central Committee of *Chosen Soren*, Volume 2, pp. 161–162.

6. In Su Choi, *People's Leader Secretary Kim Jong Il* (in Japanese). Volume 2, pp. 63–64.

7. *Chosun Jonsa* (Complete History of Korea; in Korean). Pyongyang, The People's Press of Korea, Volume 31, pp. 32–34.

8. *The Great Victory for Juche Ideology* (in Japanese), p. 205.

9. *Chosun Jonsa*. Volume 31, pp. 34–35.

10. In Su Choi, op. cit., p. 41.

11. *Chosun Jonsa* states that "this construction is a central concern of the Party." See Volume 31, p. 35.

12. *Rodong sinmun*, June 5, 1967.

13. Shuhachi Inoue, *Contemporary North Korea and Secretary Kim Jong Il* (in Japanese), p. 163.

14. *Chosun Jonsa*, Volume 31, p. 36.

15. Ibid.

16. *The Star of Leadership in the Self-Reliance Era*, pp. 275–284.

17. In Su Choi, op. cit., pp. 112–113.

18. Ibid.

19. *Encyclopedia* (in Japanese), Volume 2, p. 647.

20. In Su Choi, op. cit., p. 73.

21. Ibid., pp. 74–78.

22. Ibid., p. 77.

23. Ibid., p. 85.

24. *Chosun Jonsa*. Volume 31, pp. 272–273.

25. In Su Choi, op. cit., pp. 87–93.

26. Ibid., p. 94.

27. Ibid., p. 122.

28. Shuhachi Inoue, op. cit., 118.

29. Masashi Ishikawa, *Kim Jong Il: Personality and Achievements* (in Japanese), p. 82.

30. Shuhachi Inoue, op. cit., 153.

31. *Chosun Jonsa*, Volume 32, p. 206.

32. *Chosun Jungang Yon Kam* (in Korean; Central Yearbook of Korea, Pyongyang), 1975, p. 283.

33. Ibid., pp. 283–286.

34. *Chosun Jonsa*, Volume 32, pp. 195–196.

35. *Rodong sinmun* reported a case of this educational method as practiced in a collective farm. See its August 10, 1974 issue.

36. The First occurred on March 10-13, 1975 and the Second on March 27-April 1, 1976.

37. *Chosun Jonsa*, Volume 32, pp. 202–205.

38. *Rodong sinmun*, October 13, 1973.

39. *Rodong sinmun*, April 25, 1974.

40. The magazine reported that "Let us further reinforce our invincible revolutionary power by perfecting the self-reliance policy line."

41. He stated further that "Our party is a revolutionary party guided by the great *Juche* ideology.

42. *Rodong sinmun* carried an editorial titled "Our Party's Glorious Revolutionary Military Power and the Korean People's Army," on February 8, 1978.

43. Ibid.

8

POLITICS AND STRATEGIES FOR ECONOMIC DEVELOPMENT

SHENYING SHEN

Peking University, Beijing

Korea is a country with a history of several millennia and an abundance of natural resources. Lamentably, prolonged feudal rule impeded the country's economic development. In the twilight of the feudal society at the turn of the century, the country seemed to be at the threshold of an economic takeoff as it began dabbling in capitalism. Unfortunatley, its hope for modernization evaporated as it fell victim to aggression and occupation by Japanese imperialism. The Japanese rulers imposed a colonial rule based on militarism and fascism and embarked on massive exploitation of the country's mineral, land, forest, and human resources. For nearly half a century, the Japanese colonial rule in Korea was simply a byword for cruelty and barbarism and the country's fragile base of national capitalism was decimated in its infancy. Korea was reduced to an appendage of the Japanese economy and its economy became an anomaly as a result of lopsided development. In the meanwhile, a backward, obsolescent feudal agrarian system remained intact in the countryside under Japanese protection. In this way, Korea degenerated into a semi-feudal, colonial society.

In the aftermath of World War II, Korea was partitioned into two separate political entities locked in a bitter rivalry. Based on the socioeconomic system prevalent during various periods, the evolution of the economy in the northern half of the Korean peninsula can roughly be divided into three stages.

The first stage is known as the stage of democratic reform (1945–1948). The major developments during this stage included land reform, the nationalization of key industrial sectors (the confiscation by the government of the properties previously owned by the Japanese and their Korean collaborators), and a package of other reforms in financing, the judiciary, labor administration, and education.

The second stage is referred to as the stage of socialist transformation (1953–1958). Socialist transformation, or the transformation of the ownership of the means of production, is a process by which private ownership is abolished in favor of collective ownership. It has two dimensions, the socialist transformation of private farming and private handicraft, business, and industry.

The third stage is also known as the stage of socialist construction (1957–present). Due to space limitations, this study will primarily address itself to an examination of the lines, policies, and strategies pursued by North Korea after it had been ushered into the third stage.

The stage of socialist construction can be further subdivided into four different periods according to the objectives the country pursued in its economic endeavor:

1. The period of laying a foundation for industrialization (1957–1961);
2. The period of developing industry and agriculture (1961–1976);
3. The period of building a complete and comprehensive national economy (1976–1984);
4. The period of laying a material and technological foundation for the completion of socialist construction (1987–1993).

Together, the first three periods constituted the period of building an independent, self–reliant national economy, whereas the last period was a period for laying on economic foundation for socialism.

In addition, throughout the period of socialist construction, especially from 1960 to 1965, strenuous efforts to improve economic management emerged in response to the demands for the expansion of social productive forces. In the 1980s, North Korea once again modified, though on a limited scale, its domestic and foreign economic policies in order to adjust to a relaxed international political climate and to changes in the country's internal economic and social situations.

Towards the late 1950s North Korea embarked on a policy of building an independent national economy. In the subsequent period from the First Five-Year Plan to the Second Seven-Year Plan, the country never veered off this course in its economic development effort. According to the North Koreans, the socialist economic system was not established in North Korea until 1958, the year in which the completion of socialist transformation was witnessed. That year was a watershed; it heralded the advent of socialist construction.

During that period, the recurrent and dominant theme which resonated in North Korea's economic development policy was the building of an independent and autonomous national economy (or a self-reliant economy, as the North Koreans put it) conceived in the doctrine of self-reliance. They defined economic self-reliance as an effort to "rise to its feet with its own strength and to carry revolution and construction through to the end with its own efforts." However, it is erroneous to equate self-reliance with an objection to economic ties with foreign countries or to construe it as a rejection of foreign cooperation and assistance. On the contrary, the policy amounts to giving primacy to self-reliance and supplementing the country's own efforts with foreign cooperation and assistance.

In the North Korean political parlance, an independent, self-reliant national economy refers to an economy free from foreign control, built with domestic resources and manpower, and serving the domestic needs and the domestic people.[1] Compliance with this principle entails desisting from dependence upon foreign countries for equipment, raw materials, technical personnel support, and capital funds.[2]

After settling on a policy of economic development, the North Korean communist regime proceeded to formulate a development strategy which favored heavy industry while pushing for a simultaneous growth of light industry and agriculture. In their opinion, a strategy with emphasis on heavy industry was conducive to the speedy creation of an independent and self-reliant national economy. A system like this would be one blessed with a perfect structure, supported by a stable raw material supply base, equipped with up-to-date technology, and characterized by a reasonable sectoral balance.

The period from the First Five-Year Plan to the Second Seven-Year Plan, devoted to the accomplishment of the above mentioned goals, can be subdivided into three periods. Below is an overview of the three periods.

The first period was the period of laying a foundation for industrialization (the period of the First Five-Year Plan 1957–1961). The basic tasks during this period involved economic rehabilitation, elimination of the pernicious influence of colonialism upon the economic structure, creation of a foundation for industrialization, technological modernization of various economic sectors in preparation for industrialization, and satisfaction of the popular needs for food, clothing, and shelter.

North Korea's industrialization program allegedly got under way as early as 1947, but the effort came to an abrupt halt with the outbreak of the Korean War. The Korean War left in a shambles the country's rudimentary national economy which had barely recovered from the destruction of World War II. Production was not restored to its prewar level until after three years of intensive rehabilitation work. For this reason, the foundation for industrialization was in fact laid during the first four years of the First Five-Year Plan (1957–1960) (the Plan was fulfilled one year ahead of schedule).

Based on the basic task of the period, North Korea proposed the notion of central tasks during the First Five-Year Plan. The central tasks entailed the creation of a foundation for industrialization, the solution of the problem of feeding, clothing and housing the population, and the transformation of North Korea from a backward agrarian nation into a self-reliant industrial-agricultural country. For this reason, the development of heavy industry was geared to the needs of light industry and agriculture.

The successful fulfillment of this task, the North Korean Workers' Party contended, was contingent upon giving top priority to the basic industrial sectors of the national economy, such as the metallurgical, electrical, machine-building, coal mining, chemical, and building materials industries. The development of a machine-building industry was the highest on the planners' agenda. In addition, in anticipation of their active role in alleviating the shortage of consumer goods, the planners gave favorable treatment to some light industries which could thrive on domestically available raw materials. Rapid development of the machine-building industry was designed to assist industry in its technological renovation and upgrading efforts, and to provide equipment for agriculture, transportation, postal and telecommunication services, and the building industry.

The major production targets during the First Five-Year Plan period included 8,500,000,000 kilowatt-hours of electricity, 9,500,000 tons of coal, a 100 to 150 percent increase of steel output (approximately 400,000 to 500,000 tons if the 1956 output was 190,000 tons), 630,000 tons of chemical fertilizer, 1 to 1.5 million tons of Portland cement, 180 million meters of cotton goods, a more than 30 percent increase of aquatic products over 1956, 3.5 million tons of food grain, and half a million housing units.

During this period, capital investments amounted to 30 billion won. The bulk of the development funds were allocated for production projects, with heavy industry receiving the lion's share. The country achieved all the plan targets a year ahead of schedule. North Korean statistical data indicated that compared with 1956, its total social production in 1960 increased 124 percent, and gross national product 114 percent. Labor productivity was boosted by a big margin, 40 percent in industry and 9 percent in capital construction. The national economy also underwent structural changes. The share of industrial production in total social product rose from 40.1 percent in 1956 to 57.1 percent in 1960, while that of agriculture declined from 26.6 percent to 23.6 percent in the same time frame. Table 1 provides more detailed information in this regard.

As for the people's living conditions, North Korea achieved initial success in meeting the basic needs for food, clothing, and shelter. In 1960 the real incomes for employees of state-run enterprises in urban areas were 110 percent higher than before. The volume of retail sales was 210 percent higher than in 1956. Between 1956 and 1960 the average annual income of a farm household in terms of food grain increased from 1,616 kilograms to 2,100 kilograms. Its cash earnings rose from 95 to 300 won. In the area of housing, 6,220,000 square meters of floor space were built in cities and 5,060,000 square meters in the countryside. Free medical care became an entitlement of the whole citizenry for the first time. In 1958 compulsory secondary education was instituted throughout the country, with a total school enrollment in the vicinity of 2.53 million. The number of institutions of higher learning

TABLE 1

STRUCTURAL CHANGE OF ECONOMY (1956–1960) (IN PERCENTAGE)

	GNP	Industry	Agri-culture	Trans./Commun.	Social Indirect	Consumer Goods	Other
1956	100	40.1	26.6	4.0	12.3	10.8	6.2
1960	100	57.1	23.6	2.2	8.7	6.0	2.4

SOURCE: Various issues of *Statistics of National Economic Growth of the DPRK* (in Korean). Pyongyang, 1946–1960.

more than quadrupled, rising from 19 to 78, and their enrollment increased proportionally. (See Table 2 for detailed information on the fulfillment of targeted commodity outputs). The successful fulfillment of the first five-year plan ahead of schedule contributed to the undertaking of economic construction in the second period.

The second period was one of industrial and agricultural development (1961–1970). The basic tasks during this period were to carry out an all-around technological renovation of industry and agriculture and to raise the living standards of the citizenry. In addtition there was an effort to carry out a cultutal revolution. This task was embodied in the First Seven-Year Plan. The North Koreans devised a two-step formula for the implementation of the First Seven-Year Plan. The first three years were to be devoted to the consolidation and readjustment of heavy industry. The last four years would focus on a further expansion of heavy industry and the streamlining and modernization of its technical equipment. Under this precondition, light industry and agriculture were also to receive adequate attention. The focus of this policy also manifested itself in the pattern of capital investment. During the first three years of the Seven-Year Plan period, an overwhelmingly large proportion of the funding was earmarked for the consolidation and expansion of heavy industry (the North Korean metaphor for this process was "fleshing out the skeleton" of heavy industry) and other sectors of the economy closely associated with the people's lives, such as machine building, chemical, light industries, and fishing and agriculture. In contrast, during the last four years, the bulk of the resources were invested in the sectors which played a pivotal role in promoting industrialization. Notable among them were the energy, mining, metallurgical, machine-building, chemical, and other basic industries as well as the transportation industry.

Total state capital investment during the period was in the vicinity of 1 billion won, which represented a 130 percent increase over the previous seven years combined. Eighty-one percent of the funds were allotted for the expansion of productive capabilities, while 19 percent were intended to finance nonproductive construction projects. Industry received 58 percent of the total capital investment, of which 71 percent was invested in heavy industry. Forty-Four percent of the expenditure on nonproductive projects was invested in housing.

In order to effectively fulfill the basic tasks, North Korea's Labor Party entrusted the different sectors of the economy with the various, specific tasks.

First, the central tasks for industry were to further improve the structure of industry, to strengthen its technological foundation of industry, and to establish a diversified independent and self-reliant industrial system supported by a stable raw material base and equipped with advanced technology and facilities. In the last year of the period, total industrial output increased 220 percent. Capital goods output rose 220 percent, and consumer

TABLE 2
Production Targets and Performances

Item	Unit	First 5 Y.P. trgt	First 5 Y.P. perf 1960	First 7 Y.P. trgt	First 7 Y.P. perf 1970	6 Y.P. trgt	6 Y.P. perf 1976	Second 7 Y.P. trgt	Second 7 Y.P. perf 1984
Electricity	10 mkw	85	91	165	165	280	280	560	500
Coal	10000 tons	950	1062	2400	2750	5000	5000	7500	9000
Steel	10000 tons	45	64	235	220	390	400	760	740
Fertilizer	10000 tons	63	56	160	150	290	300	480	468
Cement	10000 tons	150	228	450	400	800	800	1300	1513
Fabrics	10 mill. meters	1.8	1.9	4.5	4	5.5	6	8	8.7
Marine Products	10000 tons	+30% (1956)	55			170	160	350	352
Grains	10000 tons	350	380	600	600	700	700	1000	900
Growth (%)			30		12.8		16.3		12.2

Following Korean sources are used: *Statistics of Economic Growth of the DPRK.* Pyongyang, 1946–1950; *Central Yearbook of the DPRK.* Pyongyang, 1971, 1978; *Rodong sinmun,* February 17, 1985; and *World Economy* (in Chinese), Peking, 1984.

goods 210 percent. Throughout the Seven-Year Plan the annual growth rate of total industrial output was 18 percent.

Total state investment in industry amounted to 10.72 billion won, of which 79 percent went to heavy industry and 21 percent to light industry.3 According to the plan, the primary mission of heavy industry was to provide complete sets of equipment for key industrial firms, and to improve and expand the heavy industry base so as to provide better and more effective support for light industry and agriculture. The primary task of light industry was to increase the variety and enhance the quality of products. It was imperative for light industry to continuously adhere to the principle of the simultaneous development of centrally and locally controlled industries through the construction of huge new light industrial complexes and the remodeling and expansion of existing plants. Mechanization of locally controlled factories was called for in order to phase out manual operation.

The central task of agriculture was technological renovation and farm mechanization aimed at boosting agricultural productivity. The transportation, postal, and telecommunication industries were to strive to increase cargo volumes transported, and to rapidly expand railroad, waterway, and highway links across the land. Arterial railroad lines were to be electrified, and total metric tonnage of cargo was to exceed 75 million.

However, because of the deterioration in the international situation and the revision of its internal policy, North Korea made a decision in October 1966 to reorient the country's economic construction strategy and to defer the completion of the Seven-Year Plan for three years until 1970. The three-year extension prevented the country from defaulting on its commitments to the Plan. Finally in 1970 North Korea pronounced all the Plan targets achieved. A perusal of the statistics released by North Korea indicated that compared with 1956, the country's 1970 total industrial output rose by a spectacular 1,060 percent. The output of capital goods increased 1,230 percent, while that of consumer goods rose 830 percent. During the period between 1957 and 1970, or the period of industrialization, the average annual rate of growth in industrial production was 19.1 percent.4 The output of major industrial products were, respectively, 16.5 billion kilowatt-hours of electricity, 27.5 million tons of coal, 2.2 million tons of steel, 1.5 million tons of chemical fertilizer, and 4 million tons of Portland cement. Obviously, most of the Plan targets were reached.5

In the sector of heavy industry, North Korea managed to fill the technical gaps and eliminate the bottlenecks in the metallurgical, chemical, machine-building, energy, building materials, and other industries and improved structural balance. The same period also witnessed the construction and expansion of power stations, mines, metallurgical, machine-building, chemical, cement plants and other key firms. In the domain of light industry, a certain percentage of plants were remodeled, expanded, or newly constructed. The technological renovation and upgrading of the firms under local jurisdiction were accelerated. As a result, a nationwide light industrial network of textile, food processing and other industries came into existence. In 1970 North Korea produced 400 million meters of textiles. Agriculture irrigation, mechanization, electrification, and chemical fertilizer became more extensively utilized than ever before. Food grain production rose to 6 million tons. In the transportation sector, the electrification of an additional 850 kilometers of railroad quintupled the extension of the country's electrified railroad lines. The tonnage of cargo vessels nearly doubled. Compared with 1950, the number of trucks increased 180 percent.

A corollary of the development of production was improved living standards of the people. By 1970 the average wages for government officials, teachers, technical personnel, and workers had increased 31.5 percent. In the meantime, the retail prices of textiles, children's apparel, and toys and over 1,000 other consumer goods were lowered. The benefits accruing from pay raises and reduced cost of living to the citizenry were estimated at more than 5 billion won. In the countryside in 1969 the average remuneration in the form of food grain for each farm household was 80 percent higher than 1960 levels and the cash compensation doubled 1960 levels. In this way, the real income of the peasantry was increased by 80 percent. Further, the construction of 800,000 housing units in both urban and rural areas during the period from 1961 to 1969 greatly relieved the pressure of a housing shortage.

The North Koreans claimed that though they had to grapple with a number of difficulties during the First Seven-Year Plan period, they could congratulate themselves upon the initial success in industrialization. They cited the following achievements as evidence of the initial success:

- First, the establishment of a fairly comprehensive and versatile heavy industry base centered on the machine-building industry and the creation of a heavy industry system capable of a variety of functions ranging from the production of raw materials to the assembly of products;
- Second, the creation of a machine-building industry with a 33.7 percent share of the total industrial output. The industry's productive capacity had been enhanced and it was now capable of turning out not only small and medium-sized but also large machines, and not only single machines but also complete sets of equipment. Its rate of self-sufficiency in equipment was a remarkable 80 percent. The industry was able to cope with the demands of different economic sectors for equipment;
- Third, the structural modernization of the national economy. In 1969 industry occupied a predominant position in the national economy. Industrial production accounted for 74 percent of the total industrial and agricultural output. By contrast, in 1956 it made up only 34 percent of the total.

In view of all this, it would not be an overstatement to assert that North Korea's impressive economic performance had qualified it for membership in the international community of industrialized nations.

The third period, or the period to establish a complete and comprehensive national economy, coincided with the periods of the Six-Year Plan (1971–1976) and the Second Seven-Year Plan (1978–1984). The basic tasks during this period were to further improve the sectoral balance of the national economy and to create an industrial system which consumed indigenous raw materials and had a 70 percent rate of self-sufficiency in raw materials. North Korea's strategy was to launch a Three Technical Revolution[6] campaign oriented toward elevating the level of technical sophistication of the national economy. Moreover, it set the target of training high-caliber manpower and fostering an indigenous science and technology personnel of 1 million. These tasks of the third period were incorporated into the basic tasks of the Six-Year Plan and the Second Seven-Year Plan.

The basic tasks of the Six-Year Plan were to consolidate and promote industrialization and to carry out the technical revolution in an extensive and deep-going way, to strengthen the material and technical base of society, and to gradually reduce the burden of manual labor for the working people. Another objective was narrowing the differentials in income and living conditions between workers and farmers and between urban and rural areas.

The major targets of the Six-Year Plan included a 120 percent increase in total industrial output from 1970 to 1976. The output of capital goods was to rise 130 percent and that of consumer goods was to double. The average annual growth rate of industrial production would be 14 percent.[7] Of the major industrial targets, electricity was to increase 110 percent, coal 80 percent, minerals 100 percent, metallurgical products 80 percent, machine tools 170 percent, ship building 260 percent, chemicals 150 percent, and building materials 90 percent. More specifically, the production of electricity would reach 28 to 30 billion kilowatt-hours, coal 50 to 53 million tons, steel 3.8 to 4 million tons, Portland cement 7.5 to 8 million tons, chemical fertilizer 2.8 to 3 million tons, food grain 7 to 7.5 million tons, housing 1 million units, reclaimed coastal marshlands 300 thousand jungbo, aquatic products 1.6 to 1.8 million tons, and textiles 500 to 600 million meters.[8]

During the Six-Year Plan period, North Korea's strategic calculus considered both the domestic and international factors and the needs of economic development when it mapped out plans for allocating capital investment and conducting its vigorous albeit small foreign trade. Such an approach paid off in a smooth implementation of the development plan. The official North Korean statistics released during this period demonstrate that the output of all major products, with the exception of steel and cement, reached the preset targets one year and four months ahead of schedule. The Plan period registered an average annual increase of 16.3 percent in total industrial output, which exceeded the targeted 14 percent. In 1976, total industrial output was increased by 150 percent over the 1970 levels. The output of capital goods increased 110 percent and that of consumer goods 150 percent. As a result, the structural imbalance of industry was redressed. Industry acquired additional capacity for the production of raw materials, energy, and power and could provide 60 to 70 percent of the needs of various sectors of the national economy for raw materials. Agriculture achieved the target of 7 million tons in food grain production. The 1976 output of vegetables, fruit, and silk were 60, 120, and 120 percent higher than the 1970 figures respectively.

Growth in agricultural production and government subsidy and other forms of assistance raised the cash earnings of the workers on collective farms above the targeted level, enabling them to enjoy a living standard equivalent to that of the erstwhile rich middle farmers. As a result, the disparity in living conditions between country people and city dwellers was narrowing. The benefits of the economic boom were also dispersed to the urban population. In the second half of 1970, the average wages for workers, technicians, and government agency employees rose 31.5 percent. That year low-income employees in all sectors of the national economy received a 10 to 24 percent pay raise.

During the Six-Year Plan period, cultural and educational institutions also experienced rapid growth. In 1975 the country implemented an eleven-year compulsory education system. The number of engineers, technicians, and experts was augmented to 1 million, and a powerful indigenous technical and managerial elite became the mainstay of the nation's ambitious economic development.

During the Six-Year Plan period, new sectoral imbalances and bottlenecks stemming from an exceedingly high economic development rate emerged. The problems that gained the highest saliency included the failure of the transportation industry to keep pace with industry and agriculture. Such was also the case with the relationship between mining and manufacturing. This gave rise to such problems as the congestion of the transportation lines and a shortage of raw materials. To redress the sectoral imbalances and eliminate the bottlenecks, North Korea decided to put a one-year moratorium on the plan. The year of 1977 was designated as a year of readjustment. An effort was made to facilitate the implementation of the subsequent economic development plans.

The second Seven-Year Plan was announced in December 1977 as an integral part of the third period and as a resumption of the effort to complete the construction of a self-reliant national economy. The basic tasks of the Second Seven-Year Plan were to enhance the independence of the national economy, to further consolidate the base of the socialist economy, and to raise the people's living standards. The main thrust of the Plan was to be directed at the development and utilization of indigenous natural resources, the establishment of new industrial sectors, the creation of a comprehensive, versatile national economy dependent on indigenous natural and human resources and characterized by a reasonable structural balance. All this revolved around the strengthening of an independent and self-reliant national economy. The approaches to the accomplishment of these goals were an all-around mechanization and automation of industry and the industrialization of agriculture. Top priority would be given to scientific research, which would speed up the improvement of production technology and managerial skills.

The major objective of the Second Seven-Year Plan was a 120 percent increase in total industrial output in 1984 as compared with 1977. The output of capital goods was to increase 120 percent, consumer goods 110 percent. The goal for the average annual growth rate for industrial production was set at 12.1 percent. More specifically, the economy was to produce 56 to 60 billion kilowatt-hours of electricity, 70 to 80 million tons of coal, 7.4 to 8 million tons of steel, 4.8 million tons of chemical fertilizer, 12 to 13 million tons of Portland cement, 800 million meters of textiles, 3.5 million tons of aquatic products, 10 million tons of food grain, and 200 to 300 thousand housing units.

In consideration of an amelioration in the international climate and the domestic economic and social needs, North Korea made a number of modifications and alterations in its internal and external policies and practices.

First, a reform of the industrial leadership system was carried out. There was a transition from subordination of the local management to control by the sectoral leadership to the domination of the local management over the sectoral authorities. There was concurrently a partial devolution of decision-making power upon lower-level agencies and a rationalized division of labor among departments and agencies.

The second reform entailed a structural readjustment of industry. For the first time, the North Koreans experimented with what they termed the revolutions of the light and service industries aimed at improving the delivery of goods and services to the population.

Third, a new, albeit limited, flexibility in internal and external policy was implemented. For instance, in the countryside, the government instituted a system of workteam responsibility, approved reclamation of wasteland and household sideline occupations by farmers, and permitted free produce markets. The regime also acquiesced in the industrial firms' marketing of the commodities produced beyond the plan quotas and gave the management more leverage in deciding the distribution of the earnings from these sales. In addition, the existing industrial wage system was rationalized to establish a linkage between remuneration and worker performance. The regime delegated more powers to industrial firms at lower levels though it was still adamant in its refusal to abolish central planning and the micromanagement of industrial operation.

During the Second Seven-Year Plan period, though beset with difficulties, North Korea achieved substantial results in its economic endeavor.

This success may be attributed primarily to the regime's wise adaptation of some of its policies to the changing times and the reconciliation of ideological indoctrination with economic work by launching the campaigns for "emulating anonymous heroes" and for carrying out the "Three Revolutions." The Second Seven-Year Plan was officially completed in 1984. During the Plan period, total industrial output increased 120 percent, with an average annual growth rate of industrial production estimated at 12.2 percent. There was some noticeable growth in agricultural production. The food grain output of 1984 was 9 million tons. The number of farm tractors rose 50 percent and weed-mowers 100 percent, greatly curtailing manual farmwork. Overall, the period registered a rise in gross national product and the real incomes of both the rural and urban population. By 1984 the gross national product was 80 percent higher than 1977 and the real incomes of workers and government employees has grown 40 percent. The government outlays on social welfare were in the vicinity of 294 million won, averaging 800 won for each household.

During this period, North Korea went on a building spree with the construction of a number of monumental structures. Notable among them were the Great People's Study Hall (or the Central Library), Man Su Dae Conference Center, Chang Kwang Boulevard, and Man Su Boulevard, which were lined with clusters of modern high-rise apartment buildings. An impressive number of rural residences on the outskirts of such cities as Nampo, Wonsan, Hamhung, Chungjin, and Danchun were renovated or remodeled. In addition, 290 medical centers for disease prevention and cure were built. Many of them were equipped with advanced, up-to-date facilities. They included Pyongyang Maternity Hospital, South Hamhung Province Stomatological Hospital, the hospital affiliated with Kang Gae Medical College, and the Kum Duk Mining Complex Hospital. The number of physicians and surgeons increased 40 percent, and the life expectancy of the citizens reached seventy-four years, thirty-six years higher than before the Communist takeover. The completion of the Second Seven-Year Plan solidified the economic base of North Korea. It could be construed as an initial success in creating a comprehensive national economy.

Through twenty-eight years and three stages of arduous economic efforts, North Korea successfully redressed the abnormalities and eliminated the bottlenecks inherent in a colonial economy. It has turned an economy mired in poverty and backwardness into a comprehensive and versatile national economy comprised of various heavy- and light-industrial sectors and self-sufficient in raw material and equipment. The country has achieved remarkable economic progress, but in its economic endeavor it has never been immune to mistakes and problems. In fact, the country has followed a tortuous course and learned many valuable lessons.

Because of a lack of experience and the tension in East-West relations during the Cold War period, Communist countries invariably opted in favor of the Stalinist development model in the early stage of economic development. In line with this model, heavy industry takes precedence over other sectors so as to create a comprehensive system of national economy. Moreover, a regimented, rigid circulation system based on a monolithic, planned, command economy and a centrally controlled resource distribution and rationing mechanism prevails. In this way, a product economy inevitably took the place of a commodity economy.

On the one hand, the communist countries' espousal of the Stalinist economic development model was motivated by a need to offset the constraints imposed by the hostile international climate of the time. On the other hand, the model demonstrated some practicality and feasibility during the initial stage of socialist construction. It was instrumental in concentrating material, financial, and human resources, overcoming the enormous difficulties, and promoting economic construction. It would also effectively assist in constraining consumption and achieving a high rate of capital accumulation, two prerequisites for a high growth rate and industrialization in socialist countries plagued by low levels of productivity.

However, the expansion of the socialist economy was inevitably accompanied by an augmentation in the scale of economic operation, an increase in the degree of specialization and division of labor, a diversification of the needs in production and life, and a rise in the frequency of socioeconomic activities. Under such circumstances, an economy will fall into disarray if the people continue to reject the market mechanisms governed by the law of value and continue to allow a few bureaucrats cooped up in their offices to exercise control by issuing administrative orders. The reason is very obvious. No matter how sophisticated, capable, knowledgeable, down-to-earth, and meticulous the bureaucratic planners may be, they can hardly cope with the complexity and fluidity of economic phenomena. This handicap on the part of the economic planners stems from a problem inherent in the planned command economy—a lack of flexibility and adaptability to respond promptly and properly to changes in the market. Therefore, the socialist countries could hardly dispense with a reform of its planned command economy at a certain stage of economic development. An overhaul of such an economy is the key element of economic reform currently underway in China and other socialist countries. The implementation of such a reform is also dictated by the needs of economic development. At certain stages of economic development, it behooves the socialist countries to reform or readjust the systems and policies incompatible with the level of the development of the productive forces and to reconcile them with the changing domestic and international situation. Socialism can thrive only on such reforms.

China's experiences reveal that at the early stage of economic development when the economy was small, the indigenous economy could be equal to the task of performing the required functions ranging from mineral extraction to the manufacturing of commodities. However, with the expansion of the economy and the improvement of technology, there will inevitably be demands for greater quantities and more varieties of raw materials, unfinished products, and spare parts. In this case, an obsessive desire to produce everything at home will prove counterproductive and disrupt sectoral balance. Such a practice will reduce the chances of improving the industrial structure because it requires no end of expansion in various sectors. This kind of expansion is a drain on the socialist economies, especially the weak and fragile ones riddled with a scarcity of resources. An oversized, overheated economy will precipitate a intersectoral scramble for capital funds, raw materials, energy and power supplies, transportation, and labor. It will also tax the economic system beyond its manpower, financial, and material capabilities. Shortfalls in raw materials and energy supply will cause the factories either to slow down or to operate below capacity. A resultant irony is that the expansion of productive capacity will not translate into an increase in production but result in the idling of production facilities.

Economic development by definition means reducing inputs to a minimum and increasing outputs to a maximum so as to add to the social wealth and to meet the needs for expanded reproduction and the ever-growing popular demands for consumption. An economy will hemorrhage excessively if the people continuously ignore the relationship between inputs and outputs and pay no heed to the economic effects or if the state and the people are not adequately rewarded for their contributions.

In the contemporary world, few if any countries still labor under the delusion that they can rely on their own efforts to provide all the required raw materials, energy, equipment and unfinished products. On the contrary, most of them strive to increase economic interaction with foreign countries while at the same time focusing their attention on the sectors in which they excel. The sectors in which they could outperform their rivals shall become the pillars of their economies. International economic specialization and division of labor and regional economic cooperation and mutual assistance will aid a country in fully tapping its strengths and overcoming its weaknesses. By availing itself of both domestic and foreign resources and markets, a country can more easily make use of the comparative advantage and will have less trouble stimulating economic growth and accelerating the process of modernization. In short, an economy pruned of its weak and inefficient limbs will surely outstrip those bogged down in a quagmire of perfectionism and excessive size.

Since 1984 North Korea has adopted a more flexible position in its economic relations with foreign countries. Its economic interactions with foreign countries have taken the forms of foreign trade, economic cooperation, joint ventures, scientific and technological cooperation, economic aid given gratis, loans and credits. At the present moment, North Korea's main thrust is directed at soliciting joint-venture partners. To this end, the government enacted and issued the "Joint-Venture Enterprise Law" in September 1984. The following year it promulgated the "Joint-Venture Enterprise Income Tax Law."

North Korea abides by the following guiding principles in its effort to develop trade with foreign countries: Steadfastly uphold the principle of geographical and product diversity and the primacy of creditworthiness; gradually raise the share of machine tools in the percentage of exports; and upgrade the composition of exports.

In observance of the principle of independence, equality, and mutual assistance, North Korea rank-ordered its partners in its foreign economic relations.

First of all, preference is given to socialist countries in economic and technical cooperation; second, North Korea will strive to cement close economic ties with developing countries in response to the call for South-South cooperation; third, it will expand trade and economic and technological interaction with capitalist countries provided they respect North Korea's sovereignty and independence. It will also augment its economic ties with countries with which North Korea does not have diplomatic ties.

The fourth period of development for North Korea was the period of laying a material and technological foundation for the completion of socialist construction (the Third Seven-Year Plan period, 1987–1993). The overriding tasks during this period were the development of science and technology, the expansion of productive capacity, the strengthening of the national economy, and a significant improvment in the living standards of the people. To this end, North Korea decided to focus its attention on the development of basic industries. It viewed such development as a prerequisite of the consolidation of the nation's economic base.

Basic industries refer to the mining, electric, metallurgical, and transportation industries. During the Third Seven-Year Plan period, the development of these industries was the highest on North Korea's economic agenda. "It is of cardinal importance for us to concentrate our resources on mining, electric, communication and transportation industries, and strive for their modernization and a drastic increase in their productive and transportation capabilities."[9] To avoid sectoral imbalances, North Korea did not neglect other industries. To raise the living standards of the people, it also exerted itself in developing light industry and agriculture.

In recent years, in view of the amelioration in the international political climate and the rapid change in the Northeastern Asian situation, North Korea has modified its foreign policy. For instance, since 1988 it has held several talks with the United States and repatriated the remains of some American soldiers killed in action during the Korean War. On September 28, 1990, North Korea signed a tripartite joint statement with Japan's Liberal Democratic Party and Socialist Party, and has since been actively seeking to normalize bilateral relations. From September to December 1990, North and South Korea held three talks at the prime-ministerial level. Though North

Korea still claims to be interested in Third World countries, its Asian neighbors now occupy a more prominent position in its diplomacy.

In response to the needs for implementing the new foreign policy seeking expanded cooperation with foreign countries, North Korea has set about improving its foreign affairs agencies and training a more competent diplomatic corps. In 1987 it established the Ministry of Joint-Venture Enterprise, thus enclosing collaboration with foreign investors and traders within the government. In February 1990, in order to strengthen the Foreign Affairs Committee of the Supreme People's Assembly, the Government appointed veteran career diplomat Hur Dam, Chairman of the Committee, and Kim Yong Soon, an expert on the Western world (also director of the International Department of the Labor Party), Vice-Chairman. In addition, a special committee in charge of the reunification policy was set up within the Supreme People's Assembly.

By the end of 1989, North Korea had conducted negotiations with more than sixty countries concerning joint-venture enterprises. Agreements on more than 100 projects had reportedly been reached. At the same time, the country was preparing to open up a special economic zone for foreign investment or joint ventures on the Hapsan Island (popularly known as the Little Gold Triangle) bordering on China and the Soviet Union. At the same time, strenuous efforts were being made to bring tourism into blossom. A plan was made to turn Kangwon Province into a province specializing in international tourism and to create tourist resorts and districts along the thoroughfares linking Kum Kang Mountain, Kaesung, and Myo Hyang San, as well as Pyongyang and Nampo.

All this notwithstanding, it is still evident from the blueprint of the Third Seven-Year Plan and related documentation that in the foreseeable future there will not be any major reversal of North Korea's economic policy. Barring a fundamental change, slow, tentative, minor amendments to the current policy are still likely. However, if there is further relaxation in the international situation, if North Korea's efforts to normalize its relations with Japan and the United States proceed smoothly, and if its economic cooperation with the "Southern" capitalist countries and regions in the form of trade and joint venture prove successful, we cannot rule out the possibility that the country will be encouraged to pursue a more flexible tentative foreign policy and embark on the road of reconciliation with other countries.

NOTES

1. Kim Jong Il: "On the *Juche* Idea," *The Central Yearbook of Korea*, 1983 edition, p. 42.
2. Kim Byung Jin: *The Experiences of Building an Independent National Economy*. North Korea, pp. 32–33.
3. National Reunification Board, South Korea: *The Second Seminar of the Promotion of Economic Interaction Between North and South Korea*, p. 10.
4. Kim Il Sung: *The Collected Works of Kim Il Sung*, Chinese version, Vol. 25, p. 190.

5. Ibid., p. 192.

6. The Three Technical Revolutions are designed to narrow the difference between light and heavy industrial labor as well as industrial and agricultural labor and to relieve women of heavy housework.

7. *The Central Yearbook of Korea*, North Korea, 1976 edition, p. 322.

8. *The Policy of Socialist Construction as Expounded by Our Great Leader Kim Il Sung.* Pyongyang: The Labor Party Press, 1974.

9. Kim Il Sung: "Strive to Bring the Advantages of Socialism in Our Country into Full Play." A speech delivered in the Ninth Supreme People's Assembly, May 24, 1990.

9

ECONOMIC CHARACTERISTICS AND PROSPECT FOR DEVELOPMENT: WITH EMPHASIS ON AGRICULTURE

MARINA YE TRIGUBENKO

The Academy of the Sciences, Moscow

In the early 1990s, the Democratic People's Republic of Korea (DPRK), commonly known as North Korea, is one of the few countries of the former world system where the traditional economic policy and a chosen adherence to socialism remain unchanged. However, as a typical example of totalitarian socialism, the DPRK feels the impact of the mistakes, deformities and distortions that were brought about by the Stalinist concepts of a new socialist society. Although not as obvious in other countries, the process of a global, all-pervading crisis is mounting in North Korea. These processes necessitate fundamental reforms in the DPRK's economy, politics, and ideology. However, the DPRK is still strong enough to retain its present economic and political system, whereas the constant military and political tensions enable it to maintain social stability and to keep in check simmering popular discontent. In addition, the DPRK is situated in the relatively stable region of Asia and the Pacific, where the tradition of totalitarian structures and so-called "iron fist" in political and economic processes are strong.

Numerous books and articles have been written about North Korea and the majority of this research has criticized *Juche*, cast doubts upon, or outright rejected the successes of North Korea in the post-colonial period. In this essay, I will size up the economic situation from a new angle and from the newer school of thought to openly admit the guilt of the USSR, its theoretical dogmas, and its actions which have deterred North Korea from holding its rightful place in world civilization which it could have achieved after Japan's withdrawal in 1945.

NEW INTERPRETATION
OF THE DIFFERENT PHASES
OF ECONOMIC POLICY

The theory of the different phases of North Korea's economic policy is strictly aligned with Leninist-Stalinist methodology: the transitional period, the building of a socialist society on its own basis, the completion of the building of socialist society, and the accession to communism. The entire complex and contradictory dialectics of such development are subordinate to one communist idea: the creation of an antipode to capitalism and, consequently, the rejection of all that has been accumulated by world civilization, including the material and cultural values of the twentieth century.[1]

Capitalism is a multiform market economy, whereas socialism in its final form is the building of a class-free planned society. The basic criterion of the transition to socialism is the domination of policy over economy and, consequently, coercive voluntarist methods of building a new society. To show the actual content of the DPRK, its economic development can be divided into four long periods, each having specific tasks. The first period was 1945–1962. This period was characterized by the Stalinist model of socialism. This model involves the coercive expropriation of the means of production, the socialist transformation's primary goal of establishing one single, state-based form of ownership, and the beginning of the cultural revolution which involved the expansion of *Juche* nationalism. The external goals of the period included the integration of the DPRK into the world socialist market. In this early phase, the Soviet Union exerted decisive influence on the formation of the economic policy of the DPRK.

The second period of development ran from 1962 to 1983. During this period the DPRK drifted away from the Soviet model and adopted the even more voluntarist Chinese methods of socialist construction. Of the many policies that the DPRK borrowed from the People's Republic of China, the principal ones were putting agriculture under state control,[2] as well as the maintenance of the consistently high rate of growth of the economy by using running battle methods in order to achieve economic peaks. This thesis was made public in 1969 in Kim's work, "On Certain Theoretical Problems in the Socialist Economy." Yet another policy included the rejection of one-man management that made industrial leaders responsible for the work of their subordinates. This system was replaced by the team system of work through which industrial management is carried out by the Communist party committee using moral and political incentives, and the brainwashing of the masses in accordance with "jonsantri" methods. In addition, the DPRK chose to follow the Chinese thesis of reliance on one's own resources. At that time, the newspapers carried editorials such as, "Let's Protect Self-Reliance." The authorities adopted the nationalist course which was formulated in these words: "independence in policy, self-reliance in the economy, self-defense."[3]

Finally, the DPRK borrowed the Chinese theory of three revolutions to start the ideological campaign of dissemination of *Juche*. The first stage involved work to create a military industrial complex. Starting in 1962, and particularly after the party conference in 1966, militarized methods of economic management were introduced. The second stage coincided with the peak of the Cold War, on the one hand, and with tremendously wasteful expenditures on the propaganda of the ideas of *Juche* and the personality cult on the other. Prerequisites took shape for the deformation and deterioration of social production for years to come.

The third period was from 1984 to 1989. During this period the economic policy was reassessed and reviewed under the influence of the economic reforms in China and the Soviet Union. The closed door policy was abandoned and in 1984 a new law on foreign investment was adopted. In addition, efforts were made for economic rapprochement with the Soviet Union, and the first limited economic reforms in industry were carried out.

New forms of foreign economic activity emerged, such as production cooperatives, joint ventures, and direct cross-border links with the Soviet Union. The government announced partial changes in its structural policy, with priority given to export and to branches of scientific and technical progress. Steps were taken to expand the sphere of consumer goods production and the sphere of services. If the government of the DPRK had deepened its innovations and developed them still further, it could very possibly have avoided the present economic crisis.

In 1990 the country entered the fourth phase of its economic policy. The earlier domestic difficulties have now been complicated by the disintegration of the world socialist economic system, the loss of gratuitous sponsors, the depletion of natural resources, and the isolation of the DPRK from the Asian and Pacific Region, which threw the country back in scientific and technological areas.

The DPRK is again toughening its domestic policy under the guise of protecting the gains of socialism: The old Tean system of work has been reanimated, and the authorities are fanning up military psychosis and war propaganda. In the fourth phase the DPRK will, in its economic policy, most likely rely on China. In its foreign economic policy it will seek to retain its traditional partners. Conceptually the authorities will seek to maintain their adherence to socialism and will not relinquish the *Juche* concept. Characteristic in this respect are Kim Il Sung's two policy-making statements made at the first session of the People's Assembly of the Korean People's Democratic Republic of the Eighth Convocation (December 30, 1986), as well as at the first session of the People's Assembly of the Ninth Convocation (May 24, 1990), and in his report on the occasion of the fortieth anniversary of the DPRK (September 8, 1988). In these speeches Kim Il Sung repeated the old theoretical precepts: To transform cooperative property into all-people's property, boost the high rates of production, strengthen the dictatorship of the proletariat, adhere to a monolithic *Juche* ideology, maintain the Tean system of work, and to continue the three revolutions: ideological, technical, and cultural.

It seemed at first that at the Seventeenth Plenary Meeting of the Central Committee of the Korean Workers' Party's Sixth Convocation in January 1990 there were some signs of change in the economic policy of the country because the problem of further growth in production linked with the task of boosting the economy and the task of adopting the achievements of scientific and technological progress. It was suggested that the volume of investment should be reduced. The Party called for the adoption of the cost-accounting method. But as it turned out, plans for economic regulation, just as before in the years of "hot" seven-year-plans, were just talk. The costly economic mechanism does not allow production to be made any more efficient or losses to be reduced. Subsidizing science, technology, and consumer goods production was put at the bottom of the list of priorities. The DPRK has a fairly well developed scientific and technological potential: 1.3 million scientific, technical personnel, two universities, 238 schools of higher learning, and 200 research centers. In addition, 10,000 North Korean specialists were trained in the USSR and other countries. A law was passed on boosting science and technology to bring to account those officials who fail to carry out plans for scientific and technological development. However, the class approach to this sphere of activity—"the working class is the hegemon, whereas the intelligentsia is second in importance," and "there is a technical mysticism among intellectuals whereas workers show initiative in making inventions"—holds back scientific and technical progress.

In his statement "On Further Development of Science and Technology" (August 1, 1985, made before senior officials of the Central Committee of the Korean Workers' Party) Kim Jong Il enumerated some of the key areas of scientific and technical progress. He attached particular significance to microelectronics, computer technology, substitutes for missing raw materials, fuels, scientific and technical progress in metallurgy and chemistry, and so on. The program of sweeping modernization of scientific and technical progress calls for extensive resources and skilled personnel, neither of which can be found in the DPRK.

LOST OPPORTUNITIES

Today we can say with a fair degree of certainty that the DPRK is pursuing a dead-end economic policy. The economic conditions and geographic position of North Korea among the most dynamic countries (Japan, the Newly Independent Country [NIC],the Association of Southeast Asian Nations [ASEAN]) and its relatively strong economy in the past enabled it to move ahead in the post-colonial period at a similarly high rate as South Korea, Taiwan, or the other NIC of Asia. Actually North Korea had a certain advantage over them in this respect.

The economic structure of colonial Korea had certain features that made it very different from other poorly developed dependent countries. On the one hand, it was an agrarian country with about 75 percent of the population engaged in agriculture and with 45,000 big landowners in the north alone. On the other hand, by the early 1940s North Korea was by far the most industrially developed colony in North-East Asia. It had modern metallurgical, extracting, military-chemical, and energy-generating facilities operating mainly in the north of the country and filling the needs of the Japanese war-oriented economy. North Korea produced over 90 percent of the metal and electric power and about 85 percent of minerals extracted on the peninsula as well as one-third of the products of its light industry. North Korea's industrial complex was closely linked with the Japanese economy. In other words, it was oriented toward the Asian Pacific Region (APR). It is true that this complex suffered from major disproportions: It had no machine-building industry, nor any modern technology. However, the old traditions of its industrial development, the existence of a workforce 2 million strong, and rich mineral and fuel and energy resources enabled North Korea in the postwar 1940s to become one of the most rapidly developing countries of North-East Asia, along with Japan. That development was halted mainly for the following reasons.

First, the communist regime (established with the direct assistance of the Soviet military command) oriented North Korea's economic development within the framework of the world economic socialist system strictly in accordance with the general directive binding on all socialist-oriented countries—the creation of a socialist economic area (a world socialist market with its own currency, prices, and administrative mechanism) isolated from the global economy. In accordance with the concept of the international socialist division of labor, each country within this world socialist area was assigned its own specific role. The DPRK—just like Cuba, Mongolia, or Vietnam—was to become the source of raw materials and cheap labor for the global economy of socialism.

Second, the international and national interests clashed almost immediately because the Stalinist doctrine of a diversified and independent economy, a doctrine that dominated the world system of socialism, was equally applied to the DPRK where, in the years of industrialization, an unscientific, dead-end concept was taking root, the concept of the simultaneous development of heavy and light industries and agriculture, with the emphasis on the heavy industry. Because of this theory, the DPRK ruled out different priorities at different stages of economic development as did the Republic of Korea starting in the early 1960s. By doing so, North Korea ruled out the possibility of developing an export-oriented economy as part of the world (and not only of the socialist) economy.

Third, the economic strategy of the DPRK was undoubtedly influenced by the complex political situation on the Korean Peninsula. Starting in 1962 (and to this day) the DPRK has pursued a policy aimed at building an economy focused on defense. North Korea's defense expenditures made up one-third of the expendable part of the budget and its army personnel increased to 1 million. The orientation toward the military industrial complex left no room for the development of civil branches and opened the way for hypertrophied development of military industries, including mechanical engineering.

Simultaneously, North Korea strengthened its military and economic links with the Soviet Union and distanced itself from South Korea, Japan, the United States, and other countries of the West as "allies in the anti-communist bloc."

By the 1970s North Korea had developed a military industrial complex that drew on military assistance from the Soviet Union. This peculiarity distinguished the DPRK from the other socialist Asian countries with their emphasis on the economic goals (rather than military), which gave their civil branches a fair reserve of strength. Even during the most difficult period (the war in Vietnam) China and Vietnam demilitarized their economies in the 1970s. The economic conversion in China enabled it to raise its general technical and technological level of industrial development and to speed up the advance of its national economy.

THE QUANTITATIVE AND QUALITATIVE CHARACTERISTICS OF THE NORTH KOREAN ECONOMY

In spite of all its efforts, the DPRK has failed to rise above the level of an average developed country with a deformed economic structure. The potential strength of any country lies in its labor resources. The level of population growth in North Korea is higher than many other countries (1.67 percent a year on average). In South Korea, by contrast, population growth is a mere 0.97 percent. At present the population of the North Korea is 22.3 million, with its active population at 6.6 million. The problem goes far beyond the shortage of jobs (according to some assessments, the excess of workforce runs 200–400 thousand) or the low professional skills, and extends to a food shortage. Suffice it to say that there is only 300 kg of food produced in North Korea per capita (not counting 30 percent of losses), which is half as much as required by health standards. North Korea has a limited gross national product and national income—19.5 billion and 18 billion won respectively, 47 percent of which (9.2 billion won) comes from industry, and 20 percent (3.9 billion won) from agriculture. In spite of the fact that 43 percent of the active population is involved in agriculture, the country cannot provide itself with farm produce and, according to some estimates, imports up to 1 million tons of grain annually.

The lopsided structure of the national economy can be illustrated by the overproduction of machines that have no foreign market (27.2 percent of the total cost of industrial output) and metal (15.3 percent). By contrast, consumer goods hold a rather modest proportion (13–14 percent).

The share of services and internal trade is miserably small. The paradoxes typical to a developing country, including an excess of labor and a shortage of a skilled workforce and 50 percent of expenditure going to capital construction, with half the existing capacities standing idle all exist. The familiar picture of wastefulness on one side and an acute shortage on the other is apparent. All of that is the result of the wasteful, ineffective system of economic management, the domination of the command system of administration, and the absence of market economic levers, money-commodity relations, and competition.

Starting in the 1970s North Korea lost out to South Korea in both the qualitative and quantitative development, and consequently in the choice of its model of development which was oriented toward a public-based type of economy, massive assistance from the socialist countries, and a closed economy. As is known, South Korea started out with and continues its economic growth under the conditions of rigid, state-controlled management, as in North Korea, but at the same time it gave wide play to private enterprise. South Korea also observed sectoral priorities and pursued a rational financial policy (prices, taxes, bank interests, credit policy). North Korea rejected the need for using commodity-money relations and ignored the economic law of cost. Its fundamental theory is a high rate of development as the principal law of the socialist mode of production. The result of this policy is economic decline and stagnation (Table 1).

As Table 1 indicates, the actual growth rates are a far cry from the target figures that, according to the plan, are to rise steadily. The current Seven-Year Plan period (1987–1993) witnessed the beginning of an industrial decline in absolute terms (Table 2).

As evidenced by Table 3, the DPRK is no longer developing faster than the Republic of Korea: While in the mid-1970s the gap was 1.6-fold, by the early 1990s it had risen to 9 plus times. Though South Korea's economy is also in a downturn, its growth rates are still fairly high.

The energy sector is North Korea's Achilles heel since this complex was geared in the DPRK to electricity generated by hydropower and thermal power stations. The DPRK has depleted their stock of these energy carriers, and problems with the generation of electricity are what explain the major industrial decline in the two last years. Today construction is beginning on 10 big and 500 small and medium-sized hydropower stations. However, the problems before the energy sector can only be resolved through the use of oil and gas (no gas or oilfields have thus far been found in the country) and the construction of a nuclear power plant, that is, through the attraction of large foreign investments. But who is willing to give loans to that country and how can it repay loans?

Data concerning the level of the DPRK economy is extremely discordant, both in terms of value and physical indicators. Also, there are differences in the calculation of the won rate in dollars. The Soviet Union uses the following exchange rates: 1.6 won per ruble and 2.1 won per U.S. dollar. The U.S. Central Intelligence Agency must use different rates, which makes for

TABLE 1

PLANNED AND ACTUAL GROWTH RATE
IN DPRK BY PLAN PERIODS (IN PERCENTAGE POINTS)

	1st 7-yr. plan pd. 1961–1967	6-yr. plan pd. 1971–1976	2nd 7-yr. plan pd. 1978–1984	3rd 7-yr. plan pd. 1987–1993
Target figure	14.6	10.3	9.6	7.9
Assessment	8.6	6.0	4.5	3.0

TABLE 2

PATTERN OF NORTH KOREAN ECONOMIC DEVELOPMENT DURING
THE 3RD 7-YEAR PLAN PERIOD (1987–1993) (IN PERCENTAGE POINTS)

Indices	1987	1988	1989	1990
GNP	1.7	2.5	-5.3	0
Industry	1.4	3.2	-10.6	0.5
Agriculture	1	-1	-1	-1.3

SOURCE: *Choson Ilbo*, December 12, 1990 and assessments by Soviet experts.

different assessments of per capita national income: 400 to 500 U.S. dollars according to Soviet experts and some 900 dollars according to the CIA (*Choson Ilbo*, December 12, 1990). Though some of the data provided by South Korean experts and contained in Table 4 (on page 150) may be challenged, in particular those on foreign trade and debt, it is of interest and, on balance, is quite accurate as regards the gap between the DPRK and South Korea.

The North Korean economic specialization determines its role and profile in the global economic ties. North Korea's exports are typically those of a developing country: It mostly exports raw resources and commodities, and its export-oriented sectors have long been technologically and morally obsolete. Among its basic export items are anthracite (2 million tons); iron ore (1 million tons); ferrous metal rolled products (400,000 tons); zinc (120,000 tons); cement (1.3 million tons); magnesite slag (600,000 tons).

North Korea has 400 engineering enterprises, including 100 big ones, but most of them service the military-industrial complex and their products are not on the global marketplace, being low-quality.

Therefore, North Korea's imports cannot become an answer to the problem of the upgrading of equipment since more than 40 percent of the value of the country's imports are crude oil and oil products (3 million tons and 150,000 tons, respectively), coke and coking coal (300,00 tons and 2.5 million tons, respectively).

Machinery and equipment account for 25 percent of the value of North Korea's imports, but the country is tied to the supplies of engineering

TABLE 3

PATTERN OF NORTH KOREAN ECONOMIC DEVELOPMENT
(IN PERCENTAGE POINTS)

Indices	1987	1988	1989	1990 (assessment)
GNP	13	12.4	6.7	9
Industry	18.8	13.4	3.7	—

SOURCE: "Korea and the World, 1990"; *Key Statistics*— Seoul, 1990, p. 27.

TABLE 4

COMPARED LEVELS OF ECONOMIC DEVELOPMENT OF NORTH AND SOUTH KOREAS IN 1989

Indices	Unit of measurement	North Korea	South Korea
GNP	billion dollars	21.1	210.1
Per-capita GNP	U.S. dollars	987	4,968
Population	million people	21.4	42.4
Annual population growth	percentage	1.64	0.97
Defense expenditures	billion dollars	4.5	9.2
Energy generation	billion kwh	30–33	94.5
Coal production	million tons	50–52	19
Crude oil import	million tons	2.6	40.4
Steel production	million tons	3.7–4	21.9
Cement production	million tons	7–8	30.1
Rice production	million tons	4	6[a]
Fish output	million tons	2	3.2[b]
Length of railways	thousand km.	5.0	6.4
Foreign trade	billion dollars	4.79	118.2
Export	billion dollars	1.95	61.4
Import	billion dollars	2.84	56.8
Foreign aid	billion dollars	6.78	29.4

SOURCE: [a] *Hanguk kendzeyi Gus Thonge*, 1990, Seoul. 1990; *Korea and the World*, 1990; *Key Statistics*. Seoul, 1990, p.27. [b] 1988

products from the USSR—which, to be sure, is true of the bulk of raw resources.

Basically speaking, the DPRK, was experiencing changes in the international cooperation environment which included the following:

1. East European nations have virtually abandoned North Korea, have cut technological aid, and have reduced their trade sharply.
2. China withheld new loans to North Korea. Also, China does not take part in the North Korean modernization effort; in fact, all it does is develop trade in limited amounts on a well-balanced basis, with strict compliance with obligations concerning individual groups of commodities.
3. The Soviet Union suggested going over to world prices and convertible currencies in international trade beginning in 1991, demands the payment of loan-repayment arrears to the tune of 2.2 million rubles, does not give loans on preferential terms, and recalls its experts. Soviet enterprises are not showing an interest in the development of direct ties with the DPRK. Imposed by ministries "from the above," cooperation in the consumer industries using Soviet raw materials to produce end products began to fold down sharply beginning in 1990. Cooperation in engineering

(the building of ships and vessels by Soviet orders) is also stalling. Finally, the construction of the only big joint venture facility in engineering, Hichchon-Gorky, has been shelved too.
4. Worsening foreign trade environment, and search for alternative sources of economic initiative.

Stagnation and industrial decline in the late 1980s and early 1990s depressed the DPRK's foreign trade in absolute terms. While in 1989 the volume of foreign trade went down by 5 to 6 percent, in 1990 the drop was 9-plus percent. (*Choson Ilbo*, December 12, 1990).

The drop was most noticeable in trade with the main partners, the Soviet Union, China, and East European nations. Trade with this group of countries dropped by 12.8 percent (export by 15 percent), including 11.8 percent for the USSR because of the folding of ties in production cooperation and the consumer industry. The USSR is North Korea's main foreign trade partner and the only country giving North Korea technological aid (the construction of the East Pyongyang Thermal Power Plant with a capacity of 200,000 kW, a 100,000-spindle textile factory, the development of a feasibility study for a nuclear power plant with a capacity of some 1.7 million kW, etc.). In addition, the USSR is the only nation among North Korea's former allies that has small joint ventures with North Korea. However, now obligations concerning trade agreements have a 20–40 percent rate of fulfillment, and the projects built with technical aid from the Soviet Union operate at 70 to 80 percent of capacity.[4]

Trade is falling with all of North Korea's main trading partners (Table 5).

TABLE 5

DPRK Trade in 1990 (in million rubles)

	Trade Volume	% of Total	1990 as % of 1989 level
Total	1980	100	87.3
USSR	1340	67.7	39.2
China	317	16.0	94.5
Czechoslovakia	85	4.3	203.8
Bulgaria	23.1	1.2	92.8
Hungary	6.3	3.2	40.2
Poland	80	4.0	74.8
Mongolia	8	0.4	97.6
Cuba	38.5	1.9	269.0
Albania	10	0.5	100.0
Romania	10	0.5	40.0
Yugoslavia	1	0.5	—
GDR	5	0.3	11.1

Source: Foreign trade statistics of the above countries.

This sharp drop in trade took place even before the transition in trade with the socialist countries for freely convertible currency. These countries account for 67 percent of all trade; capitalist ones, for 22 percent, and developing nations, for 11 percent.

Apparently, the DPRK cannot in the foreseeable future make up for the fall in the absolute figures of its trade with the countries of what was known as the world socialist system by expanding its trade with new partners from a different socialist system. This calls for making major changes to the internal course, economic reforms, the normalization of relations with the Republic of Korea that could take up much of the slack.

It is particularly disconcerting that the DPRK export level is virtually stagnant. Previously, the DPRK compensated for this by taking loans on import deliveries and keeping a chronic deficit of foreign trade, mainly by not fully meeting its delivery obligations to the USSR (Table 6).

The results of the economic development in 1990 indicate that no changes have taken place in the structural policies, despite the official protestations to the contrary. These policies continue to be based on the fuel, energy, and raw material sectors and the energy-extractive industry-engineering triad. However, the DPRK failed to expand its production of machine tools, ships, or railway carriages. For the time being, things do not go beyond verbal declarations concerning the development of electronics, information technology, computerization, and the production of robots. North Korea is to blame for marking time in the fields offering a possibility of progress: the production of numerically controlled machine tools, flexible systems, and modules manufactured by Soviet–North Korean joint ventures.

As we have noted above, cooperation for the production of end products from Soviet raw materials is being ended. The Soviet market did not receive 100 million rubles worth of goods or 25 million rubles worth of clothing because of the disruption of the supply to the DPRK of spare parts and accessories in 1990 alone (*Izvestia*, February 22, 1991).

The result is unpromising: A fall in cooperation on the basis of Soviet-supplied raw materials amounted to 50 percent (*Izvestia*, February 22, 1991).

TABLE 6

DPRK TRADE WITH THE USSR (IN BILLION RUBLES)

	1987	1988	1989	1990
Total	1.23	1.60	1.50	1.34
Export	0.43	0.54	0.56	0.49
Import	0.8	1.06	0.94	0.85

NOTE: North Korea's clearing arrears to the USSR were equal to 260 million rubles in 1990.

SOURCES: Data concerning Soviet foreign trade statistics. See: Soviet Foreign trade in 1988 and 1989; Yearbook; data for 1990, assessment by the Ministry for Foreign Economic Ties.

Due to a lack of capital investments, the export strategy was not backed up by the growth of production. Under the plan, during the current five-year period the export of nonferrous metals was to rise fivefold, that of magnesite slag, cement, vegetables, and fruit, by twofold.

Without resources for the expansion of production, the DPRK began to go over to other forms: It began to export labor extensively, first of all to the USSR, Kuzbass coal field, the Yakutia SSR, the Primorsky Territory (construction projects and agriculture), and more attention was paid to foreign tourism. An emphasis is being made on small enterprises in the services and mediation services.

CAN A NEW ROAD BE CHOSEN FOR ECONOMIC REJUVENATION?

The DPRK will have far more difficulty restructuring its economy than Vietnam and Mongolia had. The latter use their market economy to gain a margin of safety and to re-orient the structural policies for the agro-industrial era, that is, they accept the sensible alternative of self-containment in foodstuffs, accumulation at the expense of agriculture and industry processing agricultural produce, export, and, consequently, foreign currency resources.

But for the time being, the DPRK is not willing to change either its general approach (an overly centralized economy) or the traditional strategy of import substitution known as self-reliance. The task now is the need to obtain new loans from new creditors. To this end, the premier of the Administrative Council, En Hen Mun, made visits to China, Thailand, Indonesia, and Malaysia in 1990. However, these visits produced no visible results. China is preoccupied with its own economic problems. Besides, the DPRK is known to the world as an unreliable trade partner. The DPRK's total foreign debt is 4 to 5 billion rubles, including 2.2 billion rubles to the USSR (*Izvestia*, March 1, 1990). The total of its arrears to the USSR alone is 1.5 times as big as the value of the North Korean exports to this country. The USSR is raising the question that the North Korean debt should be denominated in freely convertible currency because of the transition in 1991 to payments and settlements in freely convertible currency and the current world prices (*Izvestia*, November 3, 1990).

What model for a new economy capable of coping with the economic crisis did Kim Il Sung choose? Many Western observers believe that North Korea is sure to follow the Chinese model of economic reform, that is, a planned, regulated market economy with an emphasis on an open economic policy. The North Korean leader may be fond of the Chinese model (economic rejuvenation without political reforms and the Chinese example of compromise solutions): a market economy and a rigid control on part of the state, a multisystem economy with the predominance of the state sector.

This compromise has allowed China to preserve social stability for a time, to prevent the breakdown of the command and administrative system, and to preserve the Communist Party's control of society. Kim Il Sung can reform the economy without reviewing the idea of a socialist choice of a society model without resorting to political pluralism and without sharing power with any opposition party.

The future of the North Korean economy will be determined, to an extent, by the destiny of perestroika in Russia, a republic with which the DPRK will probably preserve economic interests and by whether Russia's democrats succeed in breaking down the all-powerful command and bureaucratic machinery. Yet one should not overestimate the current influence of the USSR on the DPRK that is increasingly distancing itself from the USSR and moving closer to China, Japan, and other Asian-Pacific nations.

AGRICULTURE IN THE DPRK'S SOCIOECONOMIC STRATEGY

The national policy of containment and geography create obstacles to North Korea's self-sufficiency in foodstuffs and to its agricultures developing into a major export-oriented sector. Like the USSR, North Korea has taken the line of combatting private interest and private property in agriculture, beginning with an agricultural reform in March 1946. At that time, there was a sequestration of not only landlords' lands but also those of well-to-do peasants, monasteries, and other owners. The August 1946 Nationalization Act destroyed virtually all the sources of private initiative, including title to factories, plants, finances, various kinds of large real estate, economic resources, and the right to trade. The North Korean authorities acted on the formula of the Bolsheviks in the Great October socialist revolution of 1917: all power to the Soviets (people's committees), the land to peasants (but only to those having little land and day laborers), the factories to workers. This laid the basis for the military communism, a society devoid of any private or individual initiative. As in Russia, peasants did not own their land for long, losing the title in 1954. During three years (1954–1956) the peasantry lost all land to cooperatives of a higher socialist type that socialized labor, land, and other means of production and robbed peasants of the right to dispose of their products on their own (i.e., to sell them). These actions later received a theoretical grounding in the party's two economic programs: Economic Problems of Socialist Construction and Theses on Socialist Agrarian Question. The next step was the implementation of the Communist doctrine concerning the wiping ouy existing differences between the state and the cooperative forms of property and enhancing the latter to the level of the former. This policy of the wiping out "essential differences" included:

- construction of all facilities in the countryside at the expense of state funds, confiscation of cooperatives' internal accumulated capital as a source of their own economic initiative;
- leveling the living standards and wages and salaries in town and country. The unit of work on collective farms, the work day, became in effect a strictly egalitarian labor remuneration system; and personal plots of land, a source for the functioning of peasant markers, were virtually eliminated. Other policies of this kind include the application of army-type work methods among the peasants; the construction of housing at state expense; a ban on the choice of the place of residence and work and even on travel in the country.

Therefore, rather than being bodies stimulating collective peasant labor, cooperatives began to carry out fiscal functions. But this was still too little as the danger persisted that private peasant initiative would be revived because of the "survival" of the philosophy of private ownership among peasants. Therefore, beginning in 1974, the Workers' Party declared that it was time to develop cooperatives into different, consistently socialist, enterprises by combining what is purely peasant work with village industries, with one person working in different crafts.[5]

What was essentially the scrapping of cooperatives was theoretically rationalized as an attempt to intellectualize the peasant and remove all class distinctions since as soon as there is undivided property in the hands of the state and party apparatus, there is only one class: a socialist laborer.

This is what in effect has taken place in Korea if classes are defined regarding their relationship to different means of production and different kinds of ownership. However, even though this subject should be better dealt with in another work, a "new" class has emerged in North Korea (according to the Yugoslav scholar and politician, Gilas) that unconnected as it is with the means of production and not being a productive class, oppresses; gives instructions to, and overshadows workers, peasants, and the intelligentsia. This class is party and state elite and the bodies of repression, even though for some reason they are described in socialist countries as law-enforcement agencies (in a state not ruled by law).

AGRARIAN POLICY:
PROGRESS AND PROSPECTS

The agrarian policy of the Workers Party of Korea has been, apart from bringing all activity in this field under state control, aimed at building the material and technical base of socialism in agriculture, attaining the country's self-sufficiency in essential foodstuffs, and replenishing its export resources with farm products. Stepping up intensive farming has been the only way to enhance production in the face of a dire shortage of arable land (there are 0.12 ha of cultivated area per inhabitant, on average, the arable land constituting only 16 percent of the national territory). The achievement the DPRK has to its credit in this respect is beyond question. With half the workforce engaged in farming and less than half the crop area, it produces nearly as much food as South Korea. This is due, notably, to irrigation and application of advanced farming techniques, including chemicals. An area of 1,400,000 ha is constantly irrigated; there are 1,700 reservoirs in operation, and the total length of irrigation ditches is 40,000 km (DPRK, *Reference Book*, Moscow, 1988, p. 65). The Kiyang, Phennam, and Odhidon water-engineering systems are among the major irrigation installations.

Plans are afoot to enlarge the arable area by 25 percent by bringing into cultivation 300,000 ha of salt-marsh and 200,000 ha of new land through terracing, drainage, and by ploughing up fallow land. These are, in large measure, public works, involving manual labor and employing redundant manpower for a time. A total of around 1,000 kilometers of dikes will have to be built to make more land suitable for cultivation on the Yellow Sea shore. One example of a modern-type water-engineering development is a high dam in the Taedong River estuary, just outside the city of Nampho. The dam is 8 km long, 30 m high, on average, and 150 meters wide at the foundation. This is a project of the century hard to overestimate: It will make the river navigable for shipping of up to 20,000 ton displacement from Nampho to Pyongyang, enable fresh-water irrigation of surrounding fields. improve water supply for the Pyongyang industrial zone, ease flood control, and resolve some general transportation problems (V.I. Denisov, V.I. Moiseyev, *DPRK—40 Years*, pp. 14–15).

However, success gained in building up the material and technical base, along with strong centralized leadership, cannot resolve the main problem—that of food supply—nor forestall the flood aftermath. There was a striking case in point to note in 1990 when heavy summer flooding destroyed one-third of the rice crop and the damage caused was estimated at $1.5 billion. The DPRK appealed to international organizations for emergency aid to prevent threatened famine in some areas. It had to sacrifice some of its gold and foreign exchange reserves for grain purchases abroad. Because of a reduced grain harvest, the daily food rations had to be nearly halved. Normally, they averaged 400 grams of rice and 100–150 grams of other food.

It may be recalled that one of the long-term priorities of economic expansion, which was to have hastened the "full victory of Socialism," is to grow a grain crop of 15 million tons, including 3.9 million tons of rice and 1.5 million tons of maize. Other items of average monthly agricultural production in the 1980s were 350–370 thousand tons of potatoes and batatas; 3.5–3.6

million tons of vegetables; 450 thousand tons of fruit crops, and 170–200 thousand tons of meat. Stable low levels of agricultural production, in the absence of food imports, make derationing impossible, although the rationing has been prompted also by ideological guidelines—those of maintaining an equalized distribution of material values, relieving the population of "extra" money, and discouraging commodity-money relations. Noteworthy figures are available in respect to equalized average monthly incomes of the urban and rural household; the urban income is 180 hwan. The annual income of a peasant family is 2,400 hwan. Consequently, the monthly income is 200 hwan. This sum is reduced by an order of 30 to 50 percent through all kinds of levies and savings bank deductions (although there has been no official taxation since 1974). Thus, the disposable income, that is, the amount that remains after deductions to meet the cost of public utilities, urban transport fares, public catering, and children's day-care accommodation, is $4–5. That is the pay rate for 14–16 hours of hard work. Pension rates are 15–30 hwan which, considering the nearly total absence of a part-time farming income, means that the Korean peasant has no normal livelihood.

UPSHOT AND OUTLOOK

The DPRK had great economic potential for quickly overcoming its economic backwardness and entering the dynamically developing Pacific Rim as an equal member. Some Asian NICs which had the same or even worse starting conditions than the DPRK when they set course for dynamic growth by implementing a flexible open-market economic policy have left the DPRK far behind. It is the developing capitalism that has so far won the economic competition with socialism on Korean soil.

The main drag on economic growth in the DPRK, especially on the evolution of a docialist order of society, was the negative influence of the Great Powers, its neighbors the USSR and China. The transplanting first of Stalin's and then of Mao Zedong's methods of building a new type of society to Korean soil—as an antipode of capitalism oriented toward cooperation within the restricted economic space of the world Socialist economy—deprived the DPRK of the advantages produced by world civilization and the world's scientific and technological progress of the twentieth century.

The persisting military instability on the Korean Peninsula, artificially fostered by Communist propaganda, with a danger of the Cold War escalating into a hot one, has compounded the above mentioned abnormalities with tailoring the DPRK's economic development to the needs of the military-industrial complex, which is drawing off one-third of public spending for noncivilian ends.

The DPRK has none of the advantages it could have derived from intra-Korean economic exchange and from economic, scientific, technological, and cultural cooperation with South Korea.

The external and internal conditions for a continued commitment to the Socialist option drastically worsened at the opening of the 1990s. An economic recession set in, external economic links decreased, and there was no more economic aid on soft terms from major sponsors, former allies. The structure of the Korean economy and its standard of performance keep it hamstrung, that is, prevent it from joining the economic processes in the Asian and Pacific region without considerable foreign aid injections. Western capital is so far steering clear of the DPRK's economy for want of political guarantees. The DPRK has gone bankrupt in the world exchange market. The only way out is to look for new mutually beneficial forms of cooperation with the USSR and to advance the political dialogue with South Korea.

The DPRK is on the threshold of economic change. In all likelihood, it will draw upon the experience of the Chinese economic reform which has served to score impressive economic gains while maintaining the traditional political structures and Communist ideology readjusted in line with the "specifically Chinese" mode of building Socialism.

NOTES

1. These values are numerous and difficult to strictly define, yet they include such things as scientific and technological progress, democratization, social guarantees, and the law-based state.
2. In 1964 the Party made its agrarian program public in "Theses on the Socialist Agrarian Question in our Country."
3. The Political Programme of the Government of DPRK, 1967.
4. There was a time when the Soviet Union played an important role in the building of North Korea's industrial potential. Enterprises built with Soviet help produced basic, including export-oriented, products. In 1990 they produced: 65% of electricity, 40% of iron ore, 35 to 40% of rolled steel, 100% of aluminum, 60% of oil products, 20% of textiles, as well as 100% of enameled wire, 90% of batteries and microelectric motors, and 33% of ball bearings.
5. Significantly, Kim Il Sung said in his address to the ninth session of the DPRK's Supreme People's Assembly of the Fifth Convocation November 29, 1974, titled "Some Points Concerning the Full Implementation of Agrarian Theses:" "For long years our peasants lived under the conditions of the domination of private property, consequently, the ideology of individualism has struck deep roots in their minds. The agricultural cooperatives that will be the first to go over to a national ownership at the pilot stage must faithfully observe the socialist principle of distribution . . . . They must be administered by industrial methods. Agricultural cooperatives should be made national property at a district level . . . They must be administered by district committees for the administration of agriculture, . . ." (Ibid., Pyongyang, edition of 1979, pp. 5, 15, 17, 22.)

REFERENCES

Kim Il Sung. *On Some Theoretical Problems of Socialist Economy*, Pyongyang, 1983, 34 pp.

The Democratic People's Republic of Korea, Moscow, 1985 (edited by M.Y. Trigubenko), 272 pp.

M.Y. Trigubenko. *Agriculture of the DPRK*, Moscow, 1973, 135 pp.

Industry of the DPRK (edited by M.Y. Trigubenko), Moscow, 1977, 179 pp.

V.I. Denisov and V.I. Moiseyev. *The Democratic People's Republic of Korea Is 40 Years Old*, Moscow, 1988, 63 pp.

M.Y. Trigubenko. *People's Korea Is 30 Years Old*, Moscow, 1975, 63 pp.

M.Y. Trigubenko. "Asia Updated," *Kommunist* (journal), No. 16, 1990.

M.Y. Trigubenko. "Friendly Nations of Asia and Ourselves," *Far Eastern Affairs*. No. 6, 1990.

M.Y. Trigubenko, G. Toloraya, and A. Mansurov. "Joint Ventures in the DPRK," *Far Eastern Affairs*, No. 2, 1990.

Kim Il Sung. "Bring Out More of the Advantages of Socialism in This Country." The political speech to the first session of the Supreme People's Assembly of the DPRK (Ninth Convocation), May 24, 1990, Pyongyang, 1990, 37 pp.

Kim Il Sung. "For the Complete Victory of Socialism." The political speech to the first session of the Eighth Supreme People's Assembly of the DPRK, December 30, 1986, Pyongyang, 1987, 45 pp.

Kim Il Sung. "Holding Aloft the Revolutionary Banner of Chuchhe, Let Us Bring Off the Cause of Socialism and Communism." The report on the fortieth anniversary of the founding of the DPRK, September 8, 1988, Pyongyang, 1988, 47 pp.

Kim Chen Il. *On Advancing Science and Engineering*, Pyongyang, 1985, 25 pp.

Economic Development in the DPRK, Pyongyang, 1990, 87 pp.

10

Economic Assistance from Socialist Countries to North Korea in the Postwar Years: 1953–1963

Karoly Fendler
Budapest, Hungary

Recent sweeping and monumental changes in the international context as well as in the domestic political situation of socialist countries and their relations with one another have had major repercussions on the Far East. As a result of internal and external events, the Korean peninsula and the Korean issue are again in the forefront of international interest, of rather heated expectations, and a subject of diplomacy behind the scenes. The interest and "prognostic exercises" have particularly focused on North Korea—how long will the Democratic People's Republic of Korea (DPRK), currently struggling with a general economic crisis, be able to maintain its political system and the policy of isolation as one of the very few surviving communist countries? How long will the leadership in Pyongyang be able to preserve its extremely paternalistic personal dictatorship, and how long will the people put up with them? What impact will the phenomenal changes have on the process of unification and the relative balance of power in the Far East?

Considering the conflicting social, political, ideological, and economic systems of North and South Korea, economic relations at the moment seems to be the only viable area in which the two Korean states may approach each other, even if it is predestined to be a difficult and tortuous process (in this context I do not wish to touch upon the issue of nationalism). To assess the prospects of economic cooperation and its impact on the stabilization of the North Korean economy, it is essential to consider the existing economic conditions and structures in the DPRK. In other words, what can prospective South Korean (and foreign) investors seeking economic cooperation and joint-venture opportunities expect from this hitherto hermetically closed, xenophobic enclave enshrouded in mystery? In short, how efficient can Seoul's "North policy" (Nordpolitik), which has won international recognition and applause, be on the Korean peninsula and will any benefits be accrued from its economic pursuit? To answer these questions I believe we must first make a retrospective examination of the role of economic assistance and loans extended by socialist countries to North Korea in the postwar years. In fact, foreign economic aid has dictated and determined the structures and features of the North Korean economy and its industry, heavy industry in particular, up to the present day. Such an investigation will assist us in predicting the possible outcomes of economic cooperation with North Korea currently under consideration.

I

Economic recovery and reconstruction were the overriding tasks for victorious and defeated countries alike after World War II. For a number of countries in Eastern Europe and Asia, this task was inextricably entwined with the historic problem of economic and social modernization. It was particularly true of the underdeveloped Korea which had been liberated after forty years of Japanese colonial rule. In reality, however, the twofold task became part of, and a tool for, the evolving bipolar international politics and the confrontational strategy of the superpowers. Unfortunately, the divided Korea became the testing ground of the Cold War and remained one of the hot spots throughout the Cold War era. In the postwar decades, China and North Korea adopted the socialist or Soviet model of development which was distinctively different from other forms of modernization in Asia. Both countries, the DPRK in particular, relied on economic and financial assistance from the Soviet Union and the East European countries as a primary (and extensive) source of accumulation. Although the East European countries were much more developed than their Asian counterparts, they also had to cope with the task of modernization. However, these countries could not so much pursue an independent foreign aid policy based solely on their own economic interests as they had to defer to the Soviet intentions and influences and the prevalent spirit of "proletarian internationalism." On the other hand, however, in a hostile international environment during the early days of the Cold War, North Korea had no alternative but to turn to the Soviet Union, China, and other socialist countries for economic aid. With foreign assistance, the DPRK achieved relatively rapid and impressive economic growth and its economic situation was soon stabilized. As North Korea's economic success compared favorably with the achievements of South Korea (before 1961), the Kim Il Sung regime began to brag about the "supremacy" of socialism. It was ignored that the otherwise justified modernization and forced industrialization (i.e., the "classical" phase of the industrial revolution) took place in North Korea and several other countries.

As I have already noted, the DPRK had made relatively significant achievements by the early 1960s thanks to the economic and technical assistance of the socialist countries. Postwar industrialization brought fundamental changes in both the structure of production capacities and their geographical locations (they had originally reflected the Japanese pattern).[1] The basic needs of the people, even though at a modest level, were satisfied and adequate supplies were ensured. Economic and humanitarian assistance, expansion of foreign trade, and foreign training programs for students and specialists contributed to North Korea's integration into the international system of socialist economies. The traditional isolationism that characterized the Korean society and politics for centuries had loosened its grip on the country by the end of the 1950s. This opened up brilliant vistas for the DPRK's modernization efforts and encouraged it to pursue its development goals more vigorously even though the country's modest ambition was only to catch up with other socialist countries.

With economic development and the modernization of political power and the superstructure in sight, the question "how to move on" came to the fore in the debates within the political leadership during the second half of the 1950s. Kim Il Sung and his faction emerged triumphant in political infighting. Kim strengthened his personal power and imposed a political-administrative system based on a personality cult. Kim's dominance led to the ascendancy of isolationism. Roughly at the same time, the de-Stalinization process set in motion by the Twentieth and Twenty-second Congresses of the Soviet Communist Party caused a Sino-Soviet rift. In this context, the Pyongyang leadership decided to dissociate itself from foreign countries, mainly socialist countries, so as to defend itself against foreign intervention (to combat "shadejui," "modern revisionism," etc. in North Korean parlance). As a consequence, after the postwar aid programs expired in the early 1960s, the DPRK could hardly obtain further major economic assistance. This was especially problematic because the regime took such aid for granted when it formulated the new seven-year economic plan (1961–1967).

As a result, the internal and external resources for extensive economic development became exhausted by the mid-1960s. Even faced with such a stark reality, to safeguard its power position, the bigoted leadership adamantly refused to show any flexibility and thwarted any attempt to reformulate the political and economic concept even within framework of the given socialist model. The corollary was that the DPRK was increasingly unable to keep pace even with the East European countries in sociopolitical and economic development in spite of its advantages in terms of natural resources, labor supply and so on. Its rigid internal policy and conservatism made its political relations with other socialist countries increasingly tense although this tension was not always explicit or obvious. The DPRK's economy was further disrupted by the international tension caused by its "parallel economic and defense development" program designed to strengthen the personal power of the top leaders. The program was not only based on a totally erroneous assessment of North Korea's internal capabilities and the overall international situation but it can also be considered as a response to the emerging reform efforts in some socialist countries (Hungary, Czechoslovakia, and to a certain degree the Soviet Union). It is clear that with this program, Pyongyang embarked on a road leading to prolonged economic crises instead of modernization. This decision has been disastrous. While the North was bogged down in the quagmire of stagnation, South Korea was making tremendous progress in its modernization effort. Over the past two decades or so the military junta dominated authoritarian regime in the South has been severely criticized for its political repression. Yet, the South has made tremendous progress in its modernization efforts and effectively eliminated its traditional backwardness under such a regime. What the Communist dictatorship has brought in the North has been pathetic. Except for a limited number of prestige projects, its catastrophic policy has produced little more than prolonged crises. It has led the country to a general political and economic dead end. In North Korea, the industrialization achieved with grants from foreign countries is hardly a basis for modernization but rather serves as the economic foundation of Kim's personal power.

II

This section will provide a description of the assistance and loans extended to the DPRK and their role in the country's economic development in the postwar decades. I will first deal with the size and nature of the Soviet and Chinese assistance and give a comparative analysis of the two countries' respective contributions considering the decisive importance of the two countries. Therefore, it is necessary to discuss briefly the most important agreements on economic and financial cooperation—mainly those reached with the Soviet Union—in subsequent decades because the direction and sectoral implementation of those agreements were based on the previous aid program. The comparison of the Soviet and Chinese assistance policies will also help us arrive at certain conclusions about North Korea's policy toward these countries.

It is known to all that the Soviet Union provided the lion's share of nonrepayable assistance and loans made by socialist countries. The Soviet government provided nonrepayable assistance of 225 million rubles (1 billion old rubles) to North Korea for the postwar reconstruction of the economy as early as August 1953. At the same time, it canceled over half of the DPRK's debt on the prewar Soviet loans account and postponed the repayment of the outstanding debts on favorable terms. Upon North Korea's request, the Soviet Union granted further nonrepayable economic aid to the tune of 67.5 million rubles (300 million old rubles) in August 1956. The aid, totalling 300 million rubles, played a decisive role in the implementation of the three-year reconstruction plan (1954–1956) and the five-year economic plan (1957–1961) and helped lay a foundation for industrialization and modernization. Hence, more than forty industrial and other plants were built or rebuilt with the Soviet aid between 1954 and 1961 (see Appendix). Assistance included design and construction work provided by the Soviet side, the delivery of complex equipment and raw materials, transfer of technical documentation and technology, and training for the Korean technical staff. The bulk of economic, technical, and financial assistance provided by the Soviet Union and other socialist countries was directed to the production sector; the government of the DPRK used about one-third of the available funds to purchase complex equipment for heavy industries.

The aforementioned economic aid from the Soviet Union in 1953 and 1956 financed, among other things, the rehabilitation and reconstruction of a hydroelectric power plant in Suphun, a foundry in Chondjin, a steelworks in

Sondjin, a nonferrous metallurgical works in Nampo, a fertilizer factory in Hunnam, and the construction of a cement factory in Madong, a chemical works in Pongun, a textile works, a silk factory, a meat processing plant in Pyongyang, and a fish-canning factory in Sinpho. The same aid was used to build a veneer factory in Kildju and a furniture factory in Pyongyang and to restore the Nampo port. The Soviet Union also participated in the reconstruction of the railroad infrastructure (see Appendix). On the whole, the production capacities built or rebuilt with Soviet assistance accounted for 40 percent of electricity generation, 53 percent of coke production, 51 percent of cast iron, 22 percent of steel, 32 percent of rolling stock, 45 percent of reinforced concrete blocks, 100 percent of copper, cadmium, and ammonium sulfate, and 65 percent of cotton fabric by the end of the Five-Year Plan. Economic aid programs also helped develop and expand North Korea's export capacities and foreign trade to some extent.

Technical assistance also played an important role. Under the intergovernmental agreement of February 1955, the Soviet Union transferred more than 600 complete technical documents to the DPRK between 1955 and 1959, enabling North Korea to launch several new products in areas such as electric technology, chemical, engineering, metallurgy, and transportation within a relatively short period of time. Joint research and exploration projects were also carried out. For example, substantial ore and nonferrous metal and other mineral resources were discovered with the assistance of Soviet geologists in North Korea. Several thousand Korean experts received on-the-job and technical training in the Soviet Union and East European countries and more than 10,000 students pursued academic studies at universities and colleges in the socialist countries.

Before these Soviet aid programs were fully utilized, another major intergovernmental agreement was signed in March 1959 for Soviet technical assistance in industrial and other projects. The assistance was used for the construction of a heat power station, an ammonia plant, a polychloric vinyl factory, and two textile factories (for wool and cotton) in Pyongyang and for the substantial expansion of a metallurgical works and a textile mill in Sondjin. All of these projects were given high priority in the seven-year economic plan (1961–1967). The value of the related Soviet deliveries and technical assistance was in the vicinity of 112 million rubles (500 million old rubles) which the Korean side was supposed to repay with its general exports under the trade agreements. The Soviet Union in fact made a credit for the new "plan package." The limitations on North Korea's ability to repay its debts are evident from the Soviet Union's cancellation of the DPRK's accumulated debts of 171 million rubles as of July 1960 and the rescheduling of another 31.5 million rubles. A distinctive feature of the creditor-debtor relationship in the subsequent thirty years was continuous long-term loans extended by the Soviet Union and frequent deferral of North Korean repayment. In 1965, 1966, 1970, 1976, 1981, and other years, respectively, the debts had to be rescheduled. In sum, the Soviet nonrepayable aid and loans—most of them were subsequently canceled—went a long way toward financing the restoration, construction, and expansion of over seventy projects, more than forty of which were implemented in the industrial sectors in roughly the past thirty-five years. Those projects created the most important plants and factories in the energy, mining, primary, ferrous and nonferrous metallurgical, chemical, building, oil-refining, machine-building, textile, transportation, communication, and other sectors in North Korea. Their economic significance is evidenced by the share of these plants in overall production. They accounted for the production of 63 percent of electricity, 33 percent of steel, 11 percent of cast iron, 38 percent of rolling stock, 50 percent of petroleum products, 25 percent of coke, 20 percent of textiles, 14 percent of fertilizers and 42 percent of iron ore mining in 1982.

However, the country's forced industrialization was not accompanied by a parallel development of export capabilities. On the contrary, it left the country highly insolvent and resulted in considerable debts to both socialist and capitalist countries. According to statistics released as of November 1, 1989, the DPRK's foreign debt to the Soviet Union alone amounted to 2,234.1 billion rubles, equivalent to about half of the country's exports in one and a half or two years.[2] The annual foreign trade turnover of North Korea is in the neighborhood of 3 billion rubles, roughly 50 percent of which is with the Soviet Union.[3] Pursuant to the intergovernmental agreement of November 1990, beginning in 1991, the Soviet Union and the DPRK will settle payment accounts in convertible foreign exchange and apply international market prices in their transactions, and the same principle will apply to the amortization of the North Korean debts. In light of the economic reality in the DPRK, it seems doubtful that a major change would occur in this respect in the foreseeable future (let alone North Korea's debts to capitalist countries).

After the Korean War, the People's Republic of China also played a pivotal role in the rehabilitation of the North Korean economy. An agreement was concluded in Beijing in November 1953 whereby the Chinese government agreed to grant nonrepayable aid worth 800 million yuan to the DPRK. In addition, China canceled the North Korean debts accumulated in bilateral trade between June 1950 and December 1953 (that item alone exceeded 52 million new rubles in the 1952–53 period). The two countries also signed an agreement for economic and cultural cooperation under which the Chinese side was to provide nonrepayable technical assistance.[4] Under the 800-million-yuan aid program, China supplied coal, textiles, grain, building materials, vehicles, steel products, machinery, agricultural equipment, and fishing boats from 1954 to 1957. In addition, China assisted in the restoration of North Korea's railroad network and the construction of manufacturing plants (glass, ironware, silk, textile, etc.) (see Appendix). Further, scholarly exchange, training, and scholarship programs were offered.

In September 1958, additional intergovernmental agreements were signed—one for the "mutual supply of major materials" and one for the extension of loans. Under the second agreement, China extended a $10 million loan for the construction of a hydroelectric power station in Unbong and an additional $42.5 million for various other construction projects to be implemented from 1959 to 1962. In October 1960 China and North Korea entered into another loan agreement and an agreement "for the supply of complex equipment and technical assistance" to the tune of 96 million new rubles. The agreements were implemented between 1961 and 1964, resulting in the construction of a wheel tire factory, a wire radio factory, a paper mill and a fountain pen plant. Moreover, we cannot rule out the possibility that certain military plants were also built (for the manufacture of ammunition, and light and medium-size weapons), but no concrete data is available.

Later, Chinese aid and loans became increasingly scarce. In summer 1970, a high-level North Korean military delegation signed an agreement on Chinese assistance in Beijing but its details were not made known. In October of same year, an intergovernmental agreement on "economic and technical assistance" was concluded in Beijing but again no details were published. It is assumed that they were related to North Korea's six-year economic plan (1971–1976).[5]

There is a paucity of data concerning postwar assistance and lending by other socialist countries, but the greatest secrecy surrounds the size and amount of Chinese aid. There are no reliable statistics to show whether China totally or at least partially canceled the DPRK's debts or whether it ever agreed to reschedule repayments. Several Western studies estimate China's contributions to the economic recovery in North Korea to be half of the Soviet assistance and loans. Paige suggests that the amount may be around 1.8 billion rubles.[6] However, it is difficult to give an accurate estimate because of currency conversion and settlement problems.

As regards the East European socialist countries, about twenty-five projects were built with their nonrepayable assistance in the decade following the Korean War—two-thirds in the manufacturing and heavy industries (see Appendix). Together with technical assistance and canceled debts, the total value is estimated at 700 to 800 million rubles. It is interesting to note that Soviet literature gives different estimates of the amount of nonrepayable aid from socialist countries, varying between 500 to 800 million rubles. Pyongyang earlier reported a figure of 500 million rubles. It is a fact that for seven to eight years following the War, nonrepayable aid was a major source of annual budget revenues and accumulation. The utilization of foreign, mainly Soviet, aid was in conformity with the Stalinist development strategy of giving top priority to industry and heavy industry in particular and with the socialist economic model which Pyongyang had adopted. Pyongyang saw forced industrialization as an avenue to the country's modernization and ascendancy and maintained a high accumulation rate to the detriment of consumption for decades. As late as the early 1960s, the North Korean regime still acknowledged that sector "A" of the economy had been created with the assistance of socialist countries, making possible the utilization of domestic resources for the development of manufacturing industries and agriculture. However, that notion of international cooperation and mutual assistance was soon replaced by the concept of achieving "prosperity with our own resources." The policy of self-reliance also applied to economic development, especially after the aid program had been completed. The forced development of heavy industry and the control over consumption required that internal political tension be controlled in every possible way even if it meant the use of repressive means. Such a perceived need was also used to justify the creation of a political system centered on personal power. All this became an increasingly serious obstacle to modernization in North Korea.

As I have noted, Soviet and East European nonrepayable assistance and subsequent loans were mainly used in industry, heavy industry in particular, and this orientation was reflected in North Korea's foreign economic relations, especially with respect to the aid programs during the 1960s, 1970s, and 1980s. As for China, partly in line with its own development strategy, it concentrated on industrial plants and equipment or construction projects in North Korea which either were labor-intensive or required relatively little technology (roads, bridges, railroads, etc.). Periodic food and consumer goods supplies from China also made a significant part of the overall supply. In other words, Chinese assistance and loans were generally absorbed in the Korean economy despite the temporary and often spectacular impact they made. Production capacities built with Soviet aid, though in rapid decline, still play a significant role today. This clearly refutes the fallacy of North Korea's self-reliance and testifies to its heavy dependency on foreign aid. It shows that the DPRK can hardly dispense with foreign, especially Soviet, aid and loans in its efforts to carry out periodic economic reconstruction, to renovate or expand the existing industrial facilities, to ensure spare parts supply, or to promote technological advances.

The North Korean Communist regime has come to realize the indispensability of foreign aid. That is why the Pyongyang leadership has adopted a pragmatic approach in its foreign policy, trying very hard to strike a balance between Moscow and Beijing in the last thirty years. It is also indicated by the date of major Soviet lending and rescheduling of loans every five to six years as noted already.

In conclusion, North Korea's extensive reserves have been exhausted and its possibilities for modernization lessened. Further, convertible accounting in trade has been instituted and the nation is increasingly isolated from international politics and economics. For these reasons, its adherence to the existing model and its economic strategic potential have also become exhausted and the possibilities for balancing in international and internal politics are about to close for the Korean leadership. If the DPRK receives further foreign aid and loans, which will be inevitable and will presumably come from Japan and South Korea, they will serve a radically different political system and modernization strategy. Such assistance can, however, be effective only if the relative achievements of the modernization efforts after the Korean War and results of industrialization are taken into account. An understanding of those achievements will therefore be vital for North Korea's new economic partners.

NOTES

1. As a result of Japanese industrial strategic policy during the 1930–1944 period, 79 percent of heavy industrial establishment in Korea was concentrated in the North. See *Kyongjae Yeonku* (in Korean; *Economic Research*), Volume 8, 1957, p. 70.
2. *Izvestia*, March 1, 1990.
3. Ibid.
4. *Chosun Jungang Yeonkam* (in Korean; Korean Central Yearbook), 1954–1955, p.79.
5. Ibid., 1971, p. 360.
6. Glenn Paige, *Democratic People's Republic of Korea*. 1966, Chapter 4.

APPENDIX

PROJECTS FUNDED PARTIALLY BY AID FROM SOCIALIST SYSTEMS

Project	Unit	With Aid	Domestic	Total	Year Completed
U.S.S.R.					
1. Kim Check refinery	1000t	350	250	600	1955
steel		50	50	100	1955
cokes		400		400	1955
2. Sungjin refinery	1000t				
steel		50	50	100	1955
sheet steel		120	310	430	1959
3. Nampo	1000t				
black bronze		2.5	5	7.5	1955
bronze		2.5	4.5	7	1958
zinc		8.0	15	23	1957
4. Hungnam Chemical	1000t				
ammonia		100	28	128	1956
5. Ammonia	1000t				
ammonia		136	24	160	1958
6. Bong un Chemical I	1000t	10	30	40	1955

APPENDIX

PROJECTS FUNDED PARTIALLY BY AID FROM SOCIALIST SYSTEMS

Project	Unit	With Aid	Domestic	Total	Year Completed
7. Bong un Chemical II ammonia	1000t	10	15	25	1958
8. Madong Cement Plant cement	1000t	400		400	1959
9. Kilju Veneer veneer	1000m	17.4		17.4	1959
10. Pyongyang Furniture furniture	million rubles	20		20	1957
11. Pyongyang Textile cotton	million meters	65	15	80	1956
12. Pyongyang Silk silk	million meters	10		10	1959
13. Pyongyang Dye Plant fabric	million meters	45		45	1957
14. Pyongyang Meat Processing sausage cans	1000t	1 1		1 1	1956 1957
15. Shinpo Fish Canning Plant fish cans	1000t	4		4	1955
16. Pyongyang Reinforced Cement cement bricks		45		45	1957
17. Tracker Repair repaired		300		300	1957
18. Supoong Hydraulic Generator power	1 billion KWH	3.5		3.5	1958
19. Nampo Port					1960
20. Radio station w/2 transmitters					
21. Radio station w/4 transmitters					

APPENDIX

PROJECTS FUNDED PARTIALLY BY AID FROM SOCIALIST SYSTEMS

Project	Unit	With Aid	Domestic	Total	Year Completed
22. Railroad Shincho-Kowon					1959
23. Tuman Bridge					1959
24. Pyongyang City Hospital (600 beds)					1957
26. Jonari Cement Plant	million rubles	24		24	1956
27–32. Battery Plants					1955-58
33–40. Projects: 138, 139, 217, 261, 548, 549, 551, 573, 651					1963
China					
1. Nampo Glass	million m	6		6	1954
2. Silk Factory	1000 chu	30		30	1957
3. Consumer Goods	million won	1		1	1957
4. Enamel, Metal Cookware	million won	1		1	1954
5. Pyongyang Railroad repair					1954
6. Chongju Railroad repair					1954
7. Kowon Railroad repair					1954
8. Shin ui ju Textile	1000 chu	62.4		62.4	1959
9. Bearing Plant	million set	1.2		1.2	1960
10. Haesan Paper Mill	1000t	20		20	1963
11. Hoiryon Sugar	1000t	10		10	1963
12. Fountain Pen Factory	million	10		10	1963
East Germany					
1. Telephone Manufacturing	1000	6		6	1957
2. Hamhung Concrete	1000t	50		50	1957
3. Hamhung Housing	1000	5.3		5.3	1958
4. Hamhung Tiles	million	33		33	1959

APPENDIX

PROJECTS FUNDED PARTIALLY BY AID FROM SOCIALIST SYSTEMS

Project	Unit	With Aid	Domestic	Total	Year Completed
5. Ceramic Pipe Plant	1000m	500		500	?
6. Pyongyang Printing					1963
Poland					
1. Wonsan Auto Repair					1959
2. Pyongyang Auto Repair					1959
3. Haenam Hospital (500 beds)					1959
Hungary					
1. Pyongyang Scale Factory					1959
2. Kusan Machinery					1960
3. Bong un Paint Plant					1960
Romania					
1. Aspirin Manufacturing	ton	25		25	1958
2. Sunori Cement	1000t	200		200	1959
3. Suchon Tile Factory	million	6		6	1959
4. Pyongyang General Hospital (600 beds)					1959
Czechoslovakia					
1. Hoechon Machinery	1000		1000		1958
2. Dukchon Automobile Plant					1958
3. Wunsan Machinery					1958
4. Pyongyang Engine Factory					1958
5. Nampo non-steel minerals	1000t	12		12	1962
6. Pyongyang Cable Factory	1000t	12		12	1962
Bulgaria					
1. Forestry Industry					1956
2. Wonsan Tile Factory					1956

11

FOREIGN POLICY GOALS, CONSTRAINTS, AND PROSPECTS

BYUNG CHUL KOH

University of Illinois at Chicago

INTRODUCTION

In an increasingly interdependent world a state's foreign policy takes on an added significance: Not only does it help shape that state's ability to deal with its internal problems but it also impinges on the well-being of the rest of the world. From the standpoint of the latter the importance of a state's foreign policy is in direct proportion to its potential to disturb peace and security, either regional or global.

Viewed in this vein, the foreign policy of the Democratic People's Republic of Korea (DPRK) is a topic well worthy of scrutiny. In terms of track record and potential alike, the DPRK is a key player in Northeast Asia. Its formidable military capability and deep-seated hostility toward the Republic of Korea (ROK), coupled with the awesome military might of both the ROK and the United States arrayed against it, ensure that the Korean Peninsula will remain a potential tinderbox. Added to the above the entangling network of military alliances, both Korean states have forged with major powers. Finally, the suspicions about North Korea's nuclear weapons program further exacerbate the situation.

Although recent developments—notably the signing of two inter-Korean agreements in December 1991, one dealing with nonaggression and cooperation and the other with denuclearization of the Korean peninsula—have helped to raise the hope that the dark cloud of war hanging over the Korean peninsula has finally begun to dissipate, North Korea's attempt to adhere doggedly to its own brand of socialism in the midst of a global decline, even extinction, of socialism is both intriguing and mystifying. Will it succeed? Will it inject a sufficient measure of pragmatism in its response to the stimuli of the changing world to attain its goals, both internal and external? What are these goals? Have they remained the same over the years?

The modest aim of this article, then, is to explore some of these questions. I propose to examine three dimensions of North Korea's foreign policy, which is construed as its policy toward the rest of the world, including South Korea: (1) goals, (2) constraints, and (3) prospects.

MANIFEST GOALS

In examining a state's foreign policy, one needs to draw a distinction between its manifest goals and latent goals. The former refers to the officially stated objectives of a state's foreign policy, while the latter pertains to those objectives which can be inferred from that state's actual behavior. While the two sets of goals may coincide, they can also diverge to a striking extent.

Generally speaking, the more closed a state is, the higher the probability that its latent foreign policy goals will diverge from its manifest goals.

With this rudimentary distinction in mind, let us first examine the manifest goals of North Korea's foreign policy. In his New Year's message to the North Korean people on January 1, 1993, President Kim Il Sung said:

> The government of our Republic will continue to implement its foreign policy of [promoting] independence, peace, and friendship. We will steadfastly maintain our independence and faithfully uphold our revolutionary principles and international duties, no matter how complicated the circumstances may be. In order to attain the goal of independence for the whole world, [we] will make an all-out effort to develop friendship and cooperative relations with the peoples of the various countries of the world, including the socialist and non-aligned countries.[1]

Several things are noteworthy. First, the manifest goals of the DPRK's foreign policy are threefold: (1) independence [*chaju*], (2) peace [*p'yonghwa*], and (3) friendship [*ch'inson*]. Second, the DPRK has officially adhered to these goals for a long time; they therefore represent continuity in Pyongyang's foreign policy at the manifest level. Third, while these goals may strike the uninitiated as eminently nonideological, to trained eyes they are firmly anchored in North Korea's guiding ideology, *chuch'e sasang* (ideology of self-reliance). Fourth, the emphasis on the nonaligned countries reflects not only Pyongyang's long-held priority but also the dwindling of the ranks of socialist countries.

Before leaping to the conclusion that the three manifest goals are so general or abstract as to be meaningless, let us pause and consider whether any or all of them has any relevance for Pyongyang's actual behavior in the international arena. This in turn necessitates a brief discussion of both their sources and meanings in the context of North Korean politics or scheme of things.

The goal to which North Korea assigns the highest priority is independence, and the reasons for that are not hard to decipher. Independence happens to be the core concept in *chuch'e sasang*, which has been formally enshrined as North Korea's guiding ideology in the constitutions of the DPRK and the Workers' Party of Korea (WPK) alike. North Korea has not only extolled independence in rhetoric but also made a herculean effort to attain it. The succession of multiyear economic development plans, the permanent mobilization of the populace in economic construction, the adoption of an essentially autarkic developmental strategy, and even the development of a domestic munitions industry—all of these are emblematic of

Pyongyang's quest for independence. I should hasten to point out that despite its advocacy of independence, Pyongyang has not hesitated to seek aid from its socialist allies, particularly Moscow and Beijing. Nor can it be argued that Pyongyang either has attained or is close to attaining the goal from an economic standpoint.

Insofar as its international behavior is concerned, however, North Korea has had a fair amount of success in steering an independent course thanks largely to the fortuitous dynamics of the dispute between the former Soviet Union and the People's Republic of China (PRC). Pyongyang has also used the principle of independence as a major propaganda tool in foreign policy. In his 1991 New Year's message, Kim Il Sung proclaimed:

> The government of our Republic will strive strenuously to smash the old world order marked by domination and subjugation, build a new world order founded on independence, and develop South-South cooperation in political, economic, and other fields based on the principle of collective self-reliance.
>
> Today Asia is entering a new stage of development. If the people of Asia, who are industrious and talented, unite and cooperate closely among themselves based on the principles of independence, equality, and reciprocity, then they can attain security and common prosperity in Asia and contribute to the great task of securing world peace. . .[2]

Of special interest is Kim Il Sung's reference to "world order."[3] To him the defining characteristic of the old world order is the pervasiveness of domination and subjugation; hence a new world order must see the blossoming of independence. Compare this with the former U.S. President George Bush's vision of a new world order: a world "where diverse nations are drawn together in common cause to achieve the universal aspirations of mankind: peace and security, freedom and the rule of law" and "where brutality will go unrewarded, and aggression will meet collective resistance."[4]

North Korea's commitment to independence also helps to explain the fervor with which it pursues the goal of reunification. For, in its view, true independence will come only when the division of the Korean peninsula is terminated and Korea is made whole again. Reunification will, moreover, bolster Korea's economic power, a backbone of independence. Independence is linked to reunification in another sense as well: As far as Pyongyang is concerned, reunification must be achieved independently, a principle that has been endorsed in the North-South joint communique of July 4, 1972, as Pyongyang never ceases to point out.[5] The principle of independence, along with those of peace and national unity, were reaffirmed in the December 1991 inter-Korean agreement on reconciliation, nonaggression, and mutual exchanges and cooperation.[6] To Pyongyang, the application of the principle of independence to the process of reunifying the two Korean states mandates the removal of all foreign forces from Korea—specifically, the withdrawal of U.S. troops and arms from South Korea.

Pursuit of that goal helps to explain much of North Korea's tactics in its relations with South Korea as well as of its foreign policy, particularly policy toward the United States. Pyongyang's quest for direct negotiations with Washington and for a peace treaty with the United States can be appreciated in that light.

The second manifest goal of North Korea's foreign policy, "peace," is also tailored to advance its specific interests. As a commentary in *The Pyongyang Times* put it:

> In order to prevent war and safeguard peace, it is imperative to realize disarmament, abolish nuclear weapons and make troops and military bases withdraw from other countries and end the imperialists' armed intervention and military aggression.
>
> The Government of our Republic is working hard to frustrate the imperialist policy of aggression and war and to make the Korean peninsula a nuclear-free, peace zone and is giving full support to the anti-war, anti-nuclear peace movement throughout the world.[7]

In other words, to North Korea, "peace" is but another justification for demanding withdrawal of U.S. troops and tactical nuclear weapons from South Korea. On the other hand, its numerous proposals for reciprocal arms reduction between North and South Korea should not be dismissed out of hand as propaganda ploys pure and simple. For, given its economic difficulties, North Korea does stand to benefit measurably from reduction in its military spending as well as from a reallocation of its human resources from the military to the civilian sector.

Just as its apotheosis of independence has not prevented Pyongyang from seeking and receiving all manner of assistance from Moscow and Beijing, so its putative dedication to peace has not precluded Pyongyang from resorting to violence and terror vis-à-vis Seoul—witness the Rangoon bombing incident of September 1983 in which 16 high-ranking South Korean officials and 5 other persons were killed and the mid-air bombing of Korean Air flight 858 in November 1987 in which 115 persons were killed.[8]

The third manifest goal of North Korea's foreign policy, "friendship," too, takes on a special meaning for North Korea. As explained by a *Rodong sinmun* commentary, since North Korea not only faces the unfinished task of national reunification but also must carry out the task of socialist construction in a direct confrontation with the "U.S. imperialists who are leaders of all the imperialists in the world," it needs all the friends it can get.

"To perform these difficult and complicated tasks, we need the international support and solidarity of the world people." Only by strengthening the friendship and unity of the anti-imperialist and pro-independence forces, can we ensure the overwhelming superiority of the revolutionary forces over the counter-revolutionary forces on the world stage and crush the unified counter-revolutionary offensive of the imperialists."[9]

The preceding explanation of why North Korea seeks friendship in the world arena is consistent with its actual conduct. During the period when the United Nations served as a forum for annual debate on the Korean question, North Korea worked very hard to drum up support for its own position among UN members, and its diplomatic efforts culminated in the passage of a pro-North Korea resolution in the General Assembly in 1975. That was the first and only time the world body had ever supported Pyongyang. Although the General Assembly in effect neutralized its pro-Pyongyang vote by also passing a contradictory resolution endorsing Seoul's position, North Korea nonetheless savored its hard-won "victory," invoking the pro-Pyongyang resolution with considerable frequency in subsequent years.[10]

North Korea has continued to rely on "friends" in the Third World to generate support for its proposals on reunification and to bolster the stature of its "great leader" Kim Il Sung. While it has had a fair amount of success in eliciting verbal support in the Third World, frequently in exchange for material assistance, it has made very little headway in attaining its goal of forging an anti-imperialist (or anti-U.S.) united front.

In a word, Pyongyang's manifest goals do need to be taken seriously, provided we place them in proper context and perspective. What, then, are the latent goals of its foreign policy?

LATENT GOALS

At a relatively high level of abstraction, one can argue that North Korea has pursued three interrelated latent goals in its foreign policy over the years: (1) legitimacy, (2) security, and (3) development. These goals are sufficiently general to be applied to analysis of North Korea's domestic policy as well. A plausible case also can be made that South Korea, too, has pursued the same three goals at the latent level.[11]

The first latent goal, legitimacy, is rooted in the peculiar circumstances surrounding the Korean peninsula: its division in 1945 and the emergence of two separate states in 1948, which subsequently became engulfed in a fratricidal civil war, thus sowing seeds of mutual distrust and animosity. Since both the ROK and the DPRK claimed to be the only legitimate state on the entire peninsula, a race for legitimacy ensued. The Korean War of 1950–1953 can be viewed as Kim Il Sung's abortive campaign to settle the legitimacy issue by force. Having egregiously failed to do so, he proceeded to use diplomacy to shore up both his own image and that of the DPRK. That triggered fierce competition in the diplomatic arena between Seoul and Pyongyang—to win recognition, to have international organizations, notably the United Nations, bestow a stamp of legitimacy, and to undercut the adversary in every conceivable way.

Measured in terms of the number of states with which it has established full diplomatic relations and the number of international organizations to which it has been admitted, the DPRK has done reasonably well. On the other hand, its accomplishments are eclipsed by those of the ROK. In a word, Pyongyang has lost the race to Seoul. That Pyongyang has been able to accomplish as much as it has, it should be pointed out, owes to a significant modification of its original policy, which was to win "absolute legitimacy" in the sense of recognition by other states that the DPRK is the "only legitimate" state in all of Korea. This goal was quietly downgraded to that of "relative legitimacy," which consisted of expanding the number of states recognizing the DPRK regardless of whether they also recognized the ROK. The ROK, too, downgraded its goal in the same way. As a result, over 80 states recognize both the ROK and the DPRK today.

Security is a major goal of most states either at the manifest or latent level. That it takes on an added importance in both Korean states owes to the legacy of the civil war and the dynamics of an arms race. The latter, it is true, has much to do with Pyongyang's pursuit of reunification by any and all means. Its construction of a massive arsenal, deployment of a large proportion of its troops and equipment near the Demilitarized Zone (DMZ), digging of underground tunnels across the DMZ, and numerous other acts of provocation and terrorism have continued to reinforce Seoul's fear of renewed invasion from the North; the countermeasures both South Korea and its principal ally, the United States, have taken contribute to an unending arms race on the peninsula, precipitating a vicious circle that is counterproductive to all concerned.[12]

A concrete manifestation of concern with security in Pyongyang's foreign policy over the years has been the care with which it has cultivated ties with Moscow and Beijing. Pyongyang concluded mutual defense treaties with both in 1961 and has forged close military links with them. Until its dissolution in 1991, the Soviet Union was the principal source of sophisticated military hardware for North Korea such as MIG-23s, MIG-29s, SU-25s, IL-28 bombers, and SA-5 surface-to-air missiles. With Soviet help, North Korea has built a sizable arms industry; in the 1970s it began manufacturing tanks, armored vehicles, self-propelled artillery, submarines, destroyers, and high-speed boats. It is noteworthy that Pyongyang has "developed a new surface-to-surface missile (Rodong-1) with a range of 1,000 km." Most important, Pyongyang is widely suspected to have been working on a nuclear weapons development program.[13] Chinese contributions to North

Korea's security have been quite substantial. Most important, it was China that helped to prevent a humiliating defeat by North Korea during the Korean War, for its intervention in the war in late 1950 helped to turn the tide of the war. The only military alliance China has in the world, moreover, is with North Korea. Beijing has also provided Pyongyang with a sizable quantity of military hardware such as A-5 fighter aircraft and MIG-19s.[14]

Another example of the way in which Pyongyang's concern with security helps shape its foreign policy is its untiring pursuit of the removal of U.S. troops and weapons from South Korea. While its ulterior motive may be the removal of what it perceives as the principal obstacle to reunification on its own terms, one should not overlook the possibility that Pyongyang may feel threatened by the U.S. military presence in the South. Until their removal from South Korea in late 1991, U.S. tactical nuclear weapons had greatly magnified Pyongyang's sense of insecurity.

The third and final latent goal of North Korea's foreign policy, development, is shared by most states in the Third World. Its importance for Pyongyang, however, is accentuated by its linkage to the other two goals. Pursuit of legitimacy, by winning friends and supporters around the world, requires material resources, the production of which presupposes sustained economic development. Sheer prestige that may accompany development can, furthermore, go a long way toward shoring up legitimacy. Development is also a sine qua non for security, whether the military equipment needed to bolster it is domestically produced, purchased from other countries, or both. Theoretically, of course, it is possible to rely heavily on foreign assistance, but both Pyongyang's commitment to independence and the level of military buildup it has chosen preclude that option.

As noted, however, its policy of self-reliance has not prevented Pyongyang from actively seeking all manner of aid from Moscow and Beijing. According to Radio Moscow, the Soviet Union has helped North Korea build or reconstruct about 70 major factories. As a result, production of 34 percent of rolling products, 40 percent of pig iron, and 45 percent of petroleum products, and over 60 percent of electricity in North Korea is dependent on Soviet-supplied technology.[15] Until 1990, the Soviet Union accounted for over half of North Korea's total trade turnover.

China has served as an important source of aid for North Korea as well. According to a rare revelation by *Renmin Ribao* in October 1979, China helped North Korea to build an oil refinery, the Pyongyang subway, a thermal electric power plant, a chemical plant, and other factories.[16] For many years since the mid-1970s, moreover, China exported crude oil to North Korea at the "friendship" rate of $4.50 per barrel.[17]

North Korea suffered a major setback in September 1990, when South Korea established full diplomatic relations with the Soviet Union. It was a stunning diplomatic coup for Seoul, which had been vigorously wooing Moscow as part of its *nordpolitik* (northern policy). Seoul's achievement, it must be stressed, was owed in no small measure to dramatic change in Soviet policy initiated by Mikhail Gorbachev.

North Korea vented its anger in a *Rodong sinmun* commentary on October 5, 1990 by accusing the Soviet Union of not only having reneged on its previous commitments to North Korea but also of having literally sold out to South Korea. Noting that Seoul had reportedly pledged economic cooperation to Moscow "to the tune of 2.3 billion dollars," the commentary said that "the Soviet Union sold off the dignity and honor of a socialist power and the interests and faith of an ally for 2.3 billion dollars." It quickly added that since South Korea does not have such a huge sum of money, the money will most likely come from a "special fund of the U.S. imperialists for undermining socialism." *Rodong sinmun* accused Moscow of colluding with Washington to perpetuate the division of the Korean peninsula, warning:

> There is no change in the basic strategy of imperialism to overthrow socialist countries by means of military threats and blackmail, economic bribery and subjugation, and ideological and cultural contamination.
>
> A dignified and independent socialist country must naturally heighten vigilance against this and never fall into the trap laid by the crafty imperialists, blinded by the lure of dollars. . . .
>
> The present era is an era of independence.
>
> No matter how serious the twists and turns may be, we will go our own way to the end, overcoming whatever obstacles that may lie in our path.[18]

The new strain in Pyongyang-Moscow relations, coupled with Moscow's decision to replace barter trade with hard currency transactions beginning in January 1991, dealt a major blow to the North Korean economy, a consequence that was further aggravated by the dissolution of the Soviet Union in late 1991. North Korea has taken two measures in an apparent effort to compensate for the losses it will suffer from all this: Strengthen its ties with China and initiate negotiations with Japan for normalization of relations. Notwithstanding or, perhaps because of ever-growing economic relations between Beijing and Seoul, Pyongyang stepped up an exchange of high-level visitors with Beijing.

China, for example, was represented by Song Ping, member of the standing committee of the political bureau of the Communist Party of China (CPC), at the celebrations marking the forty-fifth anniversary of the founding of the Workers' Party of Korea in Pyongyang in October 1990, while a Soviet representative was conspicuously absent.[19] DPRK Premier Yon Hyong-muk visited China in November 1990 to conclude an agreement on economic cooperation between the two countries.[20] In January 1991 Kim Yong-sun, the WPK secretary in charge of international affairs, visited China, meeting with Jiang Zemin, the CPC general secretary and other high-ranking officials.[21]

None of this, however, could prevent a stunning development—a major setback for Pyongyang. In August 1992 the PRC and the ROK established full diplomatic relations. If Pyongyang had hoped to compensate for its diplomatic, political, and economic losses with a speedy normalization of relations with Tokyo, it was rudely disillusioned. During the first round of formal negotiations held in Pyongyang in January 1991, North Korea demanded reparations from Japan not only for colonial rule but also for damage Japan had allegedly inflicted on North Korea during the postwar period.[22] Japan not only refused even to consider the question of compensation for its alleged injury to North Korea during the postwar period, but it also insisted that North Korea lacked the legal right to demand compensation for what Japan did during the colonial period. The only thing Japan would allow would be North Korean claims for property damage. More important, Japan, in close consultation with South Korea, set a number of preconditions for diplomatic normalization—such as the settlement of the nuclear issue and progress in the inter-Korean dialogue. After holding eight rounds of talks, the two sides were hopelessly deadlocked.

Other possibilities exist for Pyongyang: An improvement of relations with Seoul has the potential to bring about significant economic benefits, since there are many complementary aspects between the economies of both. Improved relations with Washington can also open the way for trade, direct investment, and other benefits. In 1993 Pyongyang achieved its long-sought goal of holding high-level talks with Washington. Whether the talks, which were designed to deal with the nuclear issue, would be productive for North Korea in the long run remained to be seen. Meanwhile, U.S.-DPRK diplomatic contacts at the embassy political counselor level, which began in Beijing in December 1988, continued at the pace of about one every other month.[23]

CONSTRAINTS

Constraints on North Korea's foreign policy are numerous. To cite but three sets of them, they are (1) the goals of foreign policy per se, (2) internal constraints, and (3) external constraints. To begin with the goals first, some of them seem either unattainable or counterproductive or both. Take the manifest goal of independence. Laudable though it may be, the manner in which North Korea has pursued it has served to limit its options and tarnish its international image. The glaring gap between its lip service to independence on the one hand and the harsh reality of its inability to service foreign debts on the other is but one example. Pyongyang's long adherence to an autarkic developmental strategy is another, and its belated and grudging adoption of a policy that purports to open its doors slightly has thus far yielded very little results.

The latent goal of legitimacy has long since passed a point of diminishing returns. Meager returns of North Korea's multifaceted campaign to bolster its legitimacy—such as supporting solidarity groups in the Third World, conducting "invitational diplomacy," sponsoring international conferences both in Pyongyang and abroad, drumming up support in various international forums, and distributing propaganda material purporting to advertise its own accomplishments and to undercut South Korea—do not justify its prodigious opportunity costs. Many of these activities are actually counterproductive, either because they are poorly planned and executed or because they generate countermeasures from South Korea that turn out to be more effective.

Pyongyang's apparent inability either to make a sober assessment of the efficacy of its activities or to lower its sights bespeaks the stifling effects of its systemic constraints, which is the most intractable of its internal constraints. The other major internal constraint, namely the dire economic situation, is directly related to and fueled by the systemic constraints. The extreme degree to which power has been personalized at the highest level, as evidenced by the cult of personality centering on Kim Il Sung, his son and successor-designate Jong Il, and his entire clan, cannot but hamper rational decisionmaking. By demanding unquestioning obedience to the "great leader" and the "dear leader," the North Korean political system not only contradicts its own guiding ideology of *chuch'e*, which extolls self-reliance, but also stifles an airing of views in decision-making councils. A corollary of such a system is strategic rigidity in the realm of reunification and foreign policy and economic policy alike, a sluggishness in tactical adjustment, and an inability to jettison ideological blinders.

Such internal constraints serve to magnify the adverse consequences of external constraints over which North Korea has little control. The breathtaking pace with which the global political and strategic environment has been changing has caught North Korea off guard, threatening to make it a dinosaur in a world of socialist extinction.

North Korea was also slow in coming to grips with the reality of South Korea's accomplishments in economic development, political democratization, and "northern diplomacy." Buoyed by the periodic surge of opposition activity on the part of radical students, workers, and others in South Korea, North Korea clung to the hope that a revolutionary overthrow of the ROK government would soon occur. Such wishful thinking underlay Pyongyang's adherence to its sterile "united front" tactic—of trying to bypass the authorities in Seoul to establish direct contacts with people and groups outside of, and opposed to, the government in power. It also reinforced Pyongyang's reluctance to make significant concessions in its dialogue with Seoul. I should hasten to point out that progress in the inter-Korean dialogue is a function of a multitude of factors, of which Pyongyang's policy and posture is but one; Seoul, too, has shown a lack of sincerity from time to time and has been notably reluctant to take any chances, displaying symptoms of "cognitive closure."[24] On balance, however, Seoul's posture toward the dialogue and the whole range of issues in inter-Korean relations has been markedly more moderate and pragmatic than Pyongyang's. The conclusion of the inter-Korean agreements in 1991 reflected not only increased realism in Pyongyang's perceptions but also Seoul's—or the Roh Tae Woo government's—political needs.

PROSPECTS

Signs of change in Pyongyang's policy suggest that the constraints noted above need not be crippling. While the strategic goals of North Korea's foreign policy have remained remarkably resilient over the years, North Korea has nonetheless displayed a capacity for tactical accommodation from time to time. To cite some notable examples, one may point to its decision to engage in dialogue with South Korea in the early 1970s in the face of the changing strategic environment triggered by the Sino-American rapprochement; its acceptance of the Chun Doo Hwan government in Seoul as a dialogue partner in the mid-1980s after denouncing it in the harshest terms and rebuffing all overtures; its participation in prime ministerial talks in the early 1990s; its decision in May 1991 to apply for membership in the United Nations, thereby reversing its two-decades-old policy of opposing either simultaneous or separate UN membership by the two Korean states; its signing of the two inter-Korean agreements in December 1991; and its signing of an IAEA nuclear safeguards agreement in January 1992.

What, then, can one expect in the months and years ahead? Three alternative scenarios may be envisaged. First, it is conceivable that we may witness more of the same for some time to come. Pyongyang will try valiantly to cling to its own model of socialism, which features the deification of its supreme leader and glorification of his chosen successor, unrelenting ideological indoctrination, perpetual mobilization of the citizenry in economic construction, and limited experiments in market socialism. Externally, Pyongyang will continue its policy of strengthening ties with Beijing, seeking normalization of relations with Tokyo, pursuing improved relations with Washington, cultivating support in the Third World, and opening its doors slightly to foreign economic inputs. There is also a good chance that Pyongyang may cooperate with Seoul in implementing the inter-Korean agreements in an incremental and controlled fashion, taking pains to minimize their adverse political sideeffects on its political system and governing ability.

A second possibility is that Pyongyang will slowly accelerate the pace of change. A lack of notable progress in overcoming bottlenecks in economic construction, a deterioration or even a stagnation in the standard of living for the masses, and the imperative of political succession may combine to produce such an outcome. No political system is immune to shocks, and a conjunction of seemingly insoluble problems may well be tantamount to a shock potent enough to jolt the system into action. The aging of the supreme leader (born in 1912) may help enhance the policy-making powers of Kim Jong Il and his top lieutenants, most of whom appear to be technocrats. That in turn may help inject a little more rationality into policy deliberations than has been the case thus far; at the very least, calculations of costs and benefits of past policy and future options may cease to be incumbered by the intimidating presence of the Great Leader. The pressing need on the part of Kim Jong Il to shore up his legitimacy with tangible policy outputs beneficial to the masses will also play a role in inducing a reorientation of policy, both internal and external.

Finally, it is theoretically possible for even such an ossified polity as North Korea to experience cataclysmic change. A coup d'etat or a revolutionary upheaval à la Romania is within the realm of possibility. The sudden death of Kim Il Sung may possibly open the way for cataclysmic change as well. Even incremental change in policy that may make North Korean society more permeable to information and influences from the outside world, including South Korea, may over time precipitate abrupt change under popular pressure or revolution. This is precisely why the current North Korean leadership is so wary of loosening up internal controls and opening up North Korea further to the outside world.

Of the three scenarios outlined above, the least plausible is the third one for obvious reasons. The remaining two, on the other hand, are not only plausible but also mutually compatible. That is to say, there is a strong likelihood that the first scenario will unfold itself in the short term, followed by the enactment of the second scenario in the not too distant future.

In sum, change, not of the cataclysmic variety but of an incremental nature, is not only probable but already under way. Its strident rhetoric underscoring its determination to go its own way notwithstanding, Pyongyang will find it increasingly difficult to resist the winds of change. Its fear that the beginning of notable change will ineluctably mark the beginning of the end of *chuch'e*-dominated socialism, however, seems amply warranted. Once the floodgate is opened, the tide of change will eventually inundate the shores of North Korean socialism.

NOTES

1. *Rodong sinmun*, January 1, 1993.
2. Ibid.
3. Since he used the word "kukje chilson," a literal translation would be "international order."
4. *The New York Times*, January 30, 1991.
5. See *Choguk ui chajujok p'yonghwa t'ong'il rul irukhaja* (*Let Us Attain the Independent and Peaceful Reunification of the Fatherland*) (Pyongyang: Choson Nodongdang Ch'ulp'ansa, 1980), pp. 10–11. This pamphlet reproduces that portion of Kim Il Sung's speech to the Sixth Congress of the Workers' Party of Korea which pertains to reunification. It was in this

speech, made on October 10, 1980, that Kim unveiled his proposal for the establishment of the Democratic Confederal Republic of Koryo *(Koryo Minju Yonbang Konghwaguk).*

6. *Rodong sinmun*, December 14, 1991.

7. Choe Il Chol, "[The] DPRK's Foreign Policy," *Pyongyang Times*, November 3, 1990, p. 8.

8. North Korea has categorically denied responsibility for both of these incidents, calling them South Korean fabrications or "self-enacted dramas" *(chajakguk).* See *Choguk P'Yonghwa T'ong'il Wiwonhoe Sogiguk T'ongbo* [*Bulletin of the Secretariat of the Committee for the Peaceful Reunification of the Fatherland*], No. 13 (January, 1984), pp. 1–20 and No. 59 (February, 1988), pp. 15–20.

9. Ch'oe Song-guk, "Uri konghwaguk ui chaju, p'yonghwa, ch'inson ui taeoe chongch'aek" ["Our Republic's Foreign Policy of Independence, Peace, and Friendship"], *Rodong sinmun*, January, 23, 1991, p. 6.

10. For an analysis of this episode of North Korean diplomacy, see B. C. Koh, *The Foreign Policy Systems of North and South Korea* (Berkeley: University of California Press, 1984), pp. 195–198; idem, "The Battle Without Victors: The Korean Question in the 30th Session of the UN General Assembly," *Journal of Korean Affairs*, vol. 5, no. 4 (January, 1976), pp. 43–63.

11. For an elaboration of this argument, see Koh, *The Foreign Policy Systems of North and South Korea*, pp. 8–14 and idem, "Pyongyang's Foreign Policy: Continuity and Change," *Korean Studies Journal*, vol. 15, (1991), pp. 4–6.

12. For Seoul's perspective on the security situation on the Korean peninsula, see Republic of Korea, Ministry of National Defense, *Defense White Paper 1992–1993* (Seoul, 1993), especially, pp. 51–75.

13. Ibid., pp. 71–72.

14. B. C. Koh, "China and the Korean Peninsula," *Korea & World Affairs*, vol. 9, no. 2 (Summer 1985), pp. 273–274.

15. *North Korea News* (Seoul), No. 263, March, 25, 1985, pp. 3–4 and No. 561, January, 14, 1991, p. 4.

16. *Renmin Ribao*, October 19, 1979.

17. Chae-Jin Lee, "Economic Aspects of Life in North Korea," in C. I. Eugene Kim and B. C. Koh (eds.), *Journey to North Korea: Personal Perceptions* (Berkeley: Institute of East Asian Studies, University of California, 1983), p. 58. Lee's source is *Petroleum Economist*, July 1980, p. 293.

18. Nonp'yongwon [Commentator], "Ttallaro sago p'anun 'oegyo kwangye,'" *Rodong sinmun*, October 5, 1990, p. 2. An English translation of this commentary appeared in *Pyongyang Times*, October 6, 1990, p. 12. An article signed by "Commentator" reflects the view of the top leadership in North Korea. My translation is based on a comparison of both the Korean and English texts of the commentary.

19. *Pyongyang Times*, October 13, 1990, p. 2.

20. Ibid., December 1, 1990.

21. *Rodong sinmun*, January 17, 1991.

22. *Asahi shinbun*, international satellite edition, January 31 and February 1, 1991.

23. On September 15, 1993, the two sides held their thirty-fourth meeting in Beijing. *Han'guk ilbo*, September 16, 1993, evening edition.

24. "Cognitive closure" refers to the propensity of decision makers "to withold doubts about existing policies and images" even in the face of the new evidence indicating the inefficacy or inaccuracy. See Robert Jervis, *Perception and Misperception in International Politics* (Princeton, N.J.: Princeton University Press, 1973), pp. 117–118.

12

PREROGATIVES OF THE NEW FOREIGN ECONOMIC POLICY MAKING

IULI BANCHEV

Institute of World Economy and Economic Relations, Bulgaria

In recent years, the new East-West balance has provided the major impetus toward the development of a perceptible "globalization" of political detente on one side and a persistent trend towards regionalization and subregionalization of international economic relations on the other.

On the Asian-Pacific level these changes have contributed to a new mode of equilibrium, advancing the cause of peaceful coexistence and creating a sense of urgency for the rationalization of the regional economic order. Certainly, all of these trends have a direct impact on the situation in individual subregions and countries, but the most tangible effects are produced through the shifts taking place within respective larger regions.

The evolution in the intersystem relations between the North and South in the subregion of the Korean peninsula must be viewed through a conceptual framework which is inclusive of these changing factors. On one side, all major powers, including the United States and Japan, have an interest in promoting the mutual dialogues and exchanges between the two Koreas so that peaceful coexistence is accepted as a rule governing the future unification process between the North and South.

On the other side, what we are witnessing today through the North-South dialogues is that politics and ideology have too much influence over the negotiation process between the two Koreas. Therefore, the problem, paradoxically, is how to reduce political interference to stimulate the politically sensitive integration process between North and South Korea, keeping in mind that the major intra- and international political-economic changes are bound to influence the perception and formulation of security policies as well. According to former United States Secretary of State Baker, one of the possible ways to reduce political tension is to attempt to apply "systematic cooperation" in the Korean peninsula.[1] The fostering of this "systematic cooperation" in the Korean peninsula fully corresponds with the newly emerging Asian-Pacific economic order, according to which the diversification of trade relations is now imperative for all Asian countries.

While the political transformations in Northeast Asia have been quite substantial, many of the interactions which have been established as of the late 1980s have been in the economic sphere. Because of the successful development of the economies of the East- and Southeast- Asian countries other than Japan, namely South Korea, Taiwan, Hong Kong, and the ASEAN nations, the total economic size of the East- and Southeast-Asian region will equal about twice the Japanese economy by the year 2000—making the area the de facto center of the world economy at the turn of the twenty-first century. This major development in the international situation calls for an increasing interdependence among the major blocs of the region by means of international interindustry linkages and to increased competition among them.[2]

Cumulatively, in a global and regional context, the East-West balance today may be characterized by a movement toward cooperation and away from confrontation. It is unclear, however, whether the nations of Northeast Asia will move forcefully toward the creation of a more substantive concept of Pacific Basin Economic Cooperation. Formidable obstacles to an enduring peace still remain, but the building blocks for a less confrontational system are very much in evidence today. In this context, the most pressing policy question is how to define the limits to economic relations given the political impasse between the two Koreas at this stage.

South Korea has adopted the so-called "functional approach." The philosophy underlying this policy is that under the given internal and external environment, sociocultural exchange and economic cooperation are of fundamental importance to recover "national homogeneity."[3]

The marketization of politics in South Korea from 1988 forward is the major internal factor influencing the birth of the well-known Nordpolitik of the Republic of Korea. What is the political-economic logic of South Korea's Northward policy?

The more one country becomes involved in the global economy and looses control of its own economy to international market forces, the more important that country becomes in the international community, and the safer it is. The case of South Korea is an impressive contemporary example of how taking part in the global economy helps strengthen national independence. Interdependence breeds independence of a kind. That is why South Korea's Northward diplomacy, unlike North Korea's diplomacy, has easily avoided the problem neo-functionalists refer to as "spillover" typical for federalist policymakers.[4]

From that point of view, the impressive expansion of South Korea's economic and political relations with China and the former Soviet Union, as well as the East European countries, is not abstract at all, but assists in the pursuit of two major political-economic goals: First, to assure no further isolation of North Korea on the basis of South Korea's increasingly dynamic economic and political presence in the region and; second, to emphasize strongly the need to break down barriers between the two Koreas.

The goal of South Korea's Nordpolitik in the short run is the creation of a Korean economic "commonwealth," which is seen as the most adequate basis for future political unification. This explains the impressive evolution of South Korea's unification formula in the last few years from "One Country with Two Systems" to "One Country with Two Regions." Therefore, economic integration is seen as one of the major keys to the final national reunification.

Unlike South Korea, North Korea's ideological rigidness has not only hindered the development of the domestic political and economic system but has also driven the country into a state of international isolation.

Externally, North Korea failed to adapt flexibly and adequately to the major changes taking place in the international community over the last few years.

North Korean leaders have become increasingly concerned over their economic condition. Indeed, South Korea's economic development and expanded role in the international community have created unbearable challenges to Pyongyang. Furthermore, North Korea realizes that the economic factor was the main culprit in the dramatic change of East Europe and other socialist systems.

As a result of all this, Pyongyang's current paradox is that it urgently needs high levels of foreign aid and economic cooperation, especially with Japan and South Korea, in order to maintain *Juche* socialism. At this stage, therefore, the direction of political change in North Korea is twofold: system-defending and system-reforming.

The growing tension between ideological integrity and economic reality forces the North Korean leadership to separate economics from politics in its domestic and foreign policy making. This is a typical eclectic ideological approach to reforms in all totalitarian societies when leaders realize that they are slipping further behind their competitors. As Jiang Zemin explained to his guest from Pyongyang, Yon Hyong-Muk, the prime minister of North Korea, during his trip to China in November 1990, there is a "dialectical relationship" between opening to foreign capital and the survival of power and ideology, which might paradoxically bring down the system in the end.[5]

In view of the analysis above, the major problem of Pyongyang's leadership is how to ideologically support the urgency of the fast integration of the system into an international economic community largely controlled by capitalist rules and expectations. It is for this reason that we have witnessed during the last few years a very slow and cautious process of separating "pure" politics from foreign economic policy making in North Korea. The culmination of this process was the proclamation of Kim Il Sung's new five-point policy for national unification in May 1990. The second point of this policy proclaims that: "Free travel and a full-scale open-door policy must be instituted between the North and South."[6] This statement suggests that the main principles of neo-functionalism should become major prerogatives for North Korea's foreign economic policy making.

On the other side, as far as "pure" foreign policy is concerned, the "federalist" approach to Korean unification was reconfirmed by Kim Il Sung in his speech of October 10, 1990. Reiterating his three principles of national reunification, Kim promoted the creation of the Democratic Confederate Republic of Korea.

Thus seen, the reevaluation of Pyongyang's foreign economic policy making is actually eclectic, therefore contradictory. The theoretical background of this eclecticism is that North Korea is not like East Europe, where socialism "was not fruition of people's own efforts."[7] Therefore, if Kim uses Japanese and South Korean aid skillfully to restructure the economy, North

Korea can successfully imitate the South and could possibly create another economic miracle.

Recent historical experience in East European countries shows that the failure of their communist regimes was due to their adherence to the main principles of the political economy of socialism, which denies the universal character of the social and economic laws ruling both the Western and the so-called socialist societies. In this sense, the major problem of the adjustment of Pyongyang to the new internal and external environment is that the eventual acknowledgement of the objective nature of the social and economic laws of humankind would signal an admission that not only is there an urgent need for radical reforms of the economy, but also the for the establishment of a pluralist political structure in North Korean society as well.

In this context, since the type of socialism developed by Kim Il Sung is based on *Juche* ideology which combines Stalinism with the Maoist doctrine of cultural revolution, Kim, while confessing the serious problems of the North Korean economy, criticizes the economic reforms and democratization process in the former Soviet Union and Eastern European countries.

At the Supreme People's Assembly held on May 24, 1990, Kim Il Sung commented:

> The question is how to overcome the difficulties which lie on the path of advancing and continuing to undertake the great task of socialism. If socialist principles were to be abandoned and the capitalist mode to be adopted in an attempt to solve the difficulties, those difficulties would not be resolved and the excellence of socialism would be lost and plunged into confusion. Even the exploits of revolution we gained by shedding blood would be lost. Socialism could be constructed only in accordance with the socialist principles and socialist methods.[8]

North Korean socialism under Kim Il Sung raises an outright objection to the efforts of the formerly socialist East European countries to cope with their political and economic problems through liberalization (including political pluralism and market economy) on the grounds that it will disintegrate the socialist system from within because it is incapable of effectively coping with the infiltration of imperialism and alien capitalist culture.

The North Korean regime is even basically opposed to the revised formula of the market economy which introduced material incentives but is preoccupied with a dogma of socialist construction based only on political and moral incentives. According to Kim Il Sung:

> The great motive power of socialist construction in our country is, above all, the politico-ideological strength, conscious enthusiasm and creative activity of our people. This comes from the leadership of the Party which educates the people to regard the socialist cause

as genuinely their own undertaking. The collective strength and mass heroism of our people, who are promoting socialist construction, is also brought into full play by the leadership of the Party which combines the interest of individuals and those of the collective and increases the power of unity and cooperation. The creativity of our people is displayed to the full in socialist construction.[9]

In sum the continuing speed campaign plus harsh public propaganda against any possible "capitalist contamination"[10] were reminders that whatever the problems faced by formerly centrally planned economies elsewhere, the subjecting of all significant economic activity to stringent political controls over a long period of time has meant that the Pyongyang authorities simply are unable to even contemplate dealing with the contradictions that are silently multiplying: economic adjustment, reform or restructuring. North Korea's economic stagnation should be seen exclusively in the light of its nonscientific *Juche* economic policy.

For all the adverse human implications of artificially depressing consumption levels and artificially augmenting industrial production, the prevalence of such distortions in North Korea may be described as a failure. To the extent that these distortions are a result of the industrialization policy, they may be seen as the accomplishment of deliberate government action.

In the late 1960s and the 1970s, various development specialists noted that the incidence of poverty in North Korea had remained surprisingly high, despite relatively rapid rates of industrial growth. It is in this context that, during the 1980s, the North Korean government came to openly admit the shortage of such basic necessities as food, shelter, and clothing and put major emphasis on resolving the problems for the minimum subsistence of the people.

Ordinarily, the simplest method of attending to the adverse consequences of an induced distortion is to stop exerting the distorting influence. Rather than relieving distortions induced by the industrialization policy, however, basic human needs policies required the expansion of government consumption. These policies reduced the share of private consumption in local economies below already involuntary low levels and investment levels typically remained inviolate.

This pattern seems to suggest that a vast and involuntary transformation of the economy has occurred in North Korea. To judge by its output, for instance, the economy of today's North Korea would seem strangely insensitive to the needs and desires of its population. Insofar as these peculiar patterns appear to be relatively recent, it is correspondingly apparent that North Korea, on the whole, has become even less oriented toward articulating popular demand and less effective in satisfying self-assessed human needs than in earlier decades. In that fundamental sense, the distortions impressed upon the North Korean economy over the past generation may fairly be described as inhumane.

Peculiar and pronounced distortions which are referred to else-where as "industrialization without prosperity" and "investment without growth"[11] now characterize the economy of North Korea. To the extent that the contemporary economic situation in North Korea may accurately be described as a deepening crisis, it must be recognized as a crisis of *Juche* socialism as a theory and in practice.

There are several basic structural problems causing North Korea's deepening economic crisis. First, due to its almost entirely self-dependent development strategy, Pyongyang has rejected large-scale use of foreign capital and technology. As a result of this closed-economy approach, North Korea lags far behind the South in tapping outside sources of technological improvement and capital formation. Secondly, North Korea's management style is still very similar to that adopted by the USSR during the Stalin era. Because North Korea relies on the "stakhanovite" approach that puts over-whelming emphasis on the role of increased labor mobilization to expand production, the North Koreans have given technological innovation compar-atively low priority. Third, during the 1980s, North Korea placed excessive emphasis on military spending. The steady erosion of its previously strong ties with the Soviet Union, and to a lesser extent with China, has forced Pyongyang to expand its domestic arms production in order to maintain its forces aimed against South Korea. According to U.S. and South Korean mili-tary sources, North Korea is estimated to have devoted between 20 to 25 percent of its GNP, or as much as 11 to 12 billion won annually in recent years, to defense spending. The North Koreans officially admit that military expenditures accounted for only 12 percent of the national budget, or 4.3 billion won in 1989. This figure, however, excludes allocations for the defense industry and other military activities that fall under other sectors of the economy.

Although shortages of almost all basic commodities and energy plague the rest of the country, the military and arms industry appears to enjoy ready access to scarce resources. While many of the country's indus-trial plants are affected by severe energy shortages, it is estimated that Pyongyang has stockpiled more than 1 million tons of oil in case of war. The arms industry's production capabilities are both extensive and relatively sophisticated by Third World standards. There is also speculation that Pyongyang is moving toward the development of nuclear weapons capa-bility, with reports of a reprocessing facility next to a nuclear facility at Yong-byon, near Pyongyang. In addition, eight plants are believed to be engaged in the production of chemical and biological weapons. Further, more than 100 civilian factories could quickly switch to military production in an emer-gency, and much of the rest of economy is skewed to supporting the arms industry with the heavy industrial sector receiving special treatment in government priorities.

The country's arms industry is assuming growing economic impor-tance as weapons exports, in particular sales to the Middle East, are one of the few channels through which North Korea can earn foreign exchange. Since the mid-1980s, the Iranians are reported to have purchased Scuds valued at U.S. $500 million, as well as nearly U.S. $2 billion worth of other arms from the North Koreans, including artillery, tanks, and missiles. With funds earned from sales to Iraq, Libya, Nicaragua, Zimbabwe, and other African and Middle Eastern states, arms are North Korea's most valuable export. However, some of these deals were arranged on barter terms, with the Iranians exchanging oil for arms. Much of the revenue generated from arms is probably brought back into the country's arms purchases. Although North Korea has been a major recipient of Chinese and Soviet arms, usually in the form of aid or at low "friendship" prices, Pyongyang still spends several hundred million dollars on foreign arms each year. The acquisition of sophisticated Soviet equipment has significantly increased Pyongyang's arms import bill in recent years, from an average of U.S. $200 million a year in the late 1970s and early 1980s to U.S. $400 million since the mid-1980s, totaling more than US $3 billion for the decade, according to U.S. congressional estimates.[12]

The arms race on the Korean peninsula has seriously drained the North Korean economy, and analysts believe this to be the key factor forcing Pyongyang to begin talks with Seoul on the reduction of military tensions. In addition, with reduced external assistance, the North Koreans are quickly falling behind in technological advances as the South Koreans continue to acquire the latest arms from the United States.

As a result of the excessive militarization of the country, North Korea's overall economic structure is highly imbalanced. In one sense, the North Korean economy appears to be permanently on a war footing. On the other side, the negligence by the economic planners of the commodity industries and agriculture have made poverty in North Korea a chronic disease. This disease is far from being healed because these planners still tend to rely on such handicraft-style workshops as "work teams" for the production of commodities and food.

North Korean grain production in 1990 was estimated at 4.8 million tons, down 12 percent from 1989, of which some 1.9 million tons were rice. This figure indicates that the North was short some 1.6 million tons of cereals in 1990 because its annual consumption can be calculated at about 6.4 million tons based on the officially announced standard of food rationing (700 grams per day). North Korea's food shortage has worsened since the 1970s when it started cutting down four days of food rations each month for the professed purchase of building a wartime food stockpile. In 1987, food rations were again reduced by another 10 percent in the name of conservation and patriotism. A campaign is now underway to urge people to eat only two meals a day, according to a Korean-Chinese who recently wrote a travelogue about her trip to North Korea.[13]

As a result of these main structural problems and the consequently deepening distortions of North Korea's economy, revenues have been steadily dropping, according to the only official financial statistics of North Korean government: In the 1970s, the revenue increase was 10 percent but in the 1980s it dropped to the average level of 5–6 percent, indicating further that the economy is in a severe stagnation.[14]

The implementation of the rigid *Juche* model of internalized economic development in North Korea considerably cuts down the internal sources of investment. This leads to the excessive necessity of foreign financial flows, equipment, and technology. As far as North Korea's economy is inward-looking, according to *Juche's* "self sufficiency" theory, it does not have much to trade in order to pay for the foreign loans, equipment, and technology. More than 80 percent of North Korea's exports are raw materials, primarily gold or semifinished products. The weaponry it exports to developing countries is one of the few finished goods it has to offer. Foreign reserves are minimal.

One of the main obstacles preventing North Korean officials from turning the economy around is the inability of industry to produce enough goods. In late 1986, a third Seven-Year Plan (1987–1993) was finally announced. Details published in April 1987 show that as expected, the formerly touted "ten long range goals of the 1980s" have basically been rolled over into 1993, indicating further slackening of rates of growth. There are, however, some significant changes. The steel target has been slashed from 15 million to 10 million tons, suggesting serious problems in this sector—with likely knock-on effects for all of heavy industry. On the other hand, such foreign currency earners as cement, nonferrous metals, and marine products have had their targets raised, the last dramatically so (see Table 1).

TABLE 1

ADJUSTED TARGETS OF PRODUCTION

	Original Target (1980–1989)	*Performance (as of 1986)*	*Adjusted Target (set in 1987)*
Electricity	100 twh	60 twh	100 twh
Coal	120 million tons	70 m.t.	120 m.t.
Grains	15 million tons	10 m.t.	15 m.t.
Hard steel	15 million tons	7.8-8 m.t.	10 m.t.
Fertilizer	7 million tons	5 m.t.	7.2 m.t.
Cement	20 million tons	1.2 m.t.	22 m.t.
Fishery	5 million tons	31 m.t.	11 m.t.
Textile	1.5 billion meters	0.8 b.m.	1.5 b.m.
Non-steel mineral	1.5 million tons	1.5 m.t.	1.7 m.t.
Coastal area cultivation	0.3 million hectares	n.a.	0.3 m.h.

SOURCE: EZU Country Profile, *North Korea*, 1988, pp. 64–65.

The excessive militarization of the country and the prevalence of obsolete machinery and decreased labor productivity make it difficult to squeeze more out of an economy that lacks capital and resources as well as incentives for workers. For these reasons, North Korean trade cannot meet targets set under the third seven-year economic plan. The North Korean government wanted to increase foreign trade by 3.2 times during this period, with up to a fivefold growth forecast for exports of noniron metals, manganese, and machinery. The ordinance on the Third Seven-Year Plan adopted by the DPRK Supreme People's Assembly on April 23, 1987 reads:

> There shall be a large scale increase in the exports of up to date machine tools, heavy-duty wagons, ships, electric machinery, agricultural machinery, and other machines and equipment which are marketable abroad as well as non-ferrous metals, magnesia clinker, cement and other heavy industrial products. Light industry and other economic sectors shall greatly increase the export of their products, particularly processed clothing, ceramics, glassware, enamelled ironware and plastic articles for daily use.[15]

According to figures compiled by the Japan External Trade Organization, North Korea's foreign trade in 1989 dropped 13 percent to U.S. $4.8 billion. Exports fell 6.6 percent to U.S. $1.56 billion, and imports declined 20 percent to U.S. $2.52 billion, resulting in a trade gap of U.S. $960 million, more than double the deficit of four years earlier.[16]

As a result of the above mentioned major economic distortions, North Korea's foreign debt vastly expanded during the 1980s. This huge foreign debt is one important reason for North Korea's inability to alleviate its current economic stagnation. The size of North Korean debt in 1988 was U.S. $5.2 billion, but in 1989 it reached U.S. $6.78 billion. North Korea's debt to Western banks, especially those in Japan, Austria, and Germany, is U.S. $2.74, and its debt to communist countries such as the former Soviet Union and China totals about U.S. $4.3 billion.

In the early 1970s, North Korea imported equipment, bought various grains, and made commercial loans on a deferred payment basis. After the 1970s, North Korea imported, fuels, factory equipment and machinery, primarily from the Soviet Union and China. After 1976, as the time approached for North Korea to begin paying back these loans, Pyongyang could only pay back part the loans' yearly interest, and on three different occasions it made agreements with creditor countries to extend the debt repayment periods. After 1984, North Korea was not able to pay back any of the annual interest. In June 1988, North Korea frankly admitted that it lacked the ability to pay off its foreign debt and requested that two-thirds of its debt to Western banks (U.S. $880 million) be written off.[17] The Western creditors threatened to close down their embassies in Pyongyang, and they began referring to North Korea as a defaulting nation. At present North Korea has the world's worst credit standing and is widely considered nothing less than a bankrupt nation.

The deepening economic crisis in North Korea has been the product of *Juche* socialism which the ruling hierarchy developed for the purpose of safeguarding the personality cult of Kim Il Sung and the totalitarian regime under him. Under this policy, Pyongyang kept its doors tightly closed to the outside world for the past forty years, thus restricting the inflow of democracy and scientific progress.

Thus, at the present time, North Korea is trapped in an economic vice which is becoming ever tighter. For that reason, North Korea's economic emphasis during 1990, the fourth year of the continuing seven-year economic plan, was toward boosting the production of electricity, coal, steel, and foodstuffs, implying that the country is suffering most from shortages of energy, raw materials, and food. Pyongyang has staged a year-round campaign to boost production, with various articles and commentaries in newspapers and radio broadcasts repeatedly calling for attention to the task and arguing that "boosting the production of electricity, coal, and steel is the main link in socialist economic construction."[18]

Through these efforts, North Korea has been able to keep its system intact for the time being. The situation, however, is rapidly deteriorating, and the tide of history is running against the North Korean regime. The fanatic "work-harder" campaign did not appear to improve the economy. Production could not increase without technological innovation and capital investment. In addition to the inefficiency of central planning, North Korean efforts to build a self-reliant economy have hurt its growth potential. The limitations imposed by a small domestic market, limited exposure to foreign competition, and protection of industries have all contributed to the inefficiencies of the economy, and the subsequent lack of investment capital and the underdeveloped technologies have also seriously constrained economic growth. North Korea's GNP for 1989 was estimated at U.S. $21.1 billion and per capita GNP at U.S. $987, roughly one-tenth and one-fifth, respectively, of South Korea. During 1987–1989, North Korea's annual rate of economic growth averaged less than 3 percent. And resources estimated at some U.S. $5 billion were heavily invested in less productive construction activities such as the sponsoring of the Thirteenth World Youth Festival.[19]

Poor performance in the economy emerges as the most threatening factor for the socialist political system. The importance of the North Korean government in raising the people's living standard jeopardizes Kim Il Sung's advocacy of the superiority of *Juche* socialism over other systems. It seems that North Korea may be forced to undergo its own version of perestroika if the system is to survive.

On top of the widening economic gap with the South, since January 1991 North Korea has lost the preferential terms in trade with the former

Soviet republics and China. Both Moscow and Beijing are already asking for hard currency settlement for their oil and other exports to Pyongyang. The worsening economic crisis, which will further deepen under the pressure of the new unfavorable changes in North Korea's economic relations with its traditional economic partners, forced Pyongyang to turn, though cautiously, to what the Chinese refer to as "red capitalism." In fact, North Korea is encouraging joint economic ventures and has set up special economic zones for the purpose of inducing foreign involvement. These are not, however, radical reforms, but rather tactical maneuvers intended to break out of the straitjacket of economic stagnation. One diplomat in Seoul who watches North Korea closely said that "they have only taken the first cautious step. The people at the top know the danger, the risk. They are pushed by their impoverishment."[20]

Pyongyang's major problem, therefore, seems at first glance to be economic rather than political, and its recent openings to Japan and South Korea are meant to prevent an economic crisis from snowballing into political discontent. Now, in order to rescue its sinking economy and ideology, the North Korean government desperately looking for financial and diplomatic help and support from Japan as well as the United States. According to North Korean officials, "Japan could play a backup role to help the South and North get along. The strength of Japan could be of service in easing tensions (on the Korean peninsula)."[21]

The apparent contradictory nature of North Korea's foreign economic policy making is determined, on one side, by the full understanding that every significant economic policy switch can lead to fundamental political change, bolstered by global realignment and the North's desperate economic straits. The lessons of the past three years in the socialist bloc countries suggest that radical reform has a way of creating a momentum and a direction that is nearly impossible to control. On the other side, Japan and South Korea firmly state that the inevitable improvement of their economic relations with Pyongyang should develop in a way ensuring that any changes do not destablize the peninsula.

Therefore, the successful development of North Korea's economic relations with both Japan and South Korea should be regarded as a guarantee to peace and stability in the Korean peninsula. Furthermore, if we accept the presumption that the Korean peninsula presents "the strategic fulcrum of the regional balance of power system in Northeast Asia,"[22] the efficient cooperation process between North Korea, Japan, and South Korea becomes one of the major prerequisites for a new economic order in the region.

In this context, two possible stages in the evolution of Pyongyang's foreign economic policy making may be suggested. The first one, which we are witnessing already, may be identified as an aggressive foreign economic pragmatism. Pyongyang badly needs Japan's financial and economic support to give its stagnant economy a boost and to maintain its huge armed forces, but Tokyo will not grant billions of U.S. dollars in loans and credits unless North Korea signs an agreement with and adheres to guidelines of the International Atomic Energy Agency. Nor will Japan grant this aid under Pyongyang's "reparation" formula.[23] Thus seen, the bilateral economic and diplomatic talks between Pyongyang and Tokyo could be prolonged without tangible results.

One possible development of official talks between Japan and North Korea might be some kind of an effect on the practical realization of South Korea's strategic "Economic Commonwealth" policy of an inter-Korea economic integration process. South Korean policy makers want to see the two Koreas adopt phased economic cooperation. That would likely mean moving from indirect to direct trade, followed by industrial cooperation and indirect and direct investment. Swift unification along the German formula would overwhelm the South Korean economy beyond its economic capability. For this reason, the establishment of a partially integrated institutional structure of economic ties might be a necessary prerequisite for a more pragmatic settlement of Tokyo-Pyongyang economic and diplomatic negotiations.

If we assume that "Japan cannot make a move without progress in inter-Korea dialogue,"[24] as stated by Masso Okonogi, it means that North Korea may soon be forced to take a more realistic and positive neo-functionalist approach to develop economic relations with both Japan and South Korea. This would mark the beginning of the next stage in Pyongyang's foreign economic policy- aking with the discerning feature of a gradual move toward the institutional approach to economic integration with major partners on the subregional and regional levels.

In his New Year's message for 1991, President Kim already added important changes to his earlier unification-through-federation proposal and brought it closer to the South Korean proposal. President Kim called for unification through the formula of a federation system based on one people, one nation, and two systems and two governments. The premise that two governments can coexist is the most noteworthy point of his proposal because it is similar to the South Korean proposal calling for a Korean Commonwealth of two sovereign states coexisting as an interim or transition stage to unification.

Furthermore, North Korea's surprise announcement on May 28, 1991, expressing its readiness to seek separate membership in the United Nations and the ensuing entry to the international organization as a sovereign state marks a profound policy change in Pyongyang. For the first time since 1957 when Kim Il Sung went along with the Soviet proposal for parallel membership in the UN, he is accepting the reality of division on the peninsula.

The decision by the two Koreas to seek separate membership and their eventual entry to the UN will force both sides to rethink their traditional postures of mutual hostility. In Seoul, it will trigger demands for a review of policies targeting the regime of President Kim as an adversary; in

Pyongyang it raises the need for policy adjustment in favor of peaceful coexistence with the South. Clearly, Pyongyang hopes its new stand on the UN issue will be viewed as a gesture of moderation. At least, it undermines North Korea's contention that South Korea is an illegitimate regime. That shakes the foundation of Kim Il Sung's lifelong commitment to the reunification of the country under communism. Furthermore, the increasing need for accommodation with the South to arrest the worsening economy threatens to erode Kim's awesome personality cult. Kim's dilemma is how to open up the country without endangering his leadership.

In any case, it is obvious that North Korea will have to substantially change its foreign economic policy making and open its economy under the pressure of the newly emerging subregional and regional economic communities and entities among Asian-Pacific countries. The gradual opening of the national economy will permit North Korea to use more effectively the intersystem economic relations on bilateral and multilateral levels.

In turn, these new concepts should inevitably lead to more impressive intensification of inter-Korean economic ties during this period, including in a progressive way all contemporary forms of international economic cooperation. At this stage, North Korea's first and most important goal will be to lessen, if not stop, the widening gap between the two Koreas. From this point of view, North Korea's regime will manage to strengthen more or less the national economy during the next few years and further deepen the inter-Korea economic integration process. But it cannot avoid the likelihood that the increasing social and cultural interaction between North Korea and other societies will ultimately facilitate the democratization of the system. At this second stage, the deepening inter-Korean economic interaction will start to play the role of a major internal catalyzer of the overall political democratization process on the peninsula.

Of much practical use for the institutional shaping of North Korea's open-door policy, as far as inter-Korea economic relations are concerned, might also be the concept of "China's Economic Community" which shall include Hong Kong, Macao, Taiwan, and China. Despite the undoubted similarity of North Korean and Chinese responses to events in Eastern Europe, they still are divided by such basic issues as the need for and extent of economic reforms. In this context, the China-Taiwan economic integration process may be a useful analytical example for the Korean case. Taiwan seemed to lose sovereignty as China gained recognition in the 1970s, but it appears to have been winning it back as an independent state because it has shown that the world can get on with more than one Chinese state. The more Taiwan demonstrates that it can trade with China and yet retain its independence, the better chance it stands of retaining its independent posture in the international community.

The impressive economic development of Taiwan and the marketization of its policies during the last few years led its leaders to conclude that one nation can function while divided into two systems, thus, practically accepting South Korea's "One Country—Two Regions" concept. The acceptance of this concept amounts to the recognition of separate sovereignty. Taiwan denounces the Chinese Communist Party's unwillingness to abandon its obstructionist attitude toward Taiwan's efforts to develop relations with foreign countries under the banner of One-China.[25] To the extent that there is the analogy between China-Taiwan economic integration perspectives and their Korean counterpart, one could suggest that the urgent settlement of the political-economic cooperation and unification problems between China and Taiwan would have a positive effect on the inter-Korea integration process. This projection is predicated upon the premise that "economic logic will eventually win over political logic" as predicted by a rare China-born member of the opposition Democratic Progressive Party (DPP) in Taiwan.[26]

Another factor that will influence North Korea's foreign economic policy will be the formation of a new Asian economic grouping or trade block in which Japan has a definite role as the leader of the region. In this international economic environment, as one Seoul official said, "the North will be forced to make a choice—to continue its isolationist policy or to break out of it."[27] In this context, China and South Korea have moved far ahead of North Korea.

The newly shaping progressiveness of North Korea's foreign economic policy making contains contradictions and inconsistencies in which both "reds" and "experts" are voicing their preferences. It appears that while the "reds" are talking, the "experts" are working. The experts have made some progress, but the talk coming from the other side provides a major stumbling block. Nevertheless, changes are quite conspicuous in the economy, and these changes will spill over into other sectors, including the political arena. In conclusion, North Korea's new foreign economic policy making is moving, though cautiously, from the "federalist" to the "neo-functionalist" approach. If we look at this process from the point of view of the recent historical experience of the formerly socialist Eastern European countries, one can be assured that North Korea has already entered upon its last stage of transition from a totalitarian society to a version of democracy.

NOTES

1. *Sino-Soviet Affairs*, Seoul, 14, 2, 1990, p. 44.

2. Byung-Nak Song, *The Rise of the Korean Economy*, H.K., 1990, p. 216.

3. *Sino-Soviet Affairs*, Seoul, 14, 3, 1990, p. 59.

4. *The Journal of East Asian Affairs*, Seoul, Vol. IV, No. 1, Winter/Spring 1990, p. 17; *South-North Dialogue in Korea*, Seoul, 050, October 1990, pp. 8–12.

5. *Le Monte*, 9, February 1991, p. 12.

6. *Korea and World Affairs*, Vol. 14, No. 4, Winter 1990, p. 613.

7. *Far Eastern Economic Review*, Hong Kong, 29, November 1990, p. 35.

8. *Vantage Point*, Vol. XIII, No. 12, December 1990, pp. 7–8.

9. *Study of Juche Idea* (Tokyo: International Institute of Juche Idea), January 1991, No. 52, pp. 2–3.

10. *Far Eastern Economic Review, Asia 1990 Yearbook*, Hong Kong, 1990, p. 154.

11. *Journal of Economic Growth*, Washington, Summer 1989, Vol. 3, No. 4, p. 26.

12. Byung-Nak Song, op. cit., pp. 216–227; *Far Eastern Economic Review, Asia 1990 Yearbook*, Hong Kong, pp. 6–8; *Far Eastern Economic Review*, 23, May 1991, pp. 16–17.

13. *Vantage Point*, February 1991, Vol. XIV, No. 2, p. 24.

14. *Vantage Point*, November 1990, Vol. XIV, No. 11, p. 14; *EIU Country Profile, China, North Korea,* 1988–1989, L.1988, p. 75.

15. *North Korea Quarterly*, Hamburg, Spring 1987, No. 48, pp. 45–46.

16. *Far Eastern Economic Review*, Hong Kong, August 23, 1990, pp. 54–55.

17. *Vantage Point*, November 1990, Vol. XVIII, No. 11, p. 15.

18. *Asia Survey*, Vol. 31, No. 1, January 1991, p. 73.

19. *Far Eastern economic Review, Asia 1990 Yearbook*, Hong Kong, 1990, pp. 6–7; *Asian Survey*, Vol. XXXI, No. 1, January 1991, p. 72.

20. *Far Eastern Economic Review*, Hong Kong, November 29, 1990, p. 32.

21. *The Korea Herald*, February 21, 199, p. 1.

22. *Korea and World Affairs*, Vol. XIII, No. 4, Winter 1989, p. 692.

23. *Far Eastern Economic Review*, Hong Kong, February 14, 1991, pp. 20–21.

24. *The Korea Herald*, December 23, 1990, p. 5.

25. *Beijing Review*, Vol. 33, No. 46, November 12–14, 1990, pp. 14–16; *Far Eastern Economic Review*, Hong Kong, May 23, 1991, p. 26 and June 6, 1991, pp. 40–41.

26. *Far Eastern Economic Review*, August 23, 1990, p. 17.

27. *The Korea Herald*, December 15, 1990, p. 4.

13

Pyongyang's Reunification Policy

Loszek Cyrzyk

Polish Institute of International Affairs

N̲ational reunification has always been the supreme and overriding goal of the Pyongyang regime. Internal and external circumstances change, but the drive toward the country's reunification continues unabated, though different avenues for achieving that goal have been explored. Over the past forty years or so, Pyongyang has taken a number of initiatives and devised many programs in search of a viable solution for the reunification problem. The proposed solutions generally fell into four categories: (1) use of military forces; (2) general elections; (3) a confederal state; (4) a step-by-step approach based on gradual rapprochement.

Solutions based on the use of force by either side appear impossible and undesirable in the foreseeable future. Both North and South Korea have ruled out a military conquest of the other half of the Korean peninsula because it will surely provoke domestic opposition and an international uproar. Even in countries governed in a totalitarian manner, there are limits to public acceptance which a given regime must not overstep for fear of being toppled by popular insurgency. Likewise, it would be unrealistic to expect reunification through general elections. The two Korean states are now divided by too profound differences at the present to work out a common electoral law acceptable to both sides. Elections could impede rather than expedite the process of reunification. Significantly, for at least twenty years, the issue of general elections has not been raised. Since 1972, it has never come up in the North-South dialogues.

A more realistic solution would be reunification through the establishment of a confederate state, provided it does not invoke the North Korean formula concerning the Democratic Confederate Republic of Koryo. However, a confederate state could come into shape only as a result of mutual accommodation and reconciliation and as a phase of transition to complete reunification. Therefore, a step-by-step approach appears the most realistic and feasible. Aspirations for reunification are most likely to be realized in an evolutionary manner, without the risk of political upheaval which could have dire consequences for the whole nation.

Profound transformations in East-West relations due to the collapse of the socialist bloc offer an insight into a number of issues, including the issue of the divided nation. Korea's partition was a typical Cold War product. The end of the Cold War opens up new prospects for a rational reincarnation of the nation and reshaping of its future, free from foreign domination or ideological constraints imposed by totalitarian systems and regimes.

The Cold War produced an extremely adverse effect on social sciences. Compulsory adherence to official ideology often interfered with researchers' sober assessment of various problems facing the nation. The issue of reunification exemplifies limitations imposed for political and ideological reasons. A fairly large portion of literature on that topic has been flawed by bias intended to justify the position of one side in the conflict rather than to analyze realities objectively.

In hindsight, it will not be an overstatement to assert that post-World War II North-South relations in Korea abounded with mistakes and miscalculations. The domination of ideology left little room for maneuvering in the face of pragmatism. A typical example is Pyongyang's failure to reciprocate a pragmatic change in South Korea's policy concerning the cross-recognition of the two Korean states by allied countries and their simultaneous entry into the United Nations. In fact, the instance of East and West Germany has demonstrated that such policy will not necessarily perpetuate national division. On the contrary, it enhances mutual ties and the sense of national unity.

Pyongyang was reluctant to draw proper conclusions from the detente in East-West relations. It views its security mainly in military terms, while in fact the primary current threat to the stability of the country stems from it economic malaise. During the nearly twenty years of foot-dragging and interruptions, the North-South dialogues regularly encountered obstacles even as early as the stage of negotiations on the procedures. The two sides were even unable to agree on a schedule and platform for the North-South conversation. While the South preferred economic and humanitarian initiatives, the North insisted on making political and military proposals. Not surprisingly, the talks came to be known as "a dialogue of the deaf."

It seems that such a state of affairs is impossible to sustain in the long run. Disregarding the new trends in world politics will inevitably lead to isolationism. As pragmatism will eventually be a decisive factor in policy making because the survival of any regime hinges on its effectiveness, it is believed that the two Korean states will have to search for ways of readjusting to the new international climate and avoiding moves that could jeopardize national interest.

In that readjustment process, the idea of a Korean confederate state has gained much currency and provided a fresh impetus for the reunification effort. Lately this idea has been strongly reemphasized in North Korea's reunification rhetoric, as is evident from President Kim Il Sung's November 29, 1990 interview with a representative of the Nepalese Association of Journalists[1] and his 1991 New Year's Address.[2] The Seoul government's response presented a new approach to the reunification issue. This time the South Koreans did not attempt to eschew political solutions. Instead, President Ro Tae Woo proposed a Korean Commonwealth in September 1989.[3] Although the two conceptions of the confederation differ considerably with respect to proposed solutions, one can identify some convergent features, at least in the direction of thinking. Assuming that along the path of reunification there will one day be a convergence of the interests of both sides, it is worthwhile to analyze in detail Pyongyang's conception of a confederation.

The confederation of the two Korean states is perceived by many observers as a propaganda ploy pure and simple. The North Korean leaders should be held responsible for such an impression because of the frivolous and cavalier manner in which they promoted their conception, reminiscent of the proverbial "carrot and stick" approach. In this case, the carrot is the vision of the country's reunification, while the stick was the inclusion of countless preconditions which no one could meet under the circumstances. Thus, the concept of a confederate state could not serve as a basis for more deep-going dialogues between the two rivals because the proponents could not allay the suspicion that it was politically motivated to undermine the opponent's position and to disrupt its security.

The concept of a confederate state proposed by Pyongyang is topical but by no means new. Apart from a small conclave of specialists, few people realize when and in what circumstances the idea was born and what an evolution it subsequently underwent. And yet it is that evolution that fully reflects Pyongyang's real intentions. Through a manipulation of the process and successive transformations, it appears that little more than the name remains of the original confederate concept. The idea clearly evolved toward that of a federal state, which given the high level of confrontation between the North and South, could not eliminate the differences and build confidence at a stroke. However, the time is approaching when the reunification process will have to be based on more pragmatic premises. It will be necessary to renounce total confrontation and demonstrate readiness to make further compromises. Therefore, tracing the evolution of the concept of a confederal state is of not only historical but also practical value.

THE ORIGINAL CONCEPT OF CONFEDERATION (1960)

The concept of a confederation of North and South Korea was unveiled as the keystone of North Korea's reunification program in a speech delivered by Kim Il Sung on August 14, 1960, marking the fifteenth anniversary of the country's liberation.[4] In the subsequent twenty years the concept functioned solely as a general idea, because its realization is contingent first on laying down principles and setting common goals and then implementing a detailed program. If the idea itself could serve as a political instrument, the program would constitute an initial concrete move toward rapprochement and cooperation. Kim's proposal obviously represented a big stride in the direction of North-South reconciliation. However, the first North-South joint statement issued on July 4, 1972, outlining the basic principles of reunification and concerted efforts for North-South reconciliation did not even mention the possibility of a confederal system.

The idea of a confederation was formulated by North Korea as an alternative to peaceful, independent reunification through general elections without external interference. The fiasco of the Geneva Conference on Korea in the wake of the Korean War (1954) and especially the completion in North Korea in 1954 of the socialist transformation of private ownership in agriculture, retail business, and handicraft and the construction of a strong socialist economy in the northern half of the country had virtually precluded the possibility of reunification through general elections. In this context, a fresh approach was warranted. This new approach would probably break the deadlock at a time of a deepening rift between the North and South and provide a realistic formula for national reunification. An impetus was finally provided by Kim Il Sung's offer. His proposal was to the effect that should the South Korean authorities fail to agree to all-Korean elections

> for fear that the whole of South will be transformed into a communist state, it will be necessary first of all at least to take some temporary measures to resolve the questions which from the point of view of national interest are particularly urgent. We propose as such a measure the establishment of a Confederation of North and South Korea. The confederal system we are talking about would be implemented with the temporary maintenance of political systems existing in South and North Korea and the independent activities of the governments of North and South Korea through the formation of the supreme national committee composed of representatives of the two governments, which would primarily coordinate the economic and cultural development of North and South Korea.

From a legal point of view, the crucial element of the matter was the mutual recognition of the status of participants in the confederation as subjects of international law. A confederation—a grouping of states for a specific common goal based on an international agreement—would hardly be workable if the two parties challenge each other's international legitimacy and question each other's ability to acquire international rights and to assume international obligations. It would be even harder to define concrete responsibilities within the confederation relating to inter-Korean issues such as coordination of economic and cultural development.

Moreover, mutual recognition is necessary and convenient because international activities such as the maintenance of diplomatic and consular relations, participation in international organizations, conclusion of international accords, diplomatic protection, and decisions concerning citizenship and nationality, would have to remain under the jurisdiction of two separate but equal sovereign governments. In due course, a unified body politic will emerge and assume all these functions, eventually leading to the creation of a federal state from a legal point of view as a corollary of national reconciliation. For the time being, however, within the confederal system there could be no talk about any division of labor and responsibilities because such talks could be construed as an infringement upon the sovereignty of the two parties. Thus, although the North Korean platform was not explicit about the normalization of relations between the North and the South, the proposal for a confederal system was actually moving in that direction. As a matter of fact, that was precisely the way Kim's offer was understood in South Korea. The South Korean government viewed it solely as a ploy of the North to win recognition as a legitimate member of the international community, based on the assumption that a state's legitimacy as a subject of international law stems from international recognition rather than from the assertion of its right to self-determination. South Korea's foreign minister condemned the North Korean offer as "an action designed to prolong the North Korean puppet regime and to obtain for itself international recognition."[5]

For North Korea the recognition of its status as a subject of international law was not so much a legal issue as it was a political one. The Seoul regime espoused the so-called constitutive theory and equated the acquisition of the status with international recognition, whereas the North Korean government was tilted toward the declarative theory linking the status with effectiveness resulting from the new legal order. For the Seoul government effectiveness in governance primarily concerned internal relations in South Korea, that is, relations between authorities and the citizenry. Public protests and demonstrations were viewed as signs indicating a lack of effectiveness. In this context North Korea rejected the proposal for direct negotiations with the Seoul authorities. Instead, it shifted its focus to opposition political parties and social organizations in South Korea as partners in negotiations.

The primary motive behind North Korea's August 14, 1960, initiative, apart from being an attempt to provide a new impetus for the reunification efforts, was to open whatever communications channels possible between the two parts of the country. Evidence of this was the formulation of alternative proposals geared toward national reconciliation. North Korea's statement said, "If the South Korean authorities think that the confederation we are proposing is unacceptable, we once again suggest that a purely economic commission be set up, consisting of representatives of economic circles of North and South Korea with the aim of exchanging goods between the North and the South, mutual cooperation and assistance in economic development." Of course, the creation of such a commission would make it possible to bypass the sensitive issue of mutual recognition as the commission would be composed of representatives from private companies rather than from the governments. North Korea was not yet desperate enough to win broad international acceptance at all cost. It had at least just as many reasons as the South Korean authorities to avoid recognizing the center of state power in Seoul which claimed to represent all of Korea. Thus, it preferred contacts and negotiations concerning national reunification on a nongovernmental basis. For this reason, many of North Korea's reunification initiatives in theory were not sponsored by the government or parliament but by political and social organizations, though obviously masterminded by the officials of the Communist regime.

The clauses concerning the temporary maintenance of the existing political systems and independent activities of the two governments were not designed merely to allay the fear that "all of South Korea would be transformed into a communist state." It also conveyed the message that North Korea still firmly adhered to socialism and would not abandon its political system and its alliance. In 1960 North Korea unequivocally reaffirmed its commitment to world socialism. In his speech quoted above, Kim Il Sung said, "We shall continue to raise high the banner of proletarian internationalism, further strengthen friendship and solidarity with the Soviet Union and strengthen ties with all socialist countries." From this statement no one can discern even the slightest indication of the North Korean leader's tendency toward neutrality or his readiness to compromise the socialist nature of the North Korean state. "Our nation," Kim concluded, "will defend the eastern bridgehead of the socialist camp and will make its contributions to the common goal of peace and socialism." For Kim, an ideal confederation not only should preserve the status quo on both sides of the 38th parallel and ensure long-term competition between the two social and economic systems in the initial stage but also should pave the way for the victory throughout the country.

At that time North Korea's superiority over South Korea in social and economic terms was beyond dispute. On the basis of this sense of disparity in favor of the North, North Korea's Supreme People's Assembly in 1960 unveiled an all-around program on economic, scientific, cultural and sport cooperation between the two parts of the country. This was the only time that the North Korean authorities detailed so concrete an offer as it did in this proposal.[6]

THE FIRST MODIFICATION
OF THE CONFEDERATION CONCEPT (1973)

The proposal for a confederal system in Korea proved to be politically unattractive both within and outside Korea. What was more disturbing to the North Korean leaders was the fact that North Korea gradually lost its economic lead over the South. By the late 1960s, North Korea had little to offer Seoul in terms of economic cooperation. No longer able to bargain from an economically superior position, the North Korean Communist regime began to brag about its imaginary political and social superiority. The proposal for a confederation designed to coordinate the economic and cultural cooperation between the two Koreas was never formally withdrawn, but North Korea no longer promoted it as enthusiastically as it did in the early 1960s. It reverted to the concept of a confederal state, as was evident from a speech delivered by Kim Il Sung on June 23, 1973.[7]

However, this time both the letter and spirit of the reunification proposal was modified. The first proposal called for the establishment of a supreme national Committee, composed of representatives from the two governments. The confederation proposed thirteen years later would not be proclaimed by the two governments, but by a grand national assembly composed of "representatives from all walks of life—workers, working peasants, working intellectuals, young students and soldier in the North and workers, peasants, young students, intellectuals, military personnel, national capitalists and petty bourgeois in the South"—representatives of political parties and social organizations in the North and South. Who would appoint deputies to the grand national assembly and what numbers of deputies would be appointed remained an open question. Kim Il Sung proposed that externally the divided country Korea should appear as a single state under the name of the Confederal Republic of Koryo—the namesake of an ancient kingdom on the peninsula.

A new element of the confederal system as compared with its original conception was the provision that "the North and South should also work together in the field of external activities." This was actually a response to a South Korean proposal rejected by North Korea for the simultaneous entry of the two Korean states into the United Nations. The counterproposal put forward by North Korea called for the establishment of a confederation followed by joint membership in the United Nations for the two Koreas as a single country.

Two previously important provisions of the proposal—inter-Korean communications and international recognition, which in 1960 were vital ingredients of the North Korean political strategy—lost their relevance and were dropped thirteen years later. Talks between the Red Cross organizations of the two Koreas beginning in 1971 and exchange of visits by officials had opened up communication channels. Moreover, by that time South Korea had abandoned its own version of the Hallstein doctrine which had been in force for a number of years. Other factors had emerged to dictate North Korea's political strategy. They were spelled out in the so-called five-point program for speeding up the peaceful reunification of the country. The five points were: (1) a moratorium on arms races; (2) withdrawal of all foreign troops from South Korea; (3) troop reduction; (4) a ban on supply of foreign armaments; (5) an inter-Korean treaty. The program also provided for an expansion of cooperation and exchange between the North and South in the political, military, diplomatic, economic, and cultural spheres. However, the North Koreans discussed such matters only in eloquent generalities. By that time North Korea's links with the socialist bloc had been significantly weakened. In this context, North Korea no longer stressed the importance of "raising the banner of proletarian internationalism," promoting "solidarity with the Soviet Union," and strengthening "ties with all socialist countries."

In 1973 Kim Il Sung advanced a hierarchy of objectives to be pursued by North Korea, which were arranged in the following order: peace, democracy, national independence, and socialism. Solidarity with the USSR and other socialist countries was replaced by solidarity with "international revolutionary forces." The new policy also sought to expand North Korea's influence in the Third World and within the Nonalignment Movement.

THE SECOND MODIFICATION OF THE CONCEPT OF CONFEDERATION (1980)

The main hindrance to progress in North-South negotiations in the 1970s was North Korea's reluctance to accept partial solutions bypassing the basic issue of national reunification. Any suggestions for a partial solution would arouse its suspicion and be branded as a move toward the perpetuation of the partition of the nation. In fact, it was skeptical or even resentful of any formula for the reduction of the tension on the Korean peninsula that was short of an advocacy of reunification. To enlist public support, neither of the two Korean regimes could afford to abandon their reunification efforts. No matter how skeptically the outside world viewed the reunification programs, they always played a major role within the two Koreas. The North and South have long been vying with each other in exploiting the reunification issue so as to boost their images. Neither side has failed to capitalize on the popular sentiments and to maximize public support by devising appealing programs.

The reunification program unveiled at the Sixth Congress of the Korean Workers' Party held in October 1980 basically served this purpose.[8] This program expanded on and fleshed out the concept of the confederal state proposed in 1960, though it differed from its predecessor in a number of significant ways. The name of the future Korean confederal state proposed by North Korea gives some clues to what kind of reunified country the Communist regime envisioned. It insisted that the official name should be "the Democratic Confederal Republic of Koryo" (DCRK). The use of the epithet "democratic" was probably one of the greatest historical ironies because North Korea is by every standard an antithesis of a democracy. In 1948 the Kim regime proclaimed the Democratic People's Republic of Korea in the northern half of the Korean peninsula and became one of the self-styled "people's democracies." But the high-sounding name did not prevent it from evolving into one of the world's most isolated, undemocratic totalitarian countries, just as was the case with the now defunct East Germany, the so-called German Democratic Republic (GDR). But underlying the name was the North Korean Communist regime's sinister scheme. It attempted to draw an analogy between the DPRK and the new confederal state, suggesting that the reunified nation should be modeled in the image of North Korea and be dominated by the Communist regime.

Out of the ten guiding principles and objectives of the future DCRK, five (e.g., Points 2–6)were just a rehash of those elaborated in the program formulated twenty years earlier. They concerned civic freedoms, economic, scientific, cultural, and educational cooperation, North-South transportation links, the unification of transport, postal, and telegraph services as well as the stabilization and improvement of living standards. Other stipulations of the plan represented a significant expansion of the original model of the confederation. Their primary concern was the distribution of powers and responsibilities between the component parts of the joint body. The previous formula guaranteed autonomy for the two governments and restricted the scope of its jurisdiction only to the economic and cultural spheres. By contrast, the new program provided for reforms which would greatly erode the sovereignty and autonomy of the two respective governments and would in particular impose constraints on their rights to handle foreign political relations. Although both governments were allowed to establish and maintain diplomatic relations with foreign countries separately, they would be under the obligation to readjust and reorder their foreign policy goals from time to time. The DCRK should declare the abrogation of all international treaties and agreements which ran counter to the principles of national unity, including military treaties concluded by the North and South prior to the establishment of the confederation. All economic agreements would remain in force, provided they did not conflict with national interest.

In this program, economic decision-making powers would devolve upon the joint body politic. Foreign capital investments in South Korea would remain intact. In the meanwhile, however, restrictions would be imposed on private capital linked to multinational corporations. In international organizations, both Koreas would be represented by the DCRK alone. The program did not specify how the questions of citizenship and consular protection would be settled. It is only known that the DCRK would be responsible for the welfare of overseas Koreans.

The most important provision regarding domestic politics was that the two governments should surrender the control of the military and police forces. A ban would be imposed on paramilitary organizations and military training for civilians. The armies of the two parts of Korea would be integrated into a national army under joint DCRK command. Such a new distribution of powers and responsibilities leaves the impression that the confederation was a misnomer. The DCRK appeared more like a federation than like a confederation. A confederation is by definition a relatively loose union of—in this case—two independent subjects of international law. But sometimes the name did not coincide with the actual nature of the system. The constitutional framework based on the North Korean reunification plan did not fit the definition of a confederation. That is the case with Switzerland, whose official name Confederation Helvetique is not compatible with the constitutional model of that type of unions.

The next question is what kind of policy of this nominally confederate Korean state should pursue according to the North Korean program. The DCRK would have to strictly observe the principles of neutrality, implement a policy of nonalignment, maintain friendly relations with all nations on the basis of national independence, noninterference with internal affairs, equality, mutual benefits, and peaceful coexistence. Moreover, it would declare that it will not be a party nor a co-participant in any international pact of aggression. It would declare a nuclear-free zone and a zone of peace on the Korean peninsula, impose a ban on foreign troops and foreign military bases on its territory, and denounce the manufacture, deployment, and use of nuclear weapons.

The implementation of the North Korean program would require South Korea to make more concessions than North Korea. It would entail a profound political reorientation and an overhaul of South Korea's political system.

Not surprisingly, the proposal failed to receive a positive response from the Seoul government. The North Korean government did not realize that reunification through peaceful negotiations is predicated on mutual respect for each other's security concerns within the framework of the existing social order and political systems. North Korea had sent the signal that it did not have the intention of imposing its political and social system upon South Korea. But its claims were far from credible and did not jibe with reality. Given the profound differences with respect to the political systems, only parity in participation and equality in the distribution of decision-making power within the confederation provides a sufficient guarantee. North Korea insisted on such equal representation in 1960, but subsequently retracted this demand. Attempts to include a social program invariably led to a deadlock in the bilateral talks. In the 1980 proposal North Korea only made transient and oblique references to its original concept of confederation. According to its new formula the confederal state would form a supreme national assembly based on equal representation of both the North and South parliaments and adequate representation of Korean expatriates. The assembly would elect or appoint a committee which would serve in the capacity of the central government of the confederation authorized to control regional governments and administer routine affairs that fall under its defined jurisdiction. This governing body would make decisions concerning politics, national defense, foreign relations, and other affairs of mutual interest.

After the first national reconciliation plan foundered on disagreements concerning contacts between governments and social organizations, North Korea revised its strategy and searched for solutions through the parliamentary channel. Since the two Korean governments could hardly reconcile their diametrically opposed positions, it would be inevitable that the overseas Koreans would become the protagonist and play a pivotal role in the confederal assembly. As a result, parity or equal representation would be nothing but an illusion. A retrospective investigation of Pyongyang's concept of the confederal state indicates that it has undergone changes in four respects:

1. The proposed name of the unified Korean state was first the Confederation of North and South Korea (1960), then the Confederal Republic of Koryo (1973), and finally the Democratic Confederal Republic of Koryo (1980).

2. The proposed joint governing body, which would be entrusted with the task of implementing common goals, was to be composed of an equal number of representatives appointed by each government according to the first formula for reunification (1960). The second one did not specify the ratio between the representatives from the North and the South. The third formula called for equal representation from each participant but required the induction of a certain number of overseas Koreans.

3. There was a tendency toward vesting the joint governing body with broader and broader powers and functions. According to the first proposal, it could exercise jurisdiction in the spheres of economy and culture. In 1973 the jurisdiction was extended to domestic politics and foreign affairs. In the 1980 version, national defense was added.

4. The nature of the unified Korean state also evolved. The 1960 proposal called for a confederation of the two Korean states. The union envisioned by the 1980 formula apparently bore close resemblance to a federal state. But the 1973 proposal favored something in between.

The difference between a federal and a confederal state is based on legality. The legal basis for a confederal state is international agreements concluded between two sovereign states, which are independent subjects of international law, while a federal system is based on a common constitution. The point is that the Korean language does not clearly distinguish between these two forms of state system. The term "yon-bang" can be translated both as "federal" and "confederal." In Pyongyang's English language translations the word "confederal" is used. One may assume this is an intentional error. However, from the point of view of international law, a strict distinction between a confederation and a federation is essential.

THE CONFEDERAL CONCEPT TODAY

In the 1980s North Korea remained adamant in its refusal to introduce meaningful changes in its conception of the confederal state. Its confrontation with its southern rival continued unabated. In this political context, Pyongyang came to the conclusion that it was neither possible nor advisable to redefine confederation since it was not a good and opportune time for greater openness and compromises. For this reason, it is difficult for us to predict what direction the reunification process will follow in the near future. But at least one thing is clear. Neither side will be able to continue business as usual. Whatever Pyongyang's future reunification initiatives will be, they will have to take account of the new realities within and outside Korea. The Communist leadership's political calculus will have to consider the following factors:

1. The North Korean economy has been languishing deep in the doldrums, which stands in striking contrast to the booming South Korean economy. A declining growth rate has been the prevalent trend. Living standards have ceased to improve for a long time—a major breeding for massive social unrest. The regime has been caught in a dilemma as to whether to reform the system or to continue to limit civil rights.

2. Economic autarky practiced under the slogan of self-reliance has brought the country to the brink of economic catastrophe. North Korea's economy has deteriorated to such an extent that even radical reforms will not be able to reinvigorate the devastated economy without the massive infusion of foreign capital and technology. On the other hand, opening to the outside world will inevitably lead to greater dependence upon foreign countries, which the Communist regime abhors.

3. For more than thirty years, the *Juche* idea has been the foundation of state power. In totalitarian systems, the dominance of a single ideology and thecult of the state leader make it possible to maintain a semblance of national unity, though with the passage of time the foundations of such unity will be constantly eroding. Mounting public discontent with hardships in daily life has already manifested itself. However, strict adherence to *Juche* precluded the implementation of timely and necessary reforms in the system.

4. The North Korean people live in one of the most closed and isolated societies in the contemporary world. A lack of information flow makes it easier to discipline the citizenry but at the same time hampers all progress. The authorities have to choose between isolationism with stagnation and openness with development, between a facade of unity and eventual instability.

5. Until recently North Korea's policy toward its adversary in the South more or less received support from its allies in the socialist camp. It has become necessary for North Korea to reevaluate and reshape its policy toward the South in light of the phenomenal change in its relations with the USSR (now CIS), China, and the post-communist countries. North Korea has to realize that it can no longer dictate or influence these countries' behavior in the international arena and take for granted their unreserved support on the issue of reunification.

6. In the previous decade, North Korea enjoyed relatively high prestige within the Nonalignment Movement. However, the decline of

the Movement and increasing cleavages within it have weakened the North Korean position and make it increasingly difficult to use the political capital invested in the Movement to its advantage.

7. Until recently North Korea could negotiate with South Korea from a position of strength and pursue a hardline policy toward the West because of its alliance with the Communist giants the Soviet Union and China. Now it has virtually been left to fend for itself in dealing with its powerful foes.

The international climate in the 1990s has made it necessary for North Korea to adopt a new approach to settle inter-Korean disputes. By all indications, this is the only path North Korea can follow if it hopes to prevent serious internal upheaval. Keenly aware of its new vulnerabilities, it has recently been softening its position and moving toward reconciliation with the South. It has ceased to be capricious and cavalier about the reunification issue and has made some sincere efforts to explore the avenues for reunification. Proof of this is its latest move to renew and reinvigorate the North-South dialogue. For the first time in the entire postwar period direct talks between the prime ministers of the two Korean states became possible. Even if the achievements of these talks have so far been very modest, the very fact that they were held is an indication that North Korea is backing away from an unrealistic and stubborn position of seeking solutions through contacts with South Korean opposition forces while ignoring and excluding the Seoul state authorities.

Improvement in the bilateral relations is evident from the recent events such as the participation of a joint Korean team at the Eleventh Asian Games held in Beijing, exchange of athletic delegations and music ensembles, the first joint film festival in New York in October 1990, the participation of the first joint Korean team at the Forty-first International Table Tennis Tournament, and the 1992 Barcelona Olympic Games. The significance of these measures, however, should not be overstated because North Korea has not changed its fundamental position and policy on the issue of national reunification. But it would be equally erroneous to underestimate them because they might be the prelude to a viable form of cooperation and mark the beginning of permanent institutional links between the two parts of the divided country. Inadequate institutional links have caused all North-South contacts to be conducted in an ad hoc manner at the present, and each time both sides have to devote much time to search for a negotiated settlement of the disputes over procedures.

The 1980 concept of the confederal state has been modified. No longer rigidly insistent on joint representation at the United Nations, North Korea now accepts the simultaneous entry of both Pyongyang and Seoul into the United Nations. This new approach has shown that in face of the new realities in international politics, the outmoded concept has lost its relevance and North Korea has to change it. The Pyongyang regime has to live with the reality of the two Korean states and radically modify its version of a confederation. In other words, it has to adopt a more pragmatic position on the issue of national reunification. Otherwise, it will be doomed to perpetual isolation and eventually lose its already precarious position as a viable international actor as well as its ability to influence the reunification process.

NOTES

1. The full text of the interview was published in the Nepalese weekly *Arpan*, December 7, 1990; *Rodong sinmun*, December 11, 1990; *The Pyongyang Times*, December 15, 1990.

2. *The Pyongyang Times*, January 1, 1991.

3. *To Build a National Community Through the Korean Commonwealth: A Blueprint for Reunification.* Seoul: National Reunification Board, 1989, pp. 37–55.

4. Extensive excerpts of the speech were published in *Pravda*, August 14, 1969.

5. Foreign Minister Yil Hyung's statement of August 17, 1960, rejecting the confederation proposal in: *Korean Reunification: Source Materials with an Introduction*. Seoul: Research Center for Peace and Unification, 1976, p. 255.

6. Foreign Broadcast Information Service, *Daily Report—North Korea*, December 13, 1960, pp. 1–24.

7. *The Pyongyang Times*, June 30, 1973.

8. "Report to the Sixth Congress of the Korean Workers' Party on the Work of the Central Committee," *Pyongyang Times*, October 11, 1973.

14

THE CONUNDRUM OF THE NUCLEAR PROGRAM

HAN S. PARK

University of Georgia, Athens

The controversy surrounding North Korea's suspected nuclear weapons program has frustrated the United Nations, the United States, and much of the world community. North Korea has persistently refused to give in to the pressure from the international community. Pyongyang's seemingly irresponsible behavior as a signatory of the Non-Proliferation Treaty (NPT) has been widely criticized, and yet the criticism does not seem to affect Pyongyang's determination to pursue its own course. Washington's frustration stems from North Korea's unwillingness to succumb to international laws or to the power politics of the world community. As a result, the Pyongyang regime is ridiculed for being erratic, madmanlike, unpredictable, uncivilized, and irrational. This demeaning characterization of North Korea made it easier for the International Atomic Energy Agency (IAEA) and the United States to move rapidly with sanctions and punitive measures against Pyongyang until Jimmy Carter intervened in June 1994 to alleviate the mounting tension. The crisis is not expected to be resolved easily. Pyongyang will not give in and accept a full and unconditional inspection from the IAEA without considerable concessions from its adversarial parties, especially the United States. Then, what does Pyongyang want and why does it want what it does? Without understanding Pyongyang's intentions, any effort at negotiated settlement will be futile. The purpose of this article to discern North Korea's policy objectives and behavioral orientations with respect to the nuclear conundrum. The contention being made here is that without an adequate understanding of Pyongyang's behavioral motivations, negotiation efforts may only delay the process and provide North Korea with more time. On the other hand, if the United States is willing and prepared to make certain concessions in order to work out a peaceful settlement, a fuller assessment of Pyongyang's psychological dispositions and behavioral inclinations would have to be swiftly made. Such an assessment will reveal the fact that North Korea's nuclear program could be seen as a rational choice of action, and consequently, a solution may be sought on a rational ground.

North Korea's objectives as perceived by its leadership are twofold: the moral issue of justice as seen in the doctrine of *Juche* and the more pragmatic concern for national interest.

THE MORAL BASIS AND *JUCHE*

North Koreans are clear about expressing their resentment against the IAEA and the NPT as a whole. Their signing of the NPT in 1987 may have been an attempt to ease the suspicion by the world community of Pyongyang's nuclear weapons program or it may have been a result of Moscow's influence or a simple misjudgment on the part of Kim Il Sung. But what is evident is that Pyongyang has no enthusiasm for the NPT. To North Korea, the Non-Proliferation regime itself is inherently discriminatory and imperialistic. It is quite common for North Koreans of all walks of life to criticize the United States for prohibiting small nations to develop nuclear weapons while maintaining its own stockpile in large quantity. They seem to find a great sense of pride in condemning Washington for being imperialist and the IAEA for being discriminatory. North Koreans believe it to be morally unjust for any superpower to deny small countries to develop their own defense capability.

The ideology of *Juche* calls for self-defense. Kim Il Sung in articulating this ideology felt that Korea had helplessly succumbed to the imperial Japan because it had no military capability to defend itself. Kim in his autobiography attributes the colonialization of his country to the fact that Korea did not have the necessary military strength to resist the Japanese imperial forces; its plea for assistance from the United States and other foreign governments was never received with compassion or sympathy.[1] Even in the height of the Cold War system, Pyongyang refused to rely on either the Soviet Union or China for national security. It is no surprise that Kim Il Sung's government from its very inception placed the military industry at the very top of policy goals. Further, it is not accidental that the military industry and defense science are disproportionately advanced in North Korea today.

North Koreans feel that their self-defense objective will be permanently achieved when nuclear bombs are stored on their own soil to deter any potential aggressor. They have in their belief systems a strong moral and ideological rationalization for equipping themselves with weapons. If the nuclear bomb is perceived to be necessary for self-defense, Pyongyang will do anything to proceed with its development and production. On the other hand, if they believe that self-defense is viable without nuclear weapons, their willingness to compromise will increase greatly. In short, Pyongyang's persistence with respect to the nuclear issue stems in part from its belief that their self-defense is morally right and ideologically correct, and such belief is reinforced by their perception of the IAEA and the United States as being morally misplaced.

PRAGMATISM AND NATIONAL INTEREST

To say Pyongyang is unpredictable, irrational, erratic, and madmanlike is an act of irresponsibility and ignorance. North Korea has taken a course that is perfectly congruent with the desire to maximize its own comprehensive national interest. There are several areas in which Pyongyang may have positive incentives for developing nuclear weapons.

Legitimacy Interest

There are two salient concerns in the minds of North Korean leaders. First, the power succession by Kim Jong Il requires greater charismatization for the reigning leader. Unlike his father who had fought in the Manchuria area for national independence against the Japanese rule, the young Kim has little to show off. Although concerted efforts have been made to make him an almost omniscient genius in the arts and philosophy, charismatization often requires the leader's ability and contribution to defending the nation and protecting national integrity against hostile enemies. The stage is set perfectly for Kim Jong Il to build his charisma by "fighting off" the giant force of the United States. It is not accidental in this regard that Kim Jong Il had just been assigned the rank of a marshall and appointed the supreme commander of the military forces in 1992. He receives all the credit for withstanding pressures from the United States and its allies. As long as the Pyongyang regime survives, no matter how the outcome may turn out to be, it is certain that Kim Jong Il will gain a greater charisma. One must be reminded that it is not Kim Il Sung but Kim Jong Il who needs to demonstrate a leadership character. Furthermore, Kim Il Sung could afford making mistakes but Kim Jong Il cannot. In this sense Kim Il Sung's proposal to convene a summit meeting with Kim Young Sam of the South is not a big risk factor for North Korea.

Second, there is the imperative to wage a legitimacy war with the South. The demise of the former Soviet Union and the dismantling of the Eastern European socialist systems culminating in the absorption of East Germany by the West posed a threat to Pyongyang to an alarming degree. The free world expected North Korea to follow the fate of East Germany and many South Koreans were considering the collapse of North Korea to be imminent and inevitable. The Seoul government even considered the probable economic burden of absorbing North Korea to be too high to hasten the process. All the odds were against North Korea in its competition for legitimacy with the South to unify and govern the nation. It was in this opportune time that the nuclear controversy emerged.

North Korea believes that the legitimacy war with the South can be won by convincing the people that it embodies the spirit of nationalism. It also believes that students and intellectuals as well as the working class in the South will be attracted to the ideology of *Juche*, and they will be convinced that the North has greater legitimacy than the Seoul regime. Professor Seung Duk Park of the Academy of *Juche* Science in Pyongyang observed that West Germany succeeded in absorbing the East not because of its economic affluence but because of its superior legitimacy in that the Bonn regime was more self-reliant and nationalistic.[2] He indicated further that North Korea's policies of self-reliance especially in the area of defense are received favorably by the "Southern compatriots," suggesting that the North is winning the legitimacy war.

Esteem and Leverage Interests

North Koreans have been indoctrinated into believing that they are a digni-
fied people with the great mission to fight the injustices of capitalism in order
to perfect the ill-fated socialism. And yet, they are being isolated and often
ridiculed by the international community for a series of self-inflicted disruptive behaviors such as acts of terrorism. The current nuclear issue could
bring unbearable humiliation to the North Koreans if they are forced to
subject themselves to the "special inspection." Pyongyang contended that it
had complied with all the obligations as a signatory of the NPT by declaring
all the sites of nuclear energy processing activities and by allowing the IAEA
to inspect them (which the latter conducted). However, the North Korean
leadership objected vehemently to the unprecedented "special inspection"
which was applied only to Iraq following its defeat in the Gulf War.
Pyongyang thought that such an inspection would be unacceptable humiliating to a sovereign state, and has since determinantly objected to that
measure. Although the consideration of national humiliation might not have
been the primary cause of Pyongyang's objection, it nonetheless was a significant factor to the North Korean regime which was already deeply
entrenched into ultranationalism. It is unfortunate that the world had disre-
garded the "face-saving" element in dealing with Pyongyang. In this regard,
as I shall make a focused discussion later in this article the visit to Kim Il
Sung by former U.S. President Jimmy Carter had a great deal of symbolic
meaning to North Korea. It meant that the regime was given a proper recognition and Kim Il Sung was able to improve his tarnished image especially in
the last days of his life.

In any event, the nuclear issue has brought an intriguing consequence either by design on the part of Pyongyang or by default on the part
of the United States and the IAEA. And that is the enhancement of
Pyongyang's visibility and leverage in the international community. As all
nations do, North Korea also seeks an esteemed status in the international
community. The international community that Pyongyang is particularly
concerned about is the traditional nonaligned bloc of the Third World. Third
World countries that have had bitter experiences of colonialism, and maintain
a revived nationalist culture are seemingly providing North Korea with moral
support as the latter single-handedly resists the immense pressure from the
Western powers. Visitors from those countries openly praise the Pyongyang
leadership for its refusal to submit to the pressure, and North Korea's media
exploit the situation to further promote the legitimization of the system.

Pyongyang sees its possession of nuclear capability as benefiting its
leverage and bargaining power in the international community. All indications of current negotiations (and lack thereof) seem to support that perception, and North Korea has taken advantage of the "nuclear card" effectively
to achieve its policy goals. The goals in this case are twofold: Gaining the
time Pyongyang may need to further develop weapons programs and

securing concessions from the United States. North Korea has fared remarkably well in terms of these goals. It remains to be seen whether the "nuclear card" has been exhaustively used or is even likely be overused.

Economic Interest

Since 1990, Pyongyang has openly acknowledged difficulties in its economic situation, especially in the provision of basic necessities including food. Initially, Pyongyang attributed the difficulty to at least two consecutive years of poor harvests. But still having been unable to recover from a shrinking GNP, the leadership has shifted its policy emphasis to the production of light industrial goods and international trade. In October 1992, Pyongyang introduced a set of sweeping joint-venture laws designed to attract foreign capital and technology. In the 1994 New Year's Message, Kim Il Sung reiterated the importance of expanding the production of consumer goods and improving economic relations with other countries, especially with capitalist developed countries.

Defense Burden

People of all walks of life in North Korea are willing to point to the inordinately heavy defense burden as the single obstacle to their economic growth. One military officer who was assigned to a commanding post at the DeMilitarized-Zone (DMZ) indicated that "it is a matter of prioritization that forces us to absorb economic hardships." He observed that "no country will be able to maintain economic prosperity if it is burdened with a defense expenditure amounting to some 25 percent of the gross national product." Indeed, the massive defense burden for such a long period of time has denied the North Korean economy of any possibility of igniting a takeoff. Pyongyang believes that it is imperative to cut military spending if it is to promote economic growth. It is with this belief that the government has devoted its efforts to secure unconventional weapons including the nuclear bomb. In fact, once a few bombs are developed, the maintenance of defense preparedness might be far cheaper than continuously indulging in an arms race with the South.

Foreign Currency

It is ironic that the heavy concentration of resources in the defense area might be the primary reason for defense and scientific development, including but not limited to nuclear physics. For while these expenditures in defense have been a burden on the economy, their outputs currently provide North Korea with one of its only sources of foreign currency. North Korea seems to be of the opinion that it is time for the defense sector to cash in. In fact, the sales of arms is North Korea's primary source of foreign currency. It is known that Iran, Iraq, Libya, and Syria have all made trade deals with North Korea for SCUD missiles.[3] Reportedly, North Korea concluded a deal with Iran to barter SCUD missiles and related technology for oil that may have been worth several hundred million dollars.[4]

Once North Korea's nuclear capability is conceded by the international community, it will be in a position to export technology and equipment to the OPEC countries if the NPT regime should become ineffective.[5] One must consider the reality that North Korea will be left with no alternative to explore any possible avenues for economic advancement, and the avenues North Korea can explore are severely limited.

Technology Interest

Technology has a spinoff effect. Nuclear energy and nuclear weapons programs are mutually interchangeable. Technology once obtained attains its own autonomous course of improvement with a multiplying effect. North Korea asserts that the attainment of "indigenous technology" could have far-reaching beneficial consequences because it cannot be subjected to foreign sanctions and manipulations.

Although North Korea's indigenous industrial technology is not expected to be among the foremost in the region, let alone in the world, the nation has made concerted efforts to promote research and technology at all levels of education. It is commonplace at high/middle schools that students are required to participate in at least one science project. And they are calling such practice "an investment in the future." In this respect, one might observe that North Korea views weapons' technology not in isolation from overall technological development but as a part of it.

In short, North Korea has turned to the development of nuclear technology not for an irrational reason but for a number of well-thought-out "rational" considerations.

NORTH KOREA'S OPTIMAL SCENARIO

Thus far, I have discussed the behavioral motivations for North Korea with respect to the nuclear issue by focusing on the factors to which it could possibly give in. Those factors are the inducement or incentive factors that were too large for North Korea to give in to. However, if Pyongyang had been convinced that the suspected sanctions from the IAEA or the United States might threaten the very existence of the political system itself as Washington and conservative circles insisted, it might have been more conciliatory or at least more serious about negotiations. In fact, Pyongyang might have had its own ideas and perceptions about the implications and ramifications of the economic and possible military sanctions.

The Economic Sanction

At the height of the crisis, Pyongyang warned that an economic sanction would be considered as an act of aggression, and it would not hesitate to take retaliatory actions. Whether such a warning was the expression of a genuine intention or only a bluff cannot be answered with any degree of objective accuracy. But what is clear is the fact that economic sanctions would have little or no effect on altering Pyongyang's policy.

There are only a handful of countries that have any kind of noteworthy trade relations with North Korea. Among them are China, Japan, Russia, and South Korea. Practically no trade relations exist with Western systems including the United States. The volume of trade is rather insignificant. Most of the trade items are either consumer products or raw material, indicating that North Korea has little structural dependence on the external economic system. China has the greatest leverage on Pyongyang as the primary supplier of crude oil as approximately 40 percent of North Korea's oil consumption is believed to be imported from China.[6] Moreover, an undetermined amount of food and commodity items are traded across the border. Beijing has shown great reluctance to further strain its relations with North Korea by siding with the United States. On March 21 at the IAEA's board meeting, China abstained from voting on the resolution to refer the issue to the UN Security Council. Even if China does not exercise the veto power to block any resolution to sanction North Korea in the UN Security Council, it will act without enthusiasm. Given this, one might question if China can or will forcefully punish North Korea.

Then, there is Japan. Most economic activities between Japan and North Korea are carried out primarily by the pro-North Korean residents in Japan. Represented by the association of *Chosen Soren*, they have been transferring cash to North Korea in the amount of $600 million. Although Japan is anxious to prevent North Korea from becoming a nuclear power, stopping the flow of money in this case is not a simple matter given the fact that the Japanese yen is an international open currency. The suspected arrangement for petroleum import from Iran and possibly other countries friendly to Pyongyang poses yet another problem. It will take a blockage of the open sea to effect the embargo, a complicated and risky proposition. Then, there are the former socialist countries including Russia. But even a cursory examination indicates that their actual trade with North Korea has declined since late 1980s and reached an almost negligible level. Finally, there is South Korea. A handful of companies in South Korea have been trading with the North through a third party (mostly Hong Kong). But cessation of such activity would leave no dent in North Korean economic life whatsoever.

This does not mean that North Korea would be completely immune to trade sanctions. It does mean, however, that the extent to which trade sanctions may work as an effective means to induce Pyongyang's policy change is expected to be seriously limited. In this regard, one should not forget that North Korea has developed a great deal of resiliency to economic difficulties throughout the country's history. In fact, North Korean people have long been under a de facto trade embargo from Western countries and Japan, and their economic life is already in a state of poverty. The same Western countries have little leverage to exercise against North Korea when little or no economic interaction exists. The economic hardships are not new to the North Korean people, nor will they blame their own government for their misfortune. On the contrary, they believe that foreign "imperialist" powers are responsible for their difficulties, helping the government in further solidifying its power base.

Military Action

The military sanction may be the ultimate option for the United Nations. In this event, the United States and South Korea will once again be the primary actors of the UN forces. Hawkish circles in both Washington and Seoul believe that this eventuality will force the North Korean regime to dismantle either by surrendering or significantly weakening Kim Jong Il's power base, thus leading to a serious power conflict within the ruling elite. Either situation could develop but not very likely. One might presume that a massive air strike similar to the "Dessert Storm" operation against Iraq in the Summer of 1990 could destroy North Korea's military capability and in the process kill millions of people. Can we also assume that North Korea's military power will be completely incapacitated, preventing a retaliatory response?

There are a few issues that need to be brought up in this debate. First, can airstrikes achieve the goal of incapacitating North Korea so that the possibility of retaliation may be ruled out? One must be mindful of the fact that North Korea has shown the ability to dig tunnels and utilize the underground for transportation as demonstrated by the impressive subway system operated 100 meters below the surface. One should also remember that this xenophobic society has been so tightly closed to the outside world that little is known about its military situation, especially its logistics. In view of these facts, no one can be sure if the UN forces would be able to even locate all the military installations, let alone destroy them. It is most likely that North Korea would retaliate with whatever weapons it could use against the U.S. and South Korean forces.

At the same time, one should not forget that a preemptive first strike by North Korea cannot be ruled out. What would be the implications of such an occurrence? Such a strike would certainly produce millions of casualties in the South. In the event of a conflict, would the North Korean government be perceived illegitimate and lose its power base? The damage would be greater in the South than in the North. It is possible that the South Korean government could experience a serious legitimacy crisis as the people in the South might question the morality of such a costly inter-Korean conflict. The South Korean government and its system could be more vulnerable than the Northern counterpart simply because the former can be more easily subjected to criticism from the public. The North Korean leadership might experience some difficulty in maintaining power solidarity but it would not be likely to lose its ruling position.

On this issue, one should also weigh in international public opinion. The destruction of a country and the death of large number of people which would certainly be aired on the world's mass media would not win sympathy, especially among the Third World countries. Moral justification will be shaky if all North Korea did was to withdraw from the NPT; Iraq blatantly *invaded* Kuwait but the condemnation of North Korea's action would not be universally pervasive throughout the world. There might be many observers worldwide who might think that North Korea's weapons program is for its national security and national interest. We could expect that discussions of "imperialism" in the very structure of the nonprolifera-tion regime would surface, and the disruptive North/South ideological dispute would ensue. In fact, North Korea has already publicly condemned the NPT as an imperialist ploy when one diplomat questioned the moral foundation for allowing only the handful of countries that presently possess nuclear weapons to monopolize while preventing all others from possessing the same weapons. In short, the employment of military action would bring far more complicated implications for the United States and the world community.

THE CARTER FACTOR

For reasons yet to be explained fully, the former President of the United States Jimmy Carter was invited to visit North Korea in November 1992 after a series of informal contacts initiated by Pyongyang. The initial contact was made in the summer of 1992, before the presidential election in the United States when the nuclear issue had not evolved into a major foreign policy issue. At that time Governor Clinton as the nominee of the Democratic party asked Jimmy Carter to refrain from visiting North Korea before the election for such a trip could be politically damaging to the Democratic ticket. Since the inauguration of the Clinton administration, numerous efforts were made by North Korea to materialize the Carter visit and Mr. Carter himself "accepted" the invitation and sent a fact-finding mission to Pyongyang. But Mr. Clinton, then the nominee of Democratic party, asked Mr. Carter not to make that trip for possible political damage to the party ticket. It was all along Mr. Carter's intention not to do anything against his own government's desire. For this reason, the former president refused to materialize the trip until June 1994 when the Clinton administration had exhausted all other means before resorting to punitive measures against Pyongyang. The fact that Mr. Carter was in contact with high-ranking officials before making up his mind to explore the feasibility of the trip and that he was intensely briefed by the government on the eve of the trip indicates that the Clinton administrative supported the trip, and was interested in seeing what the former president could do in the deadlock.

President Carter's trip produced remarkable outcomes in both the nuclear issue and inter-Korea relations. The late President Kim Il Sung shocked the world by showing surprisingly conciliatory gestures. He offered to freeze the processing of petroleum at Yongbyun and also proposed a summit meeting with his South Korean counterpart in return for a third round of high-level talks with the United States. These measures demonstrated President Kim's desire for a negotiated settlement, in contrast to the much publicized notion that he is a "war monger." Within less than three weeks after President Carter's visit, things were evolving rapidly, reversing the previous course: The Washington-Pyongyang high-level talks started smoothly in Geneva; Seoul and Pyongyang agreed to open the first summit meeting on July 25. The Carter visit opened a new door for North Korea and it also helped the Western world in reassessing the horrible stigma of Kim Il Sung and his government which might have been founded on misinformation and disinformation. Furthermore, Mr. Carter's trip might well have preempted a possible conflict on the Korean peninsula which was certain to bring human and material devastation.

THE DEATH OF KIM IL SUNG

In the middle of the hopeful developments brought about by the President Carter's successful mission, the world was stunned by the news of President Kim Il Sung's death. He died of a heart attack on July 8, 1994. It was only two weeks and a half after President Kim received the former U.S. president in Pyongyang for a historic meeting. His death makes Mr. Carter's visit more meaningful and extremely timely. If Kim had not set the stage in motion in the last days of his life, the world would have applied economic and possibly military sanctions to which Pyongyang would have responded violently. At the same time, there would have been no channels or means of negotiation at the time of Kim's death. The world, then, might have been celebrating the misfortune of North Korea instead of sending condolescences, further aggravating the already deeply grieving people in Pyongyang. His death leaves lasting impressions of his own to the world as a reasonable and peace-seeking person. More importantly, his conciliatory policies will amount to his last wishes that the ensuing regime under the leadership of Kim Jong Il will undoubtedly pursue them.

Although there are many variables that are uncertain about the stability of the new regime, all indications are that there will be no immediate threat to its legitimacy and functional normalcy. Therefore, it would be mistaken to expect any drastic changes in policy goals or political climate. The central motivations of developing weapons of mass destruction are still intact, and their current strategies will continue to follow the same course as they did during the Kim Il Sung era.

TOWARD A NEGOTIATED SETTLEMENT

Given the preceding discussion, what is likely to happen to the nuclear issue? Pyongyang will continue to gain with the nuclear leverage the security assurance, economic cooperation, and political recognition. For the reasons discussed earlier, these same goals will be pursued for both ideological and pragmatic reasons. The United States and its allies, while showing solidarity and determination to keep North Korea nuclear free, have amply showed their willingness to make concessions for a negotiated solution to the exceedingly complex conundrum. Concessions will have to be made if Pyongyang is to be brought to the fruitful negotiation table. The issue at stake is no less than the NPT regime itself. The United States and the IAEA seem to have no other choice but to seek a negotiated settlement through making deals with North Korea. The package for negotiation is expected to include the cessation of the Team Spirit exercise, the formation of an Asia-Pacific alliance system inclusive of North Korea, economic assistance, and diplomatic recognition as possible concessions by the United States and its allies. The controversial issues of U.S. troop withdrawal along with its weapons from South Korea and the conversion of the armistice agreement to a peace treaty are to be dealt with in conjunction with the alliance system. In return, Pyongyang must make its nuclear programs transparent to the satisfaction of the IAEA. It is a mistake to assume that North Korea without Kim Il Sung will be easier to punish or it will be more irrational and unpredictable, and abandon the course set by the late president of North Korea and Jimmy Carter.

In conclusion, the whole issue of North Korea's developing weapons of mass destruction including possibly the nuclear is not unexplainable, nor is it irrational on the part of the Pyongyang regime. The expected payoffs might be too large for North Korea to give up. Furthermore, to bring Pyongyang on its knees by coercive means is infeasible not only because it has retaliatory capability but more importantly its ideology of *Juche* will not tolerate it. Given the fact that *Juche* is the lifeline for North Korea, surrendering to foreign pressures undercuts the very basis of system legitimacy itself. In this sense, Pyongyang has acted most "rationally" in accordance with the national goals and strategic interest as perceived by the leadership.

At the same time, the observation and contention made in this article in favor of a peaceful settlement through the process of bargaining and negotiations are the only rational course of action on the part of the world community.

NOTES

1. Kim Il Sung, *Saegi wa Duboro*, (*With the Century*), Pyongyang: KWP Press, 1992 (in two volumes).
2. Professor Park conveyed this observation to the author in November 1993 when the latter visited the Academy of *Juche* Science.
3. For a concise presentation of North Korea's missile trade, see Peter Hayes, "International Missile Trade and the Two Koreas," Monterey Institute of International Studies, Working Paper No. 1.
4. *Journal of Commerce*, November 16, 1993; Economist Intelligence Unit, China, North Korea Country Profile, 1992–1993, p. 87.
5. In agreement with this assessment, Richard Perle maintains that North Korea will not hesitate to sell nuclear weapons and related technology and components to other countries. See "Policy Implications of North Korea's Ongoing Nuclear Program," The U.S. House of Representatives, Subcommittee on East Asian and Pacific Affairs of the Committee on Foreign Affairs, the U.S. House of Representatives (Washington, D.C.: U.S. GPO, 1992), p. 5.
6. *Wall Street Journal*, April 2, 1993.